To Eileen,
Enjoy and have
fun with the
Best
Sylvia

More praise for *Don't Bring It to Work*

"I always thought people chose to be the way they are. Sylvia's teaching, now available in this book, showed me a whole new perspective on how my family patterns were bearing upon my interaction with others. Using her framework, I have broken through to new levels of patience and understanding in crucial relationships including my mother, fellow executives, and even my kids."

—**Andrew Cornell,** CEO, Cornell Iron Works, Inc.

"Wonderful insights for anyone who manages a business, works in a business, or leads a business. Read it now!"

—**Michael E. Gerber,** author of the *E-Myth books;* founder of E-Myth Worldwide and The Dreaming Room LLC

"Sylvia Lafair's book brings a rare view of 'systems' and 'systems thinking' that is helpful to individuals and families, as well as businesspeople working to build appreciation, cohesion, and success."

—**Frances Hesselbein,** chairman and founding president, Leader to Leader Institute

"Dr. Sylvia Lafair has written a superb book on working relationships that should be on every executive's desk and used by anyone who is in the business of depending on efficient teamwork for productivity. Her reflections on how our family systems can sabotage our working lives are brilliant and totally applicable in practical terms. This book is a must-read for all business programs, regardless of how large or small."

—**Dr. Frank Lawlis,** author of *Mending the Broken Bond*

"Through Sylvia Lafair's astute work, you will see yourself, your co-workers, and your family dynamics in an entirely new light. More importantly, this will help you change the patterns that have been keeping you from reaching your highest potential. This ranks with the best business and psychology books on the market; not only is it insightful and practical—it's a great read!"

—**Anita Sharpe,** CEO and founder of GeniusSuite; Pulitzer Prize–winning writer at the *Wall Street Journal*

"A phenomenal book! Sylvia's insights, experience, and brilliant communication style make her one of the leading experts in this field. I have had the honor of working with Sylvia over many years and can attest to the power of her methods in transforming negative patterns into positive behaviors. This really works!"

—**Eslie Dennis,** MD, vice president, Medical Head Northeast, Novartis Pharmaceuticals Corporation

"Most educators feel they are standing sentry over a system under siege on all fronts. It's exhausting! Sylvia Lafair shows us effective ways to make change happen. This seminal book provides me the Holy Grail to forge a strong team on behalf of our mission to prepare children for the future. I've been waiting for this for 35 years."

—**Linda C. Brewer,** EdD, superintendent, Derry Township School District

"Sylvia takes a highly personalized approach to leadership development. She helps each person become more aware of their personal styles and their possible origins, and raises behavior patterns to a conscious level. From awareness comes change. I found great value in applying these lessons both at work and at home to successfully balance demanding jobs, motherhood, and a two-career marriage."

—**Nancy Singer,** senior director, Global Sales and Marketing Leadership Development, Merck & Co., Inc.

"This book brings a new way of doing business. It changed the way we run our company and the results are significant. This sentence says it all: 'It is time to get out of the sandbox of childhood and gain a deeper knowledge of the fact that we are all connected and no one wins unless we all do.' This book is a 'must-have' for supervisors all the way up to the executives of the company."

—**Yvonne Cangelosi,** executive vice president, SPEX CertiPrep, Inc.

"Amazing! Sylvia Lafair tells us what every successful person already knows: that business and personal lives can never be totally separate. She destroys this myth and gives us the tools to bring people together to build great companies and deliver bottom-line results. Groundbreaking work!"

—Richard Harris, CEO, Spa Sydell

"Sylvia Lafair's life work is helping people reach their potential. Like many brilliant ideas, the pattern recognition process described in *Don't Bring It to Work* seems obvious in hindsight. Its power is the power to transform not just life in the workplace, but the total quality of human life. Vital for those working in a family business."

—Edwin Neill III, president, Neill Corporation

"Dr. Lafair is on to something that will totally change how you see yourself and others in the workplace. The PatternAware Leadership Model helps people recognize and address their core issues. This is so much more than 'dress for success' advice. Buy it, read it, apply it! It will transform you and your relationships."

—Dorene E. McCourt, vice president, Product Development & Management, MedImpact Healthcare Systems, Inc.

"Don't Bring It to Work is a wonderful tool for anyone wishing to make their work environment more successful. It addresses the baggage that we all bring to the workplace and gives wonderful revelations as to how to move forward from this and build on our strengths. It is about leadership of the highest level."

—Carole Haas Gravagno, board member, Philadelphia Orchestra

"This book distills various behavior patterns at work and helps you identify negative patterns, and then takes you through personal transformation. Every leader and manager should read this book. Wow! It's wonderful!"

—Nancy Duarte, CEO, Duarte Design; author of *slide:ology*

"This is an incisive exploration of the limiting patterns that hold us captive and sabotage our efforts to be effective leaders in our organizations. Sylvia Lafair's call is simple and practical as she sets out to offer her readers clear steps to unravel their past and transform limiting habits into pathways of success and well-being in our organizations. I highly recommend this book."

—**Amber Chand,** founder, The Amber Chand Collection:
Global Gifts for Peace & Understanding

"This book offers keen insights into how individuals process information and guides leaders in helping employees at every level become the best they can be. It is amazing how quickly conflicts can be resolved when we understand the meta-messages that lie at the core of most communication. It should be required reading for all leaders and leaders-in-training."

—**Lynn Rolston,** CEO, California Pharmacists Association

"This engaging book has a powerful core message. We're bringing family dynamics—from childhood and even from our parents' childhoods—to work, and the results are not pretty. Packed with stories of workplace dynamics gone awry—and then, amazingly enough, transformed by Lafair's compassionate approach—the book is immensely readable. You will be motivated to create change for the better."

—**Amy Edmondson,** Novartis Professor of Leadership
and Management, Harvard Business School,
Harvard University

DON'T BRING IT TO WORK

Don't Bring It to Work

Breaking the Family Patterns That Limit Success

Sylvia Lafair

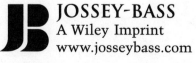

JOSSEY-BASS
A Wiley Imprint
www.josseybass.com

Published by Jossey-Bass
A Wiley Imprint
989 Market Street, San Francisco, CA 94103-1741—www.josseybass.com

Jossey-Bass books and products are available through most bookstores. To contact Jossey-Bass directly
call our Customer Care Department within the U.S. at 800-956-7739, outside the U.S. at 317-572-3986,
or fax 317-572-4002.

Jossey-Bass also publishes its books in a variety of electronic formats. Some content that appears in
print may not be available in electronic books.

Library of Congress Cataloging-in-Publication Data

Lafair, Sylvia, 1940-
  Don't bring it to work : breaking the family patterns that limit success/Sylvia Lafair.
    p. cm.
  Includes bibliographical references and index.
  ISBN 978-0-470-40436-2 (cloth)
    1. Organizational behavior.   2. Interpersonal relations.   3. Conflict management.
  4. Work and family.   I. Title.
  HD58.7.L32 2009
  650.1—dc22

                                                                          2008046855

Printed in the United States of America

FIRST EDITION
HB Printing   10 9 8 7 6 5 4 3 2 1

Contents

For my daughters,
Mikayla and Julie,
bright lights of truth and integrity,
    and, of course,
For Herb, my strong-willed and gentle husband

ACKNOWLEDGMENTS

Writing this book has been such a delight. It has been bubbling up for so many years, and it took that fateful call from my agent, Lorin Rees, who asked, "Have you ever considered putting your thoughts in book form?" to get me moving at warp speed. Thanks, Lorin, for being with me through the process.

Of course, thank you to my staff, Mary Jane Saras, Jane Evans, Lorraine Dachiel, and Shirley Sabol, who are always willing to point out and take ownership of personal patterns, the good, bad, ugly, and beautiful. What a joy to celebrate the roller coaster of life with each of you.

Our facilitators are the brave souls willing to dive deep into the core of humanness in the world of work. My thanks to Dianne Moore, with us from the beginning, always ready to take on a challenge, and to Nancy Pennebaker, John Meade, Jocelyn Goss, Connie Pheiff, Bill Drexler, Mary Wilson, Bob Roberts, Catherine Afeku, and Ben Baker for hearing the call to adventure.

Our workplace colleagues have been true pioneers, exploring the complex interface between individual contribution and collaborative efforts, between self and others, and how to find the "sweet spot" for extraordinary work relationships. It hasn't always been easy to move out of old, patterned mind-sets, yet their tenaciousness shines through. Thanks to Marty Minniti and Matt Emmens who were the first to open doors to exploring the depth of emotions that reside in the workplace. To Brian Keefe, Kathleen Belknap, Eslie Dennis, John Rex, Denise Fantuzzi, Joanne Manidis, Richard Harris, Andrew Cornell, Mats Parup, Edwin Neill, Debra Neill, Joanne LaMarca, Tyler Mathisen, Nancy Singer, Yvonne Cangelosi, Denise McNerary, Carole Gravagno, Arsalan and Arezo Hafezi, Dorene McCourt, Charlie Leing, Maria Koehler, Chester Yuan, Kathy O'Neill, Mary Vidarte, John Rooney, Billy Turner, and all the rest through the years who have dared to do it differently, thank you for giving your best. And a special thanks to Lynn Rolston, my fellow daredevil, always saying, "What if we . . ."

To the Jossey-Bass organization with its great team headed by Susan Williams, and everyone else who helped shape a bunch of words into that magical concoction called a book, thanks, and let's do it again!

To Barbara Monteiro, a superb publicist who knows how to take complex thoughts and distill them down to essence, always with a tinge of whimsy.

To the memory of Willis Harman, who kept turning me toward the workplace as the arena where real and sustainable societal change was ready to happen.

And to family, where it all begins. My love of words from my mother and my questioning of philosophy from my father are there in my writing. My yearning to go beyond the obvious comes from my older brother Jerry, who always challenged me to see the bigger picture even when I just wanted to be with the "in group." And again to Mikayla, Julie, and Mark, and those great grandkiddies, Arielle and Dylan, who are the future in present form. And to Herb, always encouraging and loving, we sure have lived a lot of life together. Thanks.

We carry our ancestors in our hearts, and sometimes on our backs.
—AUSTRALIAN ABORIGINE SAYING

INTRODUCTION

Jeanette Walters, a senior financial analyst, was an annoying person. Not just a little annoying; *very* annoying. She wore bright red lipstick and interrupted everyone. She answered every question whether she knew anything about the subject or not. She took up so much airtime that the rest of her group was suffocating. "Jeanette just doesn't get it," her boss said. "Sure, she's highly accomplished and has amazing skills. But her coworkers would love to stuff a sock in that big, red-lipped mouth. Frankly, I would too."

Every workplace has a Jeanette, or some version of her. That guy on your team who never stops complaining. The hotshot executive who steamrollers others with his ideas and never listens to people. The coworker in the next cubicle you can hear on the phone all day, spreading gossip and rumors. The board member who always challenges yet never adds anything useful.

In fact, haven't you found that just about everyone at work makes you want to stuff a sock in his or her mouth at one time or another?

Such frustrations are understandable. But what most of us, including Jeanette's boss, never really "get" is *why* people behave the way they do, and what can be done about it. The problem isn't always other people's behavior, either. How many times have you regretted something you said or did at work and thought, "Why do I always do that?"

Ever want to help your employees find out what's holding them back? Or holding you back? Ever want to kick a habit that won't let go or one you think you have mastered, only to have it boomerang with great intensity? Ever want to create a new way of relating to colleagues but haven't a clue where to start? Ever want assurance that the executive chosen to take your place when you retire can fill your shoes?

This book will help you find answers. It will help you reinvent yourself, your team, perhaps your entire organization. You'll help employees discover new, more productive ways of behaving—and be able to do the same for yourself. You'll understand conflict as a creative force that you can harness. You'll help high-potentials gain personal power as they learn what really matters about positional power. And, as a special bonus, you can take what you learn about yourself in the workplace and transfer that learning to your personal life.

But first I'd like to offer a word of caution. When you understand the essence of this approach, you will become like a magnet. People will be drawn to you, to your charisma. All sorts of possibilities will begin to open—new ideas, amazing situations, and a sense of freedom that defies description. You need to be ready to use this information for the good of everyone rather than just for your personal gain. It prepares you to take a quantum leap into an exciting and rewarding world that was always there, but that you were just not able to see. The very fact that you have chosen to read this book indicates that you are searching beyond the obvious, beyond the superficial, to become the best you can be and to help others along the way.

Once you learn how people's past family life and their work behaviors connect at a core level, you'll know where performance problems originate and conflict starts. Then you'll gain skills to do something about it. The reason most organizational programs abort is that they fail to deal with our life patterns, which are at the foundation of workplace anxiety, tension, and conflict.

Ever notice that even though companies spend billions of dollars each year on programs to enhance communication skills and team collaboration, interpersonal conflicts and disappointments continue to cause undue stress and unhappiness? We are still so frustrated when disputes waste productive time at work, and there is a sense of going round and round the merry-go-round. We all have that unsettled sense that something is missing. There are even "office politics" Web sites dedicated to assisting befuddled and confused employees. Yet not much changes.

This book helps you get to the bottom of workplace behaviors that simply don't work for you or your organization. More important, it shows you exactly what you can do about them. You'll learn practical steps you can take that improve your professional relationships and make you a better leader, a better mentor, a better teammate. You'll gain a remarkable new understanding of yourself and your colleagues almost immediately. The key is to apply the PatternAware™ Leadership Model, an approach based on my more than thirty years of experience as a leadership development consultant, executive coach, and family therapist.

Yes, I did say family therapist. I have taken the important skills from this arena into the workplace to help you learn how family baggage can derail even the smartest businesspeople and how to get back on track. **This book is all business with a human connection.** I have spent years at off-sites, in staff meetings, working with mergers and acquisitions, and in one-on-one executive coaching sessions looking for the magic bullet for fast and effective change. What I have learned I want to pass on to you. Just know that behavior patterns from our history are intimately connected with every aspect of our adult lives, not least of all our work lives. And, more important, although you can never fully leave your family behind, you don't have to bring it to work.

Now back to Jeanette. When I was asked to speak with her, I learned that this accomplished financial expert had grown up with a mother deformed from childhood polio. At a young age, Jeanette became her mother's legs, participating in track and attending college on an athletic scholarship. When she gave up track to focus on her studies, her mother was furious and rejected her, saying that running was a loftier goal than "adding and subtracting numbers." That's when Jeanette's annoying behavior began to escalate. Having given up compensating for her mother's disability to pursue her education, she now needed to compensate for her mother's rejection—so she began to prove how much she knew by talking and talking and talking.

And now for the good news: with a bit of hard work, Jeanette discovered how the pain of disability had traveled through the generations, how even though she had two perfectly capable legs, she was becoming "disabled" at work through her uncontrolled talking. She was amazed at the revelation, and her behavior began to change. Did it take effort? Of course. Was there resistance? You bet! Yet as Jeanette learned to ask more questions rather than have all the answers, she found out how deep her sadness had been during the years of watching her mother cope with daily discomfort. She was astounded when she came to the realization that she talked and talked and talked to fend off anyone seeing into her own deep anxiety, which had been there since she was a little girl. Over time, her talking became less guarded; she became more relaxed and her team more appreciative.

Hidden patterns like these wreak havoc in the workplace. They rear their ugly heads in the form of power games, "cover your ass" strategies, and a variety of disruptive behaviors. Harboring old and often hurtful memories, we react to problems with preconceived notions about how our interactions with bosses, peers, and direct reports will turn out. And these notions usually become self-fulfilling prophecies. A circle of predictability ensues that produces ineffective behavior, poor work performance, misused sick days, lawsuits, and untold time wasted rumoring and gossiping. Understanding your family patterns is more than making friends with your "inner child," more than liking or disliking your parents or the events from your childhood. **It is about claiming and taming the world of interpersonal relationships.**

This is critical learning for twenty-first-century leaders. Advanced emotional and social intelligence requires a strong comprehension of the workings of the interactive world of relationships and systems thinking. **Being "pattern aware" is an important component of mature leadership.** We can include, yet must go beyond, our personal internal worlds of likes and dislikes, hurts and disappointments. It's time to get out of the sandbox of childhood and gain a deeper knowledge of the fact that we are all connected and no one wins unless we all do.

When we break the cycle of pattern repetition, we can then discard our burdensome family baggage and replace it with renewed creative energy; we enjoy better workplace associations and, with them, more career success. I've seen it happen again and again in my coaching and in the Total Leadership Connections retreats we run. Consider the following examples.

The director of a business unit in a health care company had a tendency to behave as a persecutor, judging and micromanaging her colleagues. As she became aware of this pattern and its roots in her spoiled childhood, she was able to make the necessary adjustments. Her team excelled, and within two years she was promoted to VP of sales.

An attorney at a global electronics firm was intimidated by his boss. After recognizing that he had "inherited" from his father a tendency to play the victim, he was able to explore new, more confident ways of conducting business and was eventually offered the general counsel position.

A finance executive obsessed with obtaining the ever-elusive CFO job procrastinated on projects, afraid to make mistakes. Once she discovered that her paralyzing fear was rooted in old pressures imposed by her now deceased father, she chose to make a lateral move she would never have considered before. Successful in that role, she was asked—surprise—to become the CFO.

How would *your* world of work change if you learned to observe, understand, and transform the repetitive, patterned behaviors that drive most of your reactions, especially during times of stress and anxiety?

Don't Bring It to Work teaches you how to make the invisible visible and offers you concrete, proven tools for breaking the cycle of repetition so that you can transform the way you work at work. The message is simple: you can uncover your hidden behavioral legacies and reshape the patterns that have been limiting you.

Everything is connected—our unconscious thoughts and our behaviors, our family life and our work life. The more we as professionals gain access to the invisible, family-influenced part of our personalities, the more freedom we exercise in the workplace. And know that what you learn here is for every person in *any* family, for every individual in *any* business. These are basic building blocks of relationships, the timeless human universals that affect us all from generation to generation.

Follow the prescriptions in this book, and you open the way for a profound and wonderful transformation that begins in the workplace but does not end there. Overcoming your antiquated knee-jerk behaviors, releasing the ties that bind, you become a more caring, capable, creative, compassionate, and collaborative individual. You free yourself to reach your full potential, not merely as a professional, but as a human being. And freedom is what we all want.

UNCOVERING THE CONNECTIONS

When I first started out as a family therapist during the 1970s, I didn't appreciate the powerful connection between family life and work behavior. Actually, I wasn't focused on the workplace at all; rather, I made my living helping couples and individuals with their marriages and parenting issues. The change in my perspective occurred during the mid-1980s, when my husband, Herb Kaufman, and I opened a wellness center in suburban Philadelphia. We both felt that talk therapy, even the best, was not enough. So we added music and movement and art therapies to our foundation of family therapy. One day, a real estate executive who had attended some of our programs asked me to work with her senior management team. "They're fighting," she said.

"So what?" I said. "I'm a family therapist."

"Yeah, but you work with people who have to learn how to get along. These guys have to learn how to get along, too."

Herb and I thought about it, and we decided she was right. Families and workplaces may seem different, but they are actually quite similar. How often have you heard people say that their work group is "like one big happy family" (or, in many cases, like one big miserable family!)?

The similarity begins with the shared interests of the people involved. In the family, the shared interests are rooted in genetics, whereas in the workplace, the shared interests are rooted in economics. In either case, these shared interests give rise to *relationship systems* that interact with one another. Your past family life and your work behaviors cannot be separated, yet you can learn to bring the best of yourself into all areas of your life.

Armed with these thoughts, we decided to help the real estate executives communicate more honestly and effectively. It worked even better than we had hoped. During the early 1990s, we consulted again with the leadership team of a major pharmaceutical company. The success was more marked still. With our help, management effected changes at the corporate offices that made communication far freer and more productive. Teams in the field began to ask for our assistance. A year later, at the annual meeting, when management handed out awards to the sales force, eleven of the thirteen groups that won key awards were groups with which we had worked.

In both of these cases, I was surprised to discover that change was coming about even more quickly in the workplace than for people in traditional therapy. The key, I felt, was that people in the workplace were more willing to look at their behavior because financial success was involved. The economic factor at work proved very powerful as a stimulus to pursue change at a core behavioral level. In fact, even before coaching became widespread in the workplace, the people we encountered were willing to participate in a committed way in the context of both team building and individual development.

The other thing I learned during these early business assignments was just how powerful family experiences are in shaping workplace behavior. I'll never forget working with David, a competent, high-level sales executive who had alienated his team and was fighting with a key female direct report. When I asked him, on sheer impulse, what his relationship was like with his father, he almost threw me out of his office. In a loud, combative voice he said, "What the hell does that have to do with this?" I had to admit that I wasn't sure, and I told him so. I tend to be tenacious when these hunches come, so I asked him to humor me and just give me a sentence or two. Because his good friend had vouched for my effectiveness, he sighed and said, "OK, two sentences. One, I don't want to discuss it. Two, he was an SOB who hurt my mother and left."

Aha. It seemed that my hunch had been a button pusher. I followed up by asking him for just one more thought: What about his father had he disliked most?

"He was self-absorbed," David answered, "and needed to be the center of attention. I haven't talked to him in thirty years. Don't even know where he is. End of discussion."

It wasn't, however, the end of the revelation. Later in the conversation, when I asked David to describe the problem with the female sales executive, he said, "She's self-absorbed and needs to be the center of attention." Coincidence? I think not!

I didn't say anything then, but I realized that his conflict—and that of others with whom I was working—was not just with his colleague. The invisible battles going on, the unresolved struggle with traumas of the past, showed up in repetitive and unproductive workplace patterns. And so many people didn't recognize that they were struggling—even people who were otherwise sharp, observant, and socially aware.

It makes sense if you think about it: the original organization we join is our family. We didn't know it then, but that's when we started learning relevant workplace skills, such as how to find a role for ourselves, how to understand authority, and how to work with peers. Indeed, science is confirming just how fundamentally important the family system is in determining who we are as people. It turns out that the emotional programming provided by the family system penetrates as far down as the neurological level. Hardwired with concerns and thought processes, each generation both repeats the patterns of past generations and has the opportunity to stand on the shoulders of this past. Biologically and psychologically, we are all part of a story that began well before we were begotten, and this affects the way we behave in all situations, including at work.

Another thing I saw in my early work is that certain patterns showed up again and again, in workplace after workplace. I saw certain behavior patterns so often that they began to take on a life of their own, the way characters in mythology and fables symbolize kernels of human truth. But although most of us have never met an Olympian god or a talking mouse, these are characters familiar to anyone who has ever worked in an office, and I realized that these three patterns, along with others I eventually named, transcend gender, race, cultural background, height, weight, and whether you have curly hair, straight hair, or little hair at all.

- **The Persecutor:** humiliates work associates with finger pointing, demanding, judging, and blaming. The persecutor behaves like a bully and takes no prisoners. No resolutions occur because everyone is afraid to take him or her on.
- **The Avoider:** leaves the scene—either physically or emotionally—when the going gets tough, so that the real concerns never are faced. Meetings get short-circuited or cancelled, projects are delayed, and resolution deteriorates into superficiality.
- **The Denier:** pretends everything is perfect, out of a desire to maintain the status quo. The denier will distort facts and statistics to keep situations from changing course, and only wants "yes people" around. The denier's mantra is "Problem? What problem?"

This was the beginning of what we call The 13 Most Common Patterns™ We Bring to Work. As I identified these patterns, I realized that probing their origins was the critical step toward overcoming bad behavior at the office. The initial list was quite long, and I finally pruned it down to the thirteen in this book. Fewer than that would have undermined the essence of this work. So stick with me, and you'll learn a lot about yourself, your workmates, and your organization.

In David's case, it was clear that the disruptive behavior complained about by his coworkers adhered closely to the model of the persecutor. Determined to change this pattern, David eventually came to terms with the underlying cause, his unresolved hatred toward his estranged father. His father had been a finger-pointing, demanding type, and without realizing it, David had become just like the dad he rejected. Finally, David found and visited his now ill father. He managed to clear the air and resolve a lifetime of grievances. It was an important, albeit difficult step. He told me about the number of times he had picked up the phone to cancel his meeting with his dad only to hang up before it ever rang. And what David learned when they finally met filled him with a mixture of regret and relief.

David was shocked to learn that this man who had been such a disappointment stayed out of his life at the request of his mother. He told his son that having hurt his wife by having an affair, he wanted to do whatever she wanted. When, during an argument those many years ago, she told him never to make contact again, he agreed, even though he missed them both terribly.

Although we can't make up for lost years, when truths surface we can gain a new perspective, and often that is all it takes to make a major difference in how we view any situation and how we continue to live life. If I had a dollar for every "I never knew that" after someone has researched an area where doors formerly locked could now open, I would be up there financially with Bill Gates. For David, the change at work was profound: learning that all things are connected and that he couldn't separate work from home, David eventually transformed his persecutor pattern and reinvented himself. He became a visionary leader who is now a senior VP in his company.

BREAKING FREE

Don't Bring It to Work takes you through the same coaching process I have used to help David and thousands of others. When I began working with AstraZeneca, Microsoft, Novartis, and other leading Fortune 500 companies, and when I began facilitating Total Leadership Connections, our highly successful leadership program, I determined that there are three main steps for becoming aware of patterns and finding the way **OUT**:

- **OBSERVE** your behavior to discern underlying behavior patterns.
- **UNDERSTAND** and probe deeper to discover the origins of these patterns.
- **TRANSFORM** by taking actions to change your behavior.

In following these three steps, you are essentially reconnecting with your deepest past in a way relevant to your present challenges. You do a variation of an organizational GAP analysis, on yourself! After first identifying your current behavior patterns, you proceed to observe and analyze in considerable detail the origins of these patterns in your earlier experience. You become aware of how not just family but also culture and crises impact the choices you make day in and day out. Then you make a conscious commitment to change what no longer works. You set up a clear and actionable plan to close the gap between how you behave today and how you would like to behave. What is exciting and of great benefit is your capacity to transfer this learning to help your direct reports, your colleagues, and even, if you choose, those to whom you report. The result: deep changes in individuals and organizations that enhance strengths and eliminate barriers to success.

This book is designed to make the process of overcoming your stubbornly ingrained behavior patterns as simple and straightforward as possible. The three chapters in Part One help you understand the importance of viewing all of life from a systems perspective. You begin to explore the connections between family background, cultural influences, and sudden unexpected occurrences that constitute bona fide crises. All these milestones, all these overt as well as the subtle life markers, impact your professional as well as personal life. Then you can connect the dots to understand how these situations apply to your workplace behavior.

The two chapters in Part Two take you through the process of recognizing specific patterns in your behavior, exploring the roots of these patterns, and taking action steps to transform them. You have an opportunity to learn about the newest research in psycho-neurology. You see how early attachment and relationship patterns have a profound and lasting influence on each of us and on future generations. I describe the thirteen most common workplace patterns and show how you can transform them—using a proprietary process called Sankofa Mapping™. You are given a detailed outline of what to do and how to make this mapping process valuable for your career.

The three chapters in Part Three explore how, as you develop a new sense of self, you can mentor others and how an organization can grow. This is "where the rubber meets the road." You learn to become a change agent who can handle the underlying anxiety that accompanies the chaotic environment of modern-day business. Then you are in a strong position not just to survive but to thrive.

Throughout the book, colorful stories and cultural examples will inspire you, and exercises and probing questions will lead you carefully through an adventure that just might change your life. Coming to grips with your entrenched patterns might seem a formidable task. I won't lie to you—it is. Changing behavior in anything beyond a superficial way requires discipline, time, and commitment. As the narratives you encounter will reveal, it *is* possible to change. And when you do, the rewards are amazing—more honest communication, better relationships, optimized teamwork, better financial results, and, of course, the deep fulfillment that comes with living a more authentic life.

I have, understandably, changed both the names and industries of those whose stories I tell. I want to honor their privacy and also take this moment to let them know how much respect and appreciation I have for their commitment to growth and their willingness to be pioneers in their teams and organizations.

You can never leave home without your family patterns. Yet please remember that not all patterns are negative; in fact, some are the keys to a person's success. **What you want to do—what this book will help you do—is harness and refine the critical patterns that can help you achieve optimal results and break or transform those that block you.** Continue to build on the patterns that reinforce such virtues as respect, courage, tenacity, and altruism. Learn to prevent those that derail or ruin your life. Those are the ones you don't have to bring to work. Albert Einstein defined insanity as "Doing the same things over and over and expecting different results." Turn to the next chapter, and you'll begin to learn how to do things differently for a change—and to get the professional and personal results that spell success.

PART ONE

THE HOME-WORK CONNECTION

CHAPTER ONE

RELATIONSHIPS AT WORK AND AT HOME

Other things may change us, but we start and end with family.
—ANTHONY BRANDT

Few things seem more different than the worlds of work and home. We talk of "work-life balance" as if work and life were chunks of matter on opposite sides of a balance scale. We talk about "taking refuge" at home when work becomes stressful, and "losing ourselves in our work" when problems break out at home. Sometimes we don't talk at all, as when we consciously limit how much we reveal about our private lives to our colleagues or bosses, and about our work challenges to our spouses or partners.

From the standpoint of relationships, though, work and home are not nearly as different as they seem. Work teams and families both constitute *systems of relationships among individuals.* There are important differences—for instance, you cannot choose your family, whereas you may be lucky enough to choose your work team. (Think about it for a moment: you can have "ex-bosses," "ex-direct reports," even "ex-spouses," but you cannot have an "ex-mother," only one you choose to steer clear of. Nor can you have an "ex-father," only one you haven't talked to in years.)

Families and work groups are structurally similar, and the day-to-day workings of both groups are fundamentally the same. It's not surprising then that home and work relationships flow quite naturally into one another. Although we gain autonomy as we grow into adulthood, we don't dispose of our old relationship systems. Rather, we layer a new web of relationships—those of our work team—on top of the original family system. Family was the place where we first learned how to exist in relation to others. It was our original organization. So it makes sense that we would repeat what we learned there in our new work systems. Unfortunately, very often the result is that the now outmoded family patterns we have never addressed flare up consistently and automatically in our professional lives.

A Workplace System That Wasn't Working

The underlying similarity between work and home is never as apparent as when problems knock on the office door. Consider the situation at Bellville, Inc., a Pennsylvania-based electronics company. The firm's CEO, Martha Bellville, had a habit of making deals without considering what it would take for the firm to deliver on them. Content to regard herself as the dashing, high-flying entrepreneur, she left it to Barry Waldman, her COO and second in command, to make it all happen. Barry did what he could, yet the firm found itself in a constant state of crisis. Everyone was struggling to make good on Martha's promises to customers while forever lacking the necessary infrastructure.

The need to keep up with Martha exacted an especially heavy toll on Barry. Week after week, he flew to San Francisco to attend to an ailing business unit. The head of this unit, Wanda, seemed determined to make a bad situation even worse. Although a competent manager, she was rebellious by nature and was reacting to the challenges facing the company by spreading rumors and refusing to follow company policies. As time passed, Barry became convinced that she needed to be fired. Yet when he tried to discuss the problem with Martha, she ignored him, saying that she was too busy, that it was his job to deal with the day-to-day operation of the business. Barry left these encounters with a sinking feeling in his stomach, aware on some level that he wasn't addressing the real issues.

Barry hit an internal wall. He couldn't figure out why he stayed with the status quo and felt helpless to change the situation.

He continued cleaning up messes created by Wanda, yet he was never making any real headway. People around him were frustrated. Customers were furious about poor performance, pulling contracts from the firm. On the home front, Barry's wife was complaining that he was never home and that his kids no longer knew him. Barry wanted to do the right thing, yet he was stuck and never seemed able to find the words to talk with his boss.

Consulting to Bellville, I realized quickly that the underlying structure of its leadership team resembled nothing so much as an ineffective family. It had the irresponsible parent (Martha), the rebellious sibling (Wanda), and the good sibling expected to pick up the pieces (Barry). Doing some digging, I learned that the relationship dynamic playing out in Bellville's leadership team was actually more or less identical to that of Barry's family. When Barry was growing up, his father was always working, and his mother kept busy organizing charity events. Barry's younger brother was rebelling and getting into drugs, but every time Barry went to his mother, she made excuses for his brother and told Barry, "I'm sorry, dear, I have a meeting." Barry spent his time keeping his brother out of trouble, and when Barry's parents got divorced, he was saddled with even more responsibility, taking care of his functional, although quite troubled, brother.

I'll say it again: families and work teams are not so different after all. Reflect on some of the families you know and then think hard about your work team. Don't people in your work system play off each other the way people do in family systems? Don't you yourself behave with certain colleagues the way you might with siblings or a parent or a child?

To improve the performance of any poorly functioning group, whether a family or a business team, you cannot simply focus on the behaviors of one or two apparent troublemakers. **Nobody's behavior exists independently of his or her interpersonal relationships**. Therefore, you need to go beyond the level of the individual and examine the inner workings of the group using a systems approach. In business, just as it is in families, real, meaningful, profitable change is possible only if we start to see work teams not as a collection of disconnected parts but as living organisms that are unique and complex.

Not You and Me and He and She, but We

What is a system exactly? By one account, it is a "collection of parts . . . integrated to accomplish an overall process." The key word here is "integrated": systems are interactive; everything depends on everything else. For example, the way doctors and nurses behave in a hospital emergency room is a system. If the experienced head nurse calls in sick, all of a sudden the team starts working in a very different way. Take away the patients, and the system stops functioning altogether.[1]

Systems are not just found among social groups like work teams or families. There are biological systems, such as the human body, food chains, and the planetary environment as a whole. There are also mechanical systems—an airplane or a dishwasher—and hybrid human-mechanical systems, such as a person typing at a computer. Local and national economies are highly complex, multidimensional systems, as are state bureaucracies, supply-chain arrangements in multinational corporations, and even large networks of friends on such Web sites as Facebook or MySpace or business networks like LinkedIn.

If systems are so prevalent, how come books about workplace issues seldom talk about them? The answer is that business is still largely shaped by analytic thinking, an intellectual orientation marked by a tendency to understand living things not by looking at the organic wholes that they are, but by separating them into their component parts. Since the Renaissance, Western thinkers have tended to break the world into stark opposites—good and bad, reason and emotion, public and private, and, of course, home and work. Such thinking has given rise to everything from the Industrial Revolution to the medical profession to the division of school days into discrete hour intervals. Ever notice that corporations are broken down into supposedly distinct functions (marketing, operations, finance, and so on), each of which is in turn broken down into its own subspecialties and competencies? That's mechanistic thinking at work.

Most business leaders aren't trained to think systemically, but rather in dichotomies or dualities. When problems occur, we resort to a predictable, analytic response: sort and judge, sort and judge, sort and judge. Often we put the spotlight on the situation or the task in question or on a specific "problem" person rather than on interactions or the larger system. And it's not only business leaders who do this. Is crime a problem? Throw the drug dealers in jail, but don't address the broken homes and urban blight that produced both them and their customers. Test scores down? Crack down on underperforming schools, but don't address the larger picture, which includes stress placed on children in our fast-paced world.

Analytic thinking seems to be a natural way of understanding reality, but if you look at world civilizations, you encounter quite another orientation. Societies have for thousands of years paid homage to organisms, systems, and the connectedness of the universe. African, aboriginal Australian, and native American cultures have long taken for granted that it takes an entire community to raise a child. The ancient Chinese yin-yang symbol represents the connection of all things as a circle with dark and light segments, each containing a smaller circle of the other color to indicate that there is always some positive in the negative as well as some negative in the positive. Buddhist philosophy holds that there are no divisions and that we contain everything in the world within us. In Western society, systems thinking flourished prior to the Renaissance, showing up in the medieval idea of the "Great Chain of Being" that linked animals, humans, and the divine. Earlier still, Aristotle captured systems thinking in his famous saying, "The whole is more than the sum of its parts."[2]

What does this have to do with the way you and I behave at work? Everything! After centuries of slumber, the older, systems-oriented mode of thinking has more recently been making a comeback in the West. During the early 1940s, Harvard sociologist Pitirim Sorokin argued that industrial societies needed to transform themselves by developing a more integrated, holistic, and systemic approach to the world—what he called "creative altruism."[3] In 1956, the Society for General Systems Research was established on the premise that all phenomena can be viewed as a web of relationships; that all systems—electrical, biological, or social—have common patterns, behaviors, and properties; and that studying and understanding connections rather than just focusing on isolated units yield a dynamic understanding of our complex world.[4]

During the 1960s, systems thinking began to enter into discussion about school reform. Open classrooms began to appear. Teams of teachers worked more fluidly with groups of youngsters of different ages, and the mechanistic conventional conveyor belt that moved students from grade to grade gave way to organic "pods" in which interest groups would learn together.[5]

Education has since fallen back on more regimented, analytic approaches, but systems orientations have begun to peek through in disciplines as diverse as physics, history, medical science, climatology, and yes, even business management. Physics has given us the butterfly effect, the notion that small variations in the initial conditions of a system (a butterfly flapping its wings) can lead to tremendous long-term changes in a system (the emergence of a tornado in a faraway place).[6] Western medicine has seen the rise of cross-disciplines that look at the whole body, such as in complementary and preventive medicine. As newspaper headlines report almost daily, ecologists and climatologists have been hard at work charting the connections between seemingly unrelated things, such as carbon emissions in Indiana, urbanization in China, and melting glaciers in Antarctica.

In her book *Leadership and the New Science,* Margaret Wheatley encourages leaders to break down artificial boundaries and think more expansively and creatively; this is one of the first attempts (and there have only been a few) to apply systems thinking to organizations.[7] Shoshana Zuboff's book *In the Age of the Smart Machine* suggests that new choices can come about only by considering the interface of systems—historical, psychological, and organizational—as we include new technology in our lives.[8] Daniel Pink's book *A Whole New Mind* explores the systemic requirements for leaders as we move into the "conceptual age"; he points out, "The future belongs to a very different kind of person with a very different kind of mind—creators and empathizers, pattern recognizers, and meaning makers."[9]

If you know to look for it, you can also find systems thinking percolating up in popular culture. In 1985, the music industry's supergroup USA for Africa embraced a holistic, systems mind-set by releasing the song "We Are the World" in support of famine relief in Ethiopia. Since then we've seen any number of similar altruistic efforts, including Hands Across America (addressing hunger and homelessness) and Live Earth (global warming awareness). Systems thinking and the notion of seemingly disconnected events fitting together like pieces of a puzzle are also visible in such films as Academy Award–winning *Crash* (2005) and *Babel* (2007), which show the unfolding of apparently unrelated but linked stories. Of course, the emergence of social networking as the dominant force in Internet development has only just begun. And, most significant, systems thinking has as of this writing become virtually omnipresent in consumer culture, with global warming renewing popular environmental awareness, and companies responding by adopting sustainability practices and investing in corporate social responsibility initiatives—all in the interest of showing a heightened global consciousness.

FAMILIES AS SYSTEMS

As we've seen, systems thinking is turning out to have wide applications across fields of endeavor, and it has proved especially promising in helping us understand relationships between people. As scientific experiments and other empirical data confirm, interactions within groups cannot be understood by looking at individuals alone; rather you must take the *system of relationships* itself as the primary unit of analysis. Nowhere has this been more clearly demonstrated than in relation to the family.

The discipline of family therapy, now decades old, is essentially the application of systems thinking to psychotherapy. Traditional, individual therapy became a viable force in the twentieth century due to the pioneer work of such luminaries as Sigmund Freud and Carl Jung. Initially the focus was on treating the inner life of individuals. By the 1950s, however, psychotherapists were beginning to understand that emotional health begins in the family system as a whole, as does emotional pathology. In one classic study, it was noticed that when adult schizophrenics returned home after successful treatment, they would revert back to inappropriate behavior and soon return to the hospital. In investigating why, researchers arrived at a surprising finding: craziness was like a virus that infected the entire family. When the patient began to recover, other "healthy" siblings became depressed and had marital or work issues. Sometimes parents developed health-related or psychiatric symptoms.[10]

The lesson? When it comes to our behavior and emotional lives, we don't exist outside our personal relationships.

Subsequent work confirmed that the larger family setting could profoundly affect the health and welfare of individuals within the system. At Children's Hospital in Philadelphia, Salvatore Minuchin began to treat children with emotional problems by exploring the demands placed on the child by parents and also the mixed messages being received. To test family health or dysfunction, the entire family was seated with menus from a local Chinese restaurant in front of them as therapists observed from behind a mirror. An analysis of the family members' interactions—how they ordered their meal; how they gave each other visual, verbal, and kinesthetic cues; and who the winners and losers were—turned out to provide a quick and useful guide to where the family as a whole was stuck and, consequently, what was causing problems for specific family members.[11] Think about your own family and the subtle negotiations that go into the seemingly simple task of deciding what to order from column A and column B.

Other family therapy pioneers broadened our understanding of the evolution of family systems over time and developed therapeutic methods for working with families. Psychiatrist Ivan Boszormenyi-Nagy, with whom I collaborated for years, explored how family heritage spanning generations could influence an individual's health or dysfunction in the present day. As he argued in his influential book *Invisible Loyalties,* families experience a continuous desire to balance and rebalance injustices from the past.[12] Another psychiatrist, Murray Bowen, who founded the Georgetown Family Center, helped develop the method of treating individuals by meeting with them and their families in a safe, contained environment to explore family conflicts. The exercise of talking directly to the primary people in their life and expressing underlying hurts turned out to be rigorous, challenging, and therapeutic for individuals in the family system.[13]

Over time, evidence has mounted that the family system plays an important role in determining whether an individual is healthy or sick. Undue stress from the family environment has been shown to help produce manic episodes among people with bipolar disorder.[14] Among patients suffering from panic attacks, an overly close family system seems to play a role. In these families, extreme dependence on other family members makes disputes difficult to resolve, causing problems in the individual's progress toward autonomy.[15] Similarly, people with eating disorders often grow up in families with excessive rigidity, overprotection, and unresolved conflicts.[16] And in a study performed by researchers at the University of North Carolina, an important correlation was even found between extreme workaholics and families with low levels of intimacy. As the researchers observed, the workaholics grew addicted to work because they were unconsciously trying to re-create the distanced, uninvolved type of family they had come to know as youngsters.[17]

One illness whose link with the family system is especially striking is depression. Millions take medications as treatment, yet family therapists find that excessive sadness is often rooted not merely in a chemical imbalance in the brain but also in childhood experiences that have gone underground in the family without the opportunity for expression. When Pulitzer Prize–winning author William Styron wrote *Darkness Visible,* his powerful memoir of depression, he placed much of the blame for his illness on his alcoholism and subsequent abstinence. Yet in the last few pages of the book, he traces the roots of his illness to the death of his mother from cancer when he was a child of thirteen. Having grown up at a time when nobody talked about cancer, Styron noted that he was unable to recall his reaction to his mother's death and that his family did not grieve because "the Styrons were a dignified family." Years later, he was finally able to talk about the permanent scar that his mother's death had left on his personality. "Some of my problems I think came from a continuing anguish over my mother's death," he said in a 1990 interview.[18]

Statistical analyses of health and wellness reveal that across measures of well-being, the unit of health is not the individual, but the family.[19] Family therapists routinely help patients with anorexia by giving them autonomy over their eating choices, setting up healthy boundaries between them and their family members, and helping the entire family realign and take responsibility for the illness.[20] In a Harvard Medical School study of recovering alcoholics, more than 50 percent of those who had used couples counseling as part of their treatment remained alcohol free after the first year, as opposed to only 30 percent of those who had received counseling on their own.[21] Another study found that depression sufferers who reported improved family functioning experienced shorter bouts of the disease.[22]

GETTING BACK TO WORK

Families clearly are relationship systems, but are work teams? The answer is, "Definitely!" Quantitative evidence is admittedly scarce, as few business coaches currently use systems approaches, and few business academics have even attempted to apply systems thinking to management issues. Yet the idea of the work team as a system makes a great deal of sense. Given that the family is the original and most fundamental social group, it's logical to think that its basic structure would carry over into other, derivative social groups, such as work teams. Everyday experience bears this out. Many of you have no doubt had mentors at work who remind you of your father or mother, mentees who remind you of your children, and colleagues who remind you of older and younger siblings. Many of you have also encountered conflicts and emotions at the office that closely resemble those you've experienced in earlier or present-day family settings.

Anecdotal evidence from my years of coaching teams has confirmed again and again that work teams are full-fledged systems on the family model. As I've seen, poorly functioning work teams suffer not just from the attitudes or behaviors of one or more "difficult" individuals but from a broader interactive system in which many people working together cause the problem.

Take the special case of family businesses. I often tell those I work with in family companies that they have signed up for the "accelerated program," where they learn about the family–work group connection all day, all the time! The Stern family had for three generations operated a business that now is the nation's leading distributor of industrial cleaning supplies. Grandfather Stern had one brother with whom he started the door-to-door business. There were lots of arguments over who worked harder or brought in more money. As it turned out, resentments between them carried over across the generations, with grandsons in the now very profitable business continuing to argue over who works harder. An anxiety-filled work environment emerged in which unresolved relationship issues and destructive pressures continued to build to the breaking point until recent interventions helped the family reinvent themselves.

Even in nonfamily businesses, the situation is similar: poorly functioning work teams reflect not just the problems of individuals but a breakdown in what turns out to be a larger system of relationships among team members. At the U.S. division of a multinational technology firm I consult to, morale was at an all-time low. Employees had little trust in senior management; they perceived a schism between their leaders and units in other countries, and they felt that their leaders were sending mixed messages. Several strong performers left to work for a key competitor, and more people than usual were on short-term sick leave. What was going on?

If you listened to Brandon, the American unit's VP of sales, you'd think that the problem was with his big boss, the firm's global CEO. "You can't take him seriously," Brandon told his colleagues off-line. "So many of these guys in global just don't get it. They're worthless." The more interviews I conducted, the more I realized that Brandon's reactive behavior was a key source of the problem. He dominated meetings, holding court and consistently plotting to overthrow the powers that be. As I dug in, I realized that you couldn't pin the blame on Brandon alone. His seditious rhetoric was outrageous and counterproductive, yet his direct reports were so conflict averse that they didn't call him on it. Behind the worsening morale problems was a system that included both out-of-control egotism and, just as important, *collusion* in the egotism.

Keep in mind, ineffective systems aren't unique to senior-level work teams. At a call center for a major hotel chain, productivity was plummeting along with morale. The problem? Unhealthy dynamics in the relationships linking call center personnel. Donna and Stan were at each other's throats. Stan was telling everyone in the office what a bad person Donna was after she chose someone else to help her on a team project. Donna wallowed in self-pity, complaining constantly about how much abuse she was taking from Stan.

Rather than solve the problem, Bob, the call center manager, was spending much of his time hearing Donna's complaints. He had been to a program about "empathic listening," and that was what he thought he should do—listen. He was not aware that he had become part of a system, the Stan-Donna-Bob persecutor-victim-rescuer triangle. Life in the office was unbearable, and if nothing happened soon, there would be a mass exodus of employees. Only the intervention requested by senior management averted what would have been a catastrophic failure of the relationship system.

Which brings me to an important point: when work team systems function poorly, the costs are potentially huge, and not merely for the organization. Unhappiness at the office can leave the individuals involved suffering severe emotional and physical symptoms, just as problems in a family can. Stress and anxiety are major issues. For years, Maggie had worked at a commercial landscape company as the CEO's right-hand woman. Steve, her boss, acted like a dictator; the entire staff bent over backward to keep him happy. Maggie wanted to speak up about this unhealthy dynamic, but she was too afraid. As the months passed, the stress continued to build, and she was feeling pressure from other team members to shake things up. She suffered sleeplessness, anxiety, and constant headaches, for which her doctor prescribed powerful pain medications. As still more time passed, Maggie knew she was overdoing it on the medication and had to make a radical change. Finally her boss made one demand too many. Her fear of taking a strong stand won, and rather than face him, she decided to quit.

She took time to "get her head on straight" and explore why she was so intimidated at work. She got herself a gift—an executive coach—and began to explore the territory between her work situation and her family history. She remembered the childhood vow she had made to keep her family happy when her despondent father came home from having lost his job. She realized she had become the consummate pleaser, and the puzzle pieces began to fit together. She soon joined another company; her ailments improved, and medication was no longer necessary. She started to speak up more effectively and used the important lesson from her coach that **" 'No' is a complete sentence!"**

THE PATH TO CHANGE

Now let's address the critical question of how to *change* ineffective behavior at work. As leaders and managers, we're tempted to blame a specific individual, group, or situation when poor quality occurs on a work team. The individual becomes the sacrificial lamb, and once the sacrifice is complete, the management feels some satisfaction that it has dealt with the difficulty quickly and decisively. There's only one problem: the blame game gets you nowhere. The only way to turn dysfunction around in a deep and lasting way is to transcend blame and to review and analyze the whole system. Such analysis inevitably yields some surprising truths, including the hidden responsibility of people who seem to be "good guys." Only when the unspoken truths come out and when team members appreciate each other's perspectives more fully can the team begin to modify counterproductive habits and open the way for a new culture of change.

At Gromwell, Inc., executives were struggling to address problems that had cropped up in one of the assembly lines. The leadership team wanted to pin all the problems on one of the production managers and request his firing. Yet the CEO refused. Addressing the leadership team's concerns, he put Clayton, the production manager, on a performance improvement plan. At the same time—and this is crucial—he required that the executive team take ownership and work with Clayton to remedy the situation. In effect, this CEO understood the need to adopt a systems approach rather than a mechanistic mind-set when tackling problem behavior. In this case, the result was a healthier, better-functioning team built on a shared sense of connectedness. As the VP of sales remarked, "I was as responsible as Clayton for what happened. I talked about him but never to him. And I've already righted that wrong by offering to spend some time on the shop floor and get to hear what the folks are saying. As an added benefit, I've been thinking about my three kids. Do I really tell them what I think? Even there, I tend to talk at them rather than engage in an honest dialogue. It's a new day for me on every front."

As I mentioned earlier, a defining characteristic of systems is that a change in any one element begins to change the system as a whole. One corollary of this is that individuals have the potential to initiate positive change in the whole team simply by addressing their own unhelpful patterns.

Shirley, the executive director of a children and youth agency, had a very bad habit. She would repeat unflattering information she had heard about a colleague to someone else, rather than going right to the source. A dynamic was created that led to incredible negativity in the office. When Shirley came to her employees with juicy tidbits, no one would ever question her. After all, she had her PhD and had taught at a prestigious university.

However, Shirley needed help. Her staff was showing disrespect toward each other, slacking off at work, and not supporting her efforts. They knew something was "off," yet couldn't put a finger on the discomfort. Shirley had a great way of being a confidant. She would always start her gossip by saying, "Now let's keep this just between us, okay?"

The icy atmosphere at the agency was affecting the clients. The parents, who were in their own turmoil, were reticent to open up. The youngsters were more rebellious than normal. The system was breaking down, and lots of employees were calling in sick with this or that virus. People were infected physically and emotionally. Initially Shirley was the heroine and would attempt to smooth the ruffled feathers of her staff, without any clear understanding that she was the culprit.

Sometimes the truth has a way of hitting us over the head with a velvet hammer. Here is what happened. One of the fathers who had had a serious drug problem in the past was doing quite well and was having supervised visits with his three children in foster care. Then he slipped. He walked into the agency obviously high. No one could calm him down. He became loud and demanded to see the "bigwig" in charge. Shirley met him in the visitation office.

They sat on little kid stools with toys all around. They eyed each other until Shirley finally told him his behavior was inappropriate. He looked over and said, "Who are you calling inappropriate? Like the pot calling the kettle black, huh Dr. Shirley?" Well, who knows what really sets truth in motion. This was one of those serendipitous moments that defy explanation.

Rather than challenge him, her usual style of always being the expert, Shirley asked him what he meant. Talk about out of character! He became the teacher and told her how many times he had sat in the reception room and heard the case workers complain about how they thought Dr. Shirley's behavior was inappropriate. "They all know you split them against each other, and they are all afraid to talk to you. Why do you do that? I know why I get high, and I'm working on it. Why do you want them to hate each other?" And then this man who was just learning about his inner demons offered her a window into her own. "You know what, Dr. Shirley; I think that is your way to keep power. Divide and conquer. I saw it all the time in prison. So who is inappropriate?" And with that he got up to leave. How do we measure time? Her life changed in that moment when she shook his hand and said, "Thank you."

Until then Shirley thought she had all the answers. Coaching had been fruitless. After all, she was the expert. She helped other people; no one was needed to help her. Yet that man in that moment had become part of the larger life system, not just a client who needed help but a human being who through his own difficult journey was able to cut past the rhetoric and go to the heart of the matter.

It took courage for Shirley to share this story with her staff, yet if they were to fulfill their mandate to the community, this was one of those "physician, heal thyself" moments. Shirley told her staff that she was committed to digging deeper to find out why she was so in need of power. PhD or no PhD, she had skated over the surface of her life, and it was finally catching up with her. When she took responsibility, magic started to happen. Her relationships with other team members improved tremendously. Having dispensed with the negativity and unspoken resentments, the whole staff started to function more smoothly. They most appreciated being treated more honestly. With distractions out of the way, the agency has succeeded in many of its ongoing initiatives and become a much more viable force in its community.

Although the process of transforming a team dynamic can take time, there are also inspiring epiphanies in which team members almost instantly realize their truths, communicate them to each other, and elevate relationships to a whole new level.

That happened with the management team at a large scientific instrument company. Leslie, the regional director, had no idea that she was seen as an overbearing micromanager until Andrew, the tall, bespectacled finance guy, snapped at a meeting. Breaking his no. 2 pencil in half, he mumbled, "That's it. I can't take another minute of being treated like a five-year-old. I half expect her to wipe my face or my ass." His "mumble" was just loud enough! Everyone in the room was astonished, most of all Leslie.

During the next several weeks, as she confronted the possibility that Andrew would leave, she started taking an honest look at her behavior. She realized she had long micromanaged her reports and even her peers. It was an eye opener.

Several on the leadership team, headed by Andrew, asked if an off-site could be facilitated, and Leslie agreed. I was asked to put the program together and lead the team through this important day. The core of the meeting was a short monologue by Leslie about her new learning, titled "Micromanaging and Mentoring." She acknowledged what she had recently learned, and related how her obsession with micromanaging had brought her discomfort throughout her life, in ways she was just beginning to understand. She did not need to go into the family history that had caused the frightened little girl to become an adult "control freak." It was enough for her colleagues to know that she had learned about herself. "Alcoholism," she said, "would have been easier to spot than micromanagement, yet the broad systemic effects were similar—lack of communication, poor results, lessened creativity, and backroom discussions that wasted time and energy."

The group was riveted. None had ever heard a boss be more candid. This was truth telling from the gut, without blame, judgment, or attack. Then Andrew spoke. Watching his boss tell the truth gave him courage too. Speaking a few short sentences, Andrew was able to tell Leslie how much he valued what she had said. Leslie stood up and took out a handful of no. 2 pencils, sharpened and ready for writing. "I'd like to end this meeting by passing the baton to each of you. I commit to being a more effective leader and giving each of you way more room to do your jobs effectively and efficiently. No more looking over your shoulder." One by one, each executive received a pencil from Leslie. Although team members would spend more time processing the meeting and sorting out their own issues, the hardest work had been done, and they were set on course to do great things.

Growth such as Leslie's gives me hope. As a consultant who has worked with many teams in dozens of companies, I'll be the first to admit that it doesn't always turn out like this. Not everyone is prepared or able to acknowledge their unhelpful ways of relating and take steps to overcome them. In those cases, work teams remain as stuck as the overly enmeshed family of an anorexic whose parents refuse to take their share of responsibility.

So what should you do? If you are ready to change and other key members are not, there sometimes is no alternative to leaving the firm and seeking out a team with a healthier, more functional relationship system. Yet before you take that final step, stop and consider the role you might be playing in the existing drama.

Where families and work teams are concerned, systems thinking beats slice-and-dice analytic thinking any day. Systems thinking is at once common sense, a spiritual truth, and a moral imperative. We're all connected on this planet, in our offices, and in our families. Our home life and our work life are connected, as are our past and our present. The more we can begin to understand and act on our own membership in a multitude of overlapping systems, the happier and healthier our lives will be.

TAKEAWAYS

- Families and work teams are structurally and functionally similar: both are living systems in which each individual plays an indispensable role.
- Systems thinking makes everyone accountable, and there is no one person to blame.
- When one person is willing to be authentic, he or she gives space for others to risk telling their truth also.
- Lessons we learned about how to relate in our first organization, the family, carry over into the workplace system.
- Considering the entire work team when trying to improve performance works best.

CHAPTER TWO

UNDERSTANDING BEHAVIOR AT WORK AND AT HOME

No diet or exercise can get rid of your emotional underbelly
—SEEN ON A T-SHIRT IN BALI

Thomas's smooth manner and skill at branding had catapulted his company to the top rung of the apparel industry. They had also earned him a long-awaited promotion from VP of marketing to CEO. Thomas went into his new office with great fervor to "clean house and get things working on a faster, more efficient level." Yet this agenda wound up driving Thomas to the edge of a precipice.

Moving to bring a fresh start to the firm, Thomas passed over several of his loyal, long-term marketing colleagues for promotions to his executive team, hiring instead younger, "hotshot" talent from outside. This elicited strong feelings of confusion and betrayal within the organization. Gossip and griping broke out, and one senior colleague in marketing filed an age discrimination lawsuit.

While the suit was pending, Thomas would see his old friend in the hallway. They nodded as if nothing was out of place, yet internally they were both burning. Thomas's once trusted colleague began to criticize the decisions of the new CEO—not out loud, more with subtle innuendos. As old friends took sides with his embittered colleague, Thomas began to feel depressed and victimized, asking, "Why is this happening to me?" Meetings were a living hell, and he found himself adrift. He felt lonely and abandoned and started to have lunch brought into his office so that he didn't have to face people. He lost confidence.

When I first met Thomas, he was willing to admit that "cleaning house" might not have been such a good idea. But why had he so vigorously pursued it? Thomas didn't know—it certainly hadn't been part of the firm's long-term strategy. A little digging made the invisible visible and brought out some important truths. As a child, Thomas watched his mother move through three marriages, their living situation improving each time. To help ease the transitions, his mother would talk with her son about the path to success, exhorting him to "always leave the past behind, move on, ignore the old, and upgrade, upgrade, upgrade." Assuming the CEO position, Thomas heard his mother's voice resonating in his head. He had seen her philosophy work, and he therefore took for granted that it was always desirable to clean house and to have better "stuff." He too had become the smart and successful one.

We like to think we are rational as leaders, yet the fact is that we don't always tailor our actions to the actual demands of a situation. Instead, we fall back on old ways of responding that are emotionally laden and sometimes horrendously counterproductive. Adopting behavior we first encountered in our families, we do the same thing over and over again—even if it kills us. We remain imprisoned by our pasts, and it is in this unhappy sense that we often bring our families to work.

Family patterns aren't merely a logical possibility in the workplace, as Chapter One indicated; they are an ever-present reality. This chapter explores why, by taking a close look at how people structure their behavior in and across systems. In a family system, a person's actions are shaped by the character roles they naturally play with relatives. Over a period of time, performance of these roles prompts people to adopt the same behavior over and over again, usually without realizing it. When children leave their family system, they invariably transport their accustomed role into the new work systems they enter. This can go on for years and span entire careers, often to the individual's own detriment.

In Thomas's case, role playing modeled by a mother was transmitted to a child, who in turn took it to work upon reaching adulthood. For other professionals, siblings might provide the model for the behavior. Whatever the case, problems arise when unconscious role playing that might have served a purpose in an old, outmoded system disrupts the present-day system in which we operate.

Family Roles

Before we can make sense of role playing in the workplace, we need first to spend some time unraveling the complexities of role playing at home.

First are the roles of parent and dependent child. From the day we are born, our parents provide food, shelter, and clothing, and we are expected to follow their direction and play the role of the dependent children we are.

Then there are sibling roles. When you were growing up, you were probably stuck with a label, such as "the smart guy" or "the pretty girl" or "the rebellious one." Many of us play the role of being popular, athletic, perfect, dramatic, shy, or devious. These are sibling roles, and they exist in every family—nuclear, single parent, adoptive, extended, same sex, even foster. Sibling roles serve as survival mechanisms that help the family system maintain stability and balance, especially during stressful periods. Children with immature or ineffective parents, for instance, become the authorities at home, making decisions and taking care of every-one. These "parentified" children are often seen as the "good ones" or the "heroes." By contrast, the "problem child" or the "scapegoat" gets blamed for even minor infractions—a move that serves to excuse parents from looking at their own personal frail-ties. All roles have their own cost-benefit ledgers.

How exactly do parent-child and sibling roles arise in families? Let's start at the beginning. The family's primary function is to ensure the survival of its members. Observing our parents' verbal and nonverbal cues and also those of our siblings and other rela-tives, we embrace roles in relation to others inside and outside the family. These ways of being take root and deepen as we grow. We are increasingly expected to help with tasks necessary for survival, whether by performing chores or taking part-time jobs. We are also expected to help with other key family functions, such as providing nurturing and comfort and negotiating relationships with neigh-bors and others in the community. Such varied activities and our increasing autonomy in carrying them out enable us to practice our ways of being, to extend sibling and child roles when interacting with new people in our lives, and to experiment with new roles.

To understand how early and deeply roles are engrained, take the example of my three-year-old granddaughter. With her light curly hair and sparkling hazel eyes, Arielle is an unusually beautiful child. (And that's not just the grandma in me talking.) People come up on a daily basis and say, "Oh my God, you're so beautiful!"

I once asked Arielle what "beautiful" means, and she said, "It means pretty!"

"Well, what does 'pretty' mean?"

She shook her head. "I don't know, but that's what I am."

In other words, my granddaughter is scarcely out of diapers and already she's been labeled "the beautiful one." Her parents ask us to acknowledge her skills and her caring nature so that she won't identify herself exclusively with her pretty face, seeing her looks as the entire basis for her self-worth as a person. Her role as the beautiful one would become as much a part of who she is as her name, and that would limit her.

Those around us are not alone in defining the roles we take on; cultural norms are important, first and foremost in relation to gender. In many societies, familial roles are rigidly structured along gender lines, with boys and girls shaping their behavior differently in preparation for the distinct roles they will later be expected to play as wage earners and mothers. Traditional Japanese society allowed for property, social standing, rights, and duties to be passed down from the father to the oldest son. As a result, males today in Japanese families remain the key wage earners, while women bear full responsibility for raising children, caring for the elderly, and managing the family finances.[1] By comparison, traditional Cherokee Indian society had a matrilineal kinship system. Women dominated family life, the economy, and government in the tribe, enjoying rights and privileges unknown to their European counterparts. They served both as heads of household and as leaders in the community[2]—a very different culture and, as you might imagine, very different roles for children to perform within the family.

Our own culture is currently in the midst of a tremendous upheaval in gender norms. Power is shifting, and everywhere you look, family relationships are trending toward more equality between partners and more independence, power, and responsibility for the children. Men are able to express emotions more freely and to share household duties, women are more able to take on professional roles outside of the family, and children of both genders are able to make their personal desires known in ways unthinkable a generation or two ago.

At the same time, this loosening of gender norms prompts some people to pull back to the "family values" of the past. In their families, women continue to stay at home and submit to the control of their husbands, and more traditional sibling roles are assigned to boys and girls. What does all this mean for family roles overall? Simply this: no cultural consensus currently exists as to how boys and girls should behave. Family roles are roundly debated in magazines, films, national talk shows, and even presidential election campaigns. We are, as philosopher Jean Houston points out, "the people of the parenthesis"—caught between old family roles that no longer support us and new roles we are in the process of defining.[3]

It's worth noting that our families usually don't set out gender-specific family roles directly. Rather, we focus on certain specific gender stereotypes that percolate up within families and that are reinforced in literature, film, and television. The good girl; the saintly mother; the strong, silent type; the jock—these characters and many others like them intersect in our minds with our parent-child and sibling roles, inflecting them, giving substance to them, shaping their day-to-day expression. In playing out our family roles, we live out elements of these gender stereotypes, both in our eyes and in the eyes of others. The gender stereotypes we adopt follow us to the school and workplace; they even surface in our romantic relationships, serving as the formula for our role-playing behavior in our own families as adults.

Because gender stereotypes affect our sibling and parent-child roles so strongly, let's take a closer look at several of them:

- *The strong, silent type and the woman warrior.* Masculinity in our culture has traditionally been seen in terms of physical and emotional strength. The strong, silent type is someone who is always in charge; he acts decisively and succeeds with women.

John Wayne, James Bond, Harrison Ford as Indiana Jones, and, of course, Superman—these are but a few of the strong, silent types we know. A corresponding role, more common in recent years, is the woman warrior. She is in charge, able to make important decisions, and emotionally strong. She can cry, but she won't decompose into mush the minute trouble arises. Key examples: Oprah Winfrey, Hillary Clinton, Angelina Jolie, and Danica Patrick of NASCAR fame.

- *The bigshot and the modern goddess.* The bigshot is an arrogant, aggressive person who has all the trappings of success and will step on anyone to get what he wants. He rarely asks for advice, although he gives it freely. Gordon Gekko of the film *Wall Street* is a prime example from the 1980s; Donald Trump keeps the role relevant for today. On the other side of the fence, the modern goddess is defined by her beauty and sex appeal. She's the woman all the cosmetics companies, fashion magazines, and clothing stores salivate over. *The Devil Wears Prada* depicts the toll it takes on a person to become a modern goddess; Paris Hilton and Lindsay Lohan dramatize its excesses.
- *The jock and the cheerleader.* Who among us doesn't know stereotypical jocks and cheerleaders? Joe Namath and O. J. Simpson are classic jock "heroes," yet Namath's alcoholism and Simpson's public disgrace reveal the impossibility of living up to the role. Tom Brady of football's New England Patriots, with his model good looks and his glossy magazine cover shots, update the role in an era that has come to objectify men as well as women. Meanwhile, cheerleaders remain today what they always were: popular, attractive, always perky and happy. Doris Day practically invented the role during the 1950s and 1960s. Miley Cyrus as Hannah Montana is today's icon of cheer.
- *The buffoon-clown and the bimbo.* Clowns mean well and are lovable, yet they behave ineffectually, particularly when attempting household chores. Hardly anyone takes them seriously. *The Cosby Show, Everybody Loves Raymond, The King of Queens*—all these shows feature clowns in leading roles. As for bimbos, they giggle a lot and accomplish very little. The airhead, the dumb blonde, the Valley Girl—these throwaway women are light as air. Reality TV abounds with them, as do video games and, of course, pornography. One Internet game

called Miss Bimbo offers the following disclaimer: "We assume no responsibility or liability for any fashion faux pas, hairstyle disasters, or boob jobs incurred in real life as a result of playing the Miss Bimbo game."

As these examples suggest, gender stereotypes reflect our collective values at any given time. Buying into these values, we incorporate gender stereotypes into our own roles and the roles we assign to our children, parents, siblings, coworkers, and bosses. This is not an altogether beneficial habit. Although gender stereotypes do speak to elements of our real personalities, they are ultimately exaggerations that, when accepted uncritically, push us to extremes of behavior and to polarized positions of "too much" or "too little." To improve your performance at work and your personal happiness throughout your life, you need to move beyond the stereotyped characters with which you identified as a child. The point is not to jettison such characters wholesale, but rather to articulate new, more sophisticated expressions of them that allow for internal balance and harmony.

In discussing parent-child roles, sibling roles, and the cultural forces that inform them, we have restricted ourselves so far to modes of behavior that we can see and touch. Family members also typically embrace a number of *invisible* parent-child and sibling roles that reflect *hidden norms, emotions, assumptions, and expectations.* The whole family system colludes to keep the rules behind these roles quiet, taking care to affirm them subtly—in actions rather than words, and also in actions that *aren't* taken. Brought to the surface, the rules sound like this:

Invisible Role	Unspoken Rule
The Smart One	"You are expected to get all A's in school (even if you hate school)."
The Pretty Girl	"You are expected to be very popular and get invited to all the parties (even if you would rather study)."
The Weak One	"You are expected to fall and hurt yourself when participating in sports (even if you're well coordinated)."

Invisible Role	Unspoken Rule
The Funny One	"You are expected to make us laugh when we are down (even if you're feeling down too)."
The Bad One	"You are expected to get in trouble and never amount to anything (never mind if you're smart or talented)."
The Compliant One	"You are expected to follow all the rules (no matter if you disagree with them)."
The Good One	"You are expected to make dinner every night (even when you are overwhelmed and wish others would help you out)."
The Industrious One	"You are expected to have many outside jobs (even if you're super-stressed and just need to chill out for a bit)."
The Social One	"You are expected to meet all kinds of people (even if you'd like nothing better than to curl up at home with a good book)."

Of all the roles we play, the invisible ones are the ones that cause us the most difficulty, precisely because we are not aware of them. We can change our visible roles as our systems evolve and we enter new ones, but we can't do that with invisible roles. Residing on the edges of our consciousness, invisible roles torture us, like an annoying itch we can't scratch. Interacting with a colleague, we often find our buttons pushed, and we don't know why. After a testy encounter, we walk away saying, "What just happened here? Why did this person's behavior bother me so much?" And then we simply move on, not changing our invisible role, but rather acting it out again and again, suffering the same or worsening feelings of stress and alienation. Until we have a formula or process to make our family's unspoken expectations visible and audible, we can't do anything about them.

You might think that invisible roles persist only in families with obvious difficulties. On the contrary: *every family* places unspoken demands on its members. Even in apparently "healthy" families where everyone has dinner together, the kids get to school and sports on time, and the parents are happy and active in the community, there is an emotional underbelly, a place where people don't like to go because it's uncomfortable (at best) or painful (at worst).

Each family does whatever it must for the survival of the system. This is neither good nor bad; it is simply the way it is. Please note that in every family there is always some degree of positive ability to function; there are also the destructive places. Every family is both functional and dysfunctional! It is only when we gravitate to the extremes, either to pretend away "the dark side" or to live there all the time, that we get stuck. In this secret netherworld, invisible roles take shape, snarled in the tendrils of hurt feelings, mixed messages, lasting resentments, emotional triangles, power games, revenge, vindictiveness, competition, bullying, bribing, shaming, blaming, intimidation, and, in extreme cases, physical and sexual abuse. Because most family members avoid the emotional underbelly as if it were the Ebola virus, invisible roles enjoy free rein, surviving over decades, even jumping across the generations. The contents of the emotional underbelly continue to weigh us down until someone in the family has the skill, guts, patience, and stomach—no pun intended—to crawl down to its level and open it up for exploratory surgery.

Why do emotional underbellies exist? And if the invisible roles that they produce hurt us so much, why aren't we more successful at just laying those roles on the table so that they can be seen and dispensed with? The answer: survival and loyalty! When it comes to social systems, people seek constancy and familiarity. We are so dependent on the family for love and our personal identities that we're terrified on a deep, unconscious level to do anything that we perceive might put the family at risk. As I suggested earlier, all roles (including invisible ones) serve vital functions within a family system. They help form our self-concept and affirm our sense of connectedness. They also tend to keep the family structure stable over time. Even the "absent" family member is playing an important role by staying away so that others can either worry about or condemn him or her.

We remain loyal to the underlying directives of the family even if this limits our own personal development. For example, the great success of one family member is often balanced by the extreme failure of another member. This "see-saw" in families is called "polarized fusion" because both individuals are locked into defined roles at opposite ends of the spectrum. Although the successful one may "dress up" better than the failing one, when the layers of behavior are peeled away there is an underlying similarity of insecurity and resentment in both. We continue to play our invisible roles, even if this means holding dark secrets inside; living with feelings of frustration, alienation, and anger; and thwarting our own personal and professional growth.

The author Anaïs Nin once wrote, "And the day came when the risk to remain tight in a bud was more painful than the risk to blossom."[4] My hope for families as well as organizations is that we can go beyond surviving and begin to blossom. However, when it comes to invisible roles, many of us never see this day. Loyalty to the status quo is too strong. A client of mine, Mel, was on the verge of a bankruptcy as well as divorce. Through conversation with him, it emerged that he was tethered too closely to his mother. If only Mel could reform his long-standing role of the dutiful child, he might get some breathing room to work on his business and his marriage. So I asked Mel to call his mother and talk about creating better boundaries. Mel appeared hopeful about the situation, as if he were ready to risk becoming a blossom. He looked defeated when he later told me about the conversation. Mel's mother explained that when Mel's father died, she felt as if she could not go on, and had turned to him, her then seven-year-old son, as a source of strength. He remained her "lifeline" ever since. Before they hung up, Mel's mother said, "Darling, you are my life. Why can't you stay with me? You've always been such a good boy."

I went to open a window while Mel went to the bathroom. When he returned, he looked at me and said, "I have to stay and take care of my mother, and that is that." Mel's invisible role was too powerful. His need for stability in his family of origin had apparently overwhelmed all else, even his relationship with his wife and his success at work. As adults, we're so frequently trapped, held back, and often we don't even know why.

ROLE PLAYING IN THE WORKPLACE

Visible and invisible roles exist not only in families but also in other social systems, most notably work teams. Just as you have parent-child and sibling relationships in a family, so in work teams you have vertical, leader-follower bonds and lateral relationships with your peers. In both cases, you also have a *need* for role playing. As in the family, role playing at work serves to endow team members with a sense of identity and connectedness within the larger organizational culture. It also keeps the team together, especially in times of hardship or turmoil.

Within work team systems, evidence of parent-child roles is not hard to find. Take communication. If it's difficult for a child to talk to her parents, it's also difficult for her to tell her boss what she really feels or thinks. I often watch junior colleagues text-message each other across a room about their boss's behavior. "They're just like siblings," I think, "commiserating about their father's annoying behavior." It's especially interesting to watch employees complain when bosses disregard their judgment, discipline them, or hold them to protocols. Usually such complaints carry echoes of stern, overprotective parents. On a recent very long plane ride, the flight attendant and I began to talk about the weather and ended up talking about his boss. He complained to me about his new CEO, whom he called "the Banker." Morale was down, and not just because of economic issues. The CEO regarded his employees and everything else at the airline as mere dollars in the bank. "He has taken away any autonomy, and we have been infantilized," the airline attendant told me. "We can't even give out a free headset or complimentary drink without permission. Sometimes I think part of our uniforms should be a pacifier."

Just as we crave affirmation from parents, so too do employees crave affirmation from their bosses. One of the teams I worked with had two stellar years in a row. They topped all the lists for sales, community involvement, and excellence in customer service. At an off-site, someone remarked, "For all the great press, you would think that the CEO or someone from corporate would want to come out here to the Southwest and find out what our magic is."

My response was both a question and a dare: "If they aren't asking you, why don't you suggest they come out and pay a visit?"

The room went surprisingly silent. "You can't do that," someone murmured.

"Why not?"

"It's just not done."

"Says who?"

Another person piped in. "We could get fired or be derailed for promotion if we became that demanding."

I smiled. "Or maybe sent to your rooms and grounded for a week?"

The whole room erupted in laughter and then fell into an uncomfortable silence. A week later, the CEO, a personal friend, called me to ask what was up; he had received ten e-mails and as many voice messages requesting that he come to the Southwest territory. "It's all about growing up," I said. Martin, a very accomplished CEO, replied that he knew what I meant. From then on, he made it his own best practice to encourage the "children" to act as the adults they were and be more candid about what really mattered to them.

A widespread expression of parent-child roles in the workplace is paternalism, commonly defined as a way of treating or governing people in a fatherly manner, especially by providing for their needs without assigning any rights or responsibilities. Paternalism has a long history in business and politics, as any number of corporate and government welfare policies suggest. Although many such policies have withered away in recent years, individual bosses continue to approach their jobs by framing their responsibilities as "command and control." One president of a retail clothing company told me he made a habit of applying at the office the same rules that had worked at home. "I correct mistakes as I see them, teaching my employees the right way to behave. It works, except with my younger crew, the twenty-somethings. They don't listen too well. Can you believe that one guy, after being on the job for six weeks, asked for two weeks of vacation? When I said no, he got angry. I realized I would have to be the parent who would help him learn discipline and to 'color inside the lines,' because obviously his parents didn't teach him!" Such "tough love" tactics are a stark expression of paternalism.

Parent-child roles are not the only roles you see in the office; sibling roles also make a grand appearance. The smart one, the lazy one, the "hotty"—they're all there. The smart one is always telling everyone how to do his or her job better. The lazy one is always procrastinating on assignments. The hotty is the guy who "innocently" flirts to get attention.

Such behavior often strikes people who witness it as immature and out of place, not to mention tiring and even annoying. The behavior *is* immature and out of place—literally—and the reason is that the roles we play at work are almost always similar or identical to those we played in our families of origin. So why do we bring these familiar roles to work? Well, consider this: as children, we played our parts, and our relatives played theirs, and together we kept the lid on all the stuff that threatened to pull us apart. As adults, we make similar collective agreements to behave with our work teams in certain ways and also not to talk about undercurrents of conflicts and emotions. Therefore it is natural that we fall back on our older ways of being.

After all, we've already mastered our family roles. Some of these roles served us well since we were infants or toddlers. We might even feel that in parting with our scripted familial roles we would be left adrift without a compass. In other words, we bring our family roles to work for the same reasons that we maintain them in the family: because of our comfort with the status quo and our loyalty to the way it always was. Above all, we don't want to rock the boat because we need to survive emotionally. "Better safe than sorry" is a message we got from our parents and one we continue to tell ourselves.

In the case of invisible roles, we have no choice but to play them out. If we lived in a purely rational world, we would enter a work system and tailor new roles to fit the specific personalities and goals of the team. We'd spend time sizing up the new system and figuring out how it was similar to and different from our old system. Then we'd arrive at new roles that would allow us to meld seamlessly with our bosses and colleagues while also remaining true to our positive self-image. In the real world, however, most people are too bound up by fear and emotional attachments to undertake such an exercise. When conflict breaks out at work, we tend to fall back on our past behavior, regardless of how unhelpful it is given our present-day work relationships. Thus we invariably bump up against our colleagues. We push each other's buttons, we fail to perform at our best, and teamwork breaks down.

RELIVING AND MENDING OUR PATTERNS

When a role repeatedly makes the leap across the barrier between family and work systems, the behavior associated with it becomes what I refer to as an *ingrained pattern*. Please remember, not all patterns are negative. We have internalized patterns to access creativity, altruism, courage, and candor. We have all seen and can integrate patterns of respect, gentleness, inventiveness, and zest. At the same time, we have also internalized a number of defensive patterns linked to blame, shame, and egotism. These destructive patterns are the ones that give us the most trouble as we travel the rocky road of relationships and career development. What helped us survive as children is not necessarily the best way to handle situations as we grow into adulthood.

Destructive patterns are like old friends who have gone to the dark side yet still want to reside with us, guiding us and becoming a part of every encounter, even as they stifle us. As the years pass and our work teams come and go, patterns become our trademark, our branding. If a pattern could talk, it would sound rather like this:

> Hey, buddy, I have been with you since you were born, serving as part of your emotional arsenal. When life was tough, I kept you and your family from exploding. You are here now and still alive, so you can see that I'm worth keeping around. You may think you don't need me anymore, that you have outgrown me, and that you can be better and stronger without me. That's bullshit. You need me as much as I need you. I'm not letting you abandon me. Not without a fight. I'll play dirty if I have to, and I'll take you down with me. Don't you know anything about loyalty? Loyal to the future, you say. How dare you! I am your future, your self-fulfilling prophecy. I *am* you.

As I've learned in my career, individuals act on the advice of this "old friend" in their heads, even when the patterns cause great harm. Jack, a middle manager at a retail store, just couldn't shake the victim role. Feeling as if he could never please anyone, he didn't have the confidence to step up and request a promotion—so of course he didn't get one. By contrast, Dennis Koslowski did get promotions. Constantly running away from his impoverished childhood, the ex-Tyco CEO followed the pattern of behaving in ways that were self-indulgent and overentitled. This continued until Koslowski threw caution to the wind and lavished a $2 million birthday party on his wife using company funds. He wound up not merely jailed and disgraced but also financially ruined—just as impoverished as he had been when growing up.[5]

We don't need to have major traumas in our lives to become trapped by our patterns. Just the fact that we are alive and breathing is a great indicator that we will experience the residuals of these playful and dangerous dragons. In Native American lore, the trickster is always there to show you your vulnerabilities. In his classic book *Island*, Aldous Huxley talks about an island where parrots sit in trees saying, "Stay Awake."[6] Perhaps we should invest in a similar system for our work environments. The good news and the bad news are the same: no one is left out, there is no special club, we are all in it together. And that means everybody. From the guy taking your ticket on the toll bridge to the powerful motivational speaker who can pump up a crowd, we're all in it together.

I've seen it happen again and again. Controlled by patterns, otherwise outstanding performers feel "stuck" in their jobs and unhappy with their marriages. They feel that they are not living up to their potential, and it bothers them. Then there are the others who do get the promotions, yet it is never enough. No car, no house, no toy satisfies. They are the proverbial Pac-Man gobblers who consume whatever they can, yet the hungry ghost inside is always demanding more.

Greg Scott was a prominent business leader in the greater Boston area who had gotten in the habit of seeking gratification outside his marriage. When a scandal involving him and a prostitute hit the front pages of the Boston papers, Greg retreated to his family's compound on Cape Cod and drank himself into a stupor. His wife, Sandra, took the bottles of expensive liquor and flushed them down the toilet. Free from the media's hostile glare, the couple sat and talked—or rather, they shouted at each other about the shame Greg had brought to the family. As dawn light began to glimmer through the curtains and the reality of his situation hit him, Greg turned to Sandra and, with an edge of frustration in his voice, pointed to the numerous portraits of male ancestors lining the walls. "This is all crap. All I did was get caught. My father and my grandfather and the rest of these old guys were fucking prostitutes for generations. It's in my genes."

"Then why were you stupid enough to get caught?" Sandra asked.

Greg was silent for a long time. "Maybe I want to end the bullshit of all these corrupt ways of relating, and I just don't know how."

Greg finally did "end the bullshit" the following week. He overdosed on prescription drugs.

The great tragedy of this story is that Greg didn't have to suffer enchained by his patterns. By becoming aware of our old family roles, we can defuse them, realizing in the process personal growth as well as an easing of the very serious consequences wrought by dysfunctional relationships. And because a change in the role played by one person affects the system as a whole (and vice versa), individuals have the potential to change an entire poorly functioning system, whether at home or at the office.

Compare Greg's story with that of another pillar of the Boston community, Webster Hammed, a partner in a prestigious law firm. Webster had come from a family of privilege and had gone to the same schools as Greg, only five years later. In Webster's family, many relatives had played the role of denier, repressing conflict, propping up an outward veneer of happiness and confidence, and losing themselves in drugs and alcohol. Webster adopted this as his own life pattern, taking excessively long martini lunches and then embracing the seemingly sophisticated habit of snorting coke. Alarmed at the escalating addiction, his wife, Catherine, went to Webster's three law partners and asked for their help. They refused at first, insisting that it was none of their business.

Catherine did finally manage to convince the partners that it *was* their business to help Webster. On a cold, snowy Boston morning, the three partners, the head of HR, and an addiction specialist came to Webster's home. The intervention took several hours, the breakthrough coming when all four men, looking worn and relieved, admitted that yes, they all had a variation of a substance problem. Any of them, they agreed, could have been in the "hot seat" that Webster was now occupying. They all were drinking too much, and one of the others had also grown too comfortable with cocaine. With these truths out on the table, the partners each entered an outpatient rehab program that included their spouses.

All of them got back on track, coming to grips with their destructive patterns. Their families benefited, and so did the firm. Having survived and grown through their addictions, the senior partners came alive as leaders. Reevaluating their notions of success, they imparted a more hospitable, more compassionate, more human culture to the entire firm, making it a place where people enjoyed coming to work.

In other cases that I've seen, one person's effort to deal with his or her patterns has brought about a measurable improvement in an entire team's performance. Philip was a manager of Chinese descent whose pattern was to avoid problems. He would deflect conflict by telling his direct reports to check in with each other, read a book, get information from the Web—do anything so long as he was not asked to help solve the difficulties. His group was disillusioned, and productivity was mediocre.

When Philip and I worked together in a coaching relationship, I was initially struck by Philip's need to constantly tell me how "American" he felt. I never said much until one day when I asked how old he was when he learned English. His accent was pronounced, and often there were word slippages that, if he were not so embarrassed by them, would be quite charming.

Sometimes just one sentence at the right time can open the floodgates. I sat for the next hour and was swept into a tale of how family, culture, and crises interface to form a life.

Philip, born in mainland China, was three when his father, outspoken about the Communists, fled to Hong Kong. His mother received a message to meet her husband as soon as possible, because the border would be closed. A painful and difficult decision was made. She would take the oldest son, who was five, and the baby, who was seven months old. Philip would stay with his grandparents. He had a vague memory of crying and hugging. Later, when he was already in bed, his mother ran back into the house to get him and his few belongings, and he was whisked into the cart with his two brothers.

The story he heard when he was older was that because his mother came back for him, the border was already closed when they got there. She took the little money she had for the rest of the trip and gave it to a man who smuggled them across under a bale of hay and rags. They arrived in Hong Kong and were drawn into the throng of refugees. Philip remembered hearing his mother scream with delight when a neighbor saw her and took them to his father.

They ended up in Taiwan and eventually the United States when he was almost fourteen years old. His father, an engineer, was rarely around to care for his family that had now grown to seven children. They knew no English when they arrived in the United

States, and Philip and his siblings watched hours of television and practiced sounding like the cowboys on the shows they loved.

When he finished this story, Philip turned to me and said, "Well, that was a long-winded answer to how old was I when I learned English."

His resentment of China was intense. His love for his mother, who came back to retrieve him, was huge. His attitude toward his father was ambivalent. His father was steeped in Chinese philosophy and customs, so Philip pulled in the opposite direction by turning to his adopted home of America. He asked me not to talk about China and didn't want to discuss his roots again. I honored his request, and we focused on his business unit, which was just above the midpoint in sales at the midpoint of the year.

That was until the off-site. The entire team was actually functioning quite well by now, so this was more a quality pick-me-up than a serious makeover. During the meeting, Philip's team requested more personal mentoring from him. When we returned to the hotel after the team dinner, I mentioned to Philip that he had received lots of validation with so many folks requesting his time. He looked thoughtful as he responded, "I guess this is how my father felt when all of us kids wanted his attention, and he was working twelve-hour days to keep his family above water."

The next morning, I received a very early call from Philip requesting a quick breakfast away from the group. Something had happened. He wouldn't tell me what, just that something had happened. We met at a little coffee shop around the corner. He looked exhausted and was angry and confused.

Here is the "something" that happened. He had a dream that for him was more like a nightmare. He was walking through an old apartment that had high ceilings and lots of mahogany. He entered the library, where there were many books, and at the far end of the room was a man sitting at a desk with his head bowed. When Philip got closer, he saw that the man was doing calligraphy, and when the man looked up, Philip was looking into his own face.

"I feel confused. This dream had a strong impact on me, yet I don't know what it means." He looked to me for some help. I was deeply touched by what I had just heard.

"I think, Philip, that you are reconnecting with an aspect of yourself you have resisted, the beautiful Chinese part you have been fighting because your father already made claim to it." It was just the salve he needed to gain some clarity for himself.

We sat quietly sipping coffee. Then he said, "I think I finally understand all my reluctance to being there for my team. I didn't want to disappoint them the way I always thought my father had disappointed me, so I stayed the reluctant leader. However, I don't think I want to tell them about the dream." I reminded him that according to the agreement we had concerning the way we worked together, he should tell them whatever he thought would make the best difference for himself as well as for his colleagues. Truth is an art form that requires grace and discipline.

What he did share had all the meaning it needed. He was able to tell the team that he wanted to be available to them in a stronger mentoring capacity and was overwhelmed that they really valued his input even though at times he wondered if he was able to make himself clear because of his poor-quality English. He also told them that part of his Chinese heritage was to wait to be asked rather than to jump in, that speaking up could mean danger, and that his tendency toward avoidance was one that he would make a strong effort to correct.

His colleagues were not sure what to say. They knew something was different, yet it was hard to describe. In short order, the work environment improved dramatically. Whereas Philip's unit had until then been in the middle of the pack, by the end of the fiscal year it was leading the company in sales.

There is a P.S. to this story that is "so Philip." He was able to make peace with his heritage and with his father. For his father's eighty-fifth birthday, Philip, of all the siblings, had come up with the idea of having a birthday cake in the shape of the Great Wall of China with eighty-six candles lighting the path. He laughed heartily when he said, "We had to help dad blow the candles out, or the fire brigade would have been at the house."

So you see, it's never too late to grapple with your patterns; even after years of working with the same people, you can still reinvent relationships and bring about incredible change. As an illustration of all that can be accomplished in the complicated context of a work team, I want to close the chapter by telling a story that unfolded at Turnwood Inc., a global commercial building company I work with.

Ron, the VP of engineering, was frustrated with the silo mentality of his company. He wanted the entire firm to embrace a more systems-oriented approach. The place to start, he thought, was his own department of three hundred. He began lecturing his top lieutenants on the virtues of a strategic approach versus a tactical one, and indicated that he was going to hold them accountable for how creative and systemic their thinking was. This brought him into direct conflict with Edgar, the firm's manager of plant engineering and Ron's long-standing colleague. Edgar was highly skilled at tactics, but he had little talent for big-picture thinking and even less respect for it. As time passed, Ron realized that Edgar was actively working to undermine his leadership, making silo-type decisions based on what was good for him and his group rather than the entire company. Tension between the two simmered, contributing to a hostile, even poisonous environment.

Tensions came to a head at a staff meeting to discuss—what else?—systems perspectives. Ron began to lecture, and as the minutes ticked away, it became clear that Edgar was seething; every few minutes he interrupted the discussion with an unhelpful comment. Finally, Ron couldn't take it any longer and gruffly told Edgar to shut up. Edgar rose from his chair and moved to the door, but Ron—a big, strong guy—physically blocked him from leaving. Edgar sat down, and a shocked silence settled over the room.

Two weeks later, the entire team participated in an off-site to work things out. As the facilitator, I helped set the stage by giving each individual time to say what he or she wanted to get from the meeting. Then we developed a list of agreements about proper communication boundaries: no sidebars, no "zingers," and no "voting" to get others to agree with a particular position. We discussed the importance of letting there be silence and not filling the time with unnecessary chatter. We talked about the discipline required not to "rush to solution" and to give each other an opportunity to respond in his or her own timely fashion. With some effort, we created an atmosphere of openness, and team members finally felt free to air some of the things that had been bothering them. Ron's reports, including Edgar, revealed that in their eyes Ron was too dictatorial, shooting down their ideas and not creating a safe environment for them to speak out. By the time the group left, Ron saw that the recent turmoil was not all

Edgar's fault; that he, Ron, had been at least partly—and probably mostly—responsible. After all, Ron could lecture his group all he wanted about thinking systemically and creatively, but if he made them too uncomfortable to contribute, he was sabotaging his own cause. Ron also learned that the team's problems were far greater than he had thought. Morale was terrible, and his efforts to move his vision and the company forward were failing.

During the next several months, Ron did some soul searching. He came to realize that he had been too heavy-handed in how he was leading his team and that this behavior reflected a pattern he had carried with him since childhood. Ron had always been extremely driven and success oriented, and not especially good at collaborating with others. While huddling with his high school football team, he had played the role of the passionate one, shouting directions at his teammates but not taking the time to listen. During his early years at Turnwood, he would stay until ten o'clock every evening, and his colleagues made fun of him for trying to be "rookie of the year." Analyzing these experiences, Ron tied it all back to his father's lectures: "My father instilled in me the idea that team sports were worthless because when push came to shove, you couldn't really depend on other people. The solo person can wrestle others to the ground to win—it's not about getting everybody to play together and play nice. I should note that I finished third in the state in wrestling."

Armed with his new self-knowledge, Ron resolved to change. He understood now that his passion and willfulness were not enough to make things happen, so he focused on listening more and eliciting feedback from others. He experimented with giving up control, something that was difficult for him, because it went against his super-achiever grain. He also made it a priority to understand Edgar better. Encouraging Edgar to communicate openly, Ron learned that his colleague had been playing the role of the rebel, the little kid on the back of the bus who was always giving the bus driver a hard time. As a child, Edgar had had an intense rivalry with his older brother, and had fallen into a habit of always taking the opposing point of view. Thanks to his conversations with Ron, Edgar discovered that his rebel life pattern was clashing bitterly with Ron's super-achiever pattern. It wasn't the two of them that were at odds; it was their patterns.

Ron and Edgar patched things up and developed a far more productive working arrangement. Not surprisingly, the team started to turn around. With Ron's dictatorial inclinations firmly in check, the team opened up and actually started talking. For the first time, they had a chance to make decisions, and it felt good. Team members reported that they were learning from watching the "new" Ron. They also learned to ask more questions, tolerate silence and moments of chaos in a meeting, and not come to solutions too hastily.

Thinking back on all the change, Ron concludes that he has grown immensely. "I'm not a perfect leader, but I've learned some important lessons. First, it's not good to rely too much on yourself. You have to help your colleagues grow, and to learn from them along the way. I now ask open-ended questions to inspire others to think." For the first time in his life, Ron feels that he is free to apply his talents to the fullest without being hemmed in by an invisible role given him by his father. "I've learned how to be myself around my colleagues and my family in a much fuller way. I feel energized, like anything is possible."

Ain't that the truth? If you take on your patterns—really spend the time understanding and working with them—then the world suddenly seems to sparkle with possibility. You open yourself up to opportunities and ways of being that you never considered before. You learn to capitalize on your inner strengths. You start to meet people on their terms, to learn from them, to be present with them in the fullest sense.

DON'T BRING IT TO WORK

When I ask executives about their families, their childhoods, and their pasts, they ask, "What does that have to do with my job?" The answer, surprisingly, is "Everything!" Take a long, hard look at the difficult behavior in the office—really *talk* to the offending party—and you find that unresolved issues are often at work, playing themselves out over and over again.

The fact is that people in systems don't interact with each other in random, disconnected ways; rather, they interact in structured ways, just like actors in a very elaborate play. Our behavior tends to remain fairly stable over time, if only because we fear the potential disruption that a fundamental change in interpersonal roles might mean. These concerns run so deep that we carry our family roles into new systems as we age, performing the same behavior again and again, even though the results may not be what we'd like. For some people, there is no escape, but for most of us, there is. We can transform our patterns and reap the benefits—invigorated relationships, career success, and deep personal happiness—all by coming to terms with our past and owning up to our hidden patterns. Steel yourself, take a risk, and descend into that seamy underworld where your annoying patterns reside. It may not be easy, but if you take this one step toward authenticity, I know it will pay off.

TAKEAWAYS

- Problems can arise at work when invisible roles that served a purpose in our original family system disrupt the present-day system in which we operate.
- We all grow up playing parent-child roles and sibling roles that maintain the stability of the family, along with roles defined by cultural norms and gender stereotypes.
- As in the family, role playing at work serves to endow team members with a sense of identity and of connectedness within the larger firm culture. It also keeps the team together, especially in times of hardship or turmoil.
- Often we play out at work the same parent-child, sibling, and invisible roles we developed in our family of origin.
- By taking the time to understand and work on patterns, you open yourself up to opportunities and ways of being that you never considered before.

CHAPTER THREE

UNDERSTANDING WORKPLACE CRISES AND CONFLICTS

You can't shake hands with a clenched fist.
—INDIRA GANDHI

You've seen anecdotally that family baggage goes with you whether you want it or not, and that these unresolved family patterns lead to a number of ills, including personal upset, thwarted careers, strained professional relationships, and team difficulties. It's no secret that disputes between colleagues inflict tremendous direct and indirect damage on organizations; that's why firms spend so much on coaching and other HR interventions. But with only a sketchy and superficial understanding of the nature of conflict, most leaders lurch from crisis to crisis, applying Band-Aid solutions, not really changing or improving anything.

In contrast to this approach, systems thinking offers a path to real change in the form of a deep, cohesive, and comprehensive interpretation of problem relationships. Further, I believe that HR departments are primed to be key movers and shakers in bringing systems thinking into the business world. This is an exciting time for HR to develop and implement programs through which individuals and teams become aware of the interdependent and reciprocal impact all parts of the system have on each other. **Patterns of behavior become the focus of attention instead of the blaming of individuals.** Systemic solutions will ultimately save organizations from the wasted energy of lawsuits, disengaged employees, and excessive time spent putting out fires in the gossip mill.

This chapter addresses several questions that will help you understand the hidden emotional mechanisms at work in a typical office environment and learn to recognize and prevent conflict in its early stages, before it causes great harm. Once you learn to "embrace" conflict to spark positive change, you can help turn interpersonal tension into growth opportunities for teams and the organization as a whole. In answering these questions, the chapter offers discussion and practical guidelines for how organizations can better act to prevent, remediate, and transform conflict and thus make the most of office environments.

1. Why is conflict almost universal in workplaces?
2. Why does conflict seem to arise almost immediately in work relationships, before colleagues have even gotten a chance to know one another?
3. Why do interpersonal crises seem to flare up with no warning, and at the very worst of times?
4. Why does conflict so often fester and worsen rather than burn itself out on its own?
5. Why do HR interventions fail to reduce the level of conflict in workplaces?

Universal Conflict

Why is conflict almost universal in workplaces?

Let's begin by taking a moment to reflect on just how big a problem workplace conflict has become. The vast majority of twenty-first-century workplaces are rife with negativity and tension, and the costs are huge. Consider the following:

- Fortune 500 HR executives spend up to one-fifth of their time dealing with litigation activities, and a full 30 percent of a typical manager's time is spent dealing with conflict.[1]
- A whopping 93 percent of workers report being "negatively affected by [an] inability to deal with conflict on the job"; 69 percent avoid "confronting co-workers on issues of accountability."[2]
- More than half of HR professionals report experiencing conflict at least once a week at work; 10 percent of employees in

the retail, food, and leisure industries claim to experience hostility at work every day.[3]

- Senior executives have been spending over half their time resolving "staff personality conflicts," about double the time spent during the 1980s.[4]
- According to the *Journal of Occupational and Environmental Medicine,* health care expenditures are about 50 percent higher for workers reporting high stress levels. According to many studies, stress is created by a conflict-ridden work environment.[5]

As far as costs to businesses go, higher health expenditures and the time spent by managers dealing with conflict when it occurs are only a small part of the picture. To get a full sense of the financial hemorrhaging, you need to factor in other big-ticket items, such as the cost of defending harassment or wrongful termination lawsuits, the cost of employee turnover (estimated at 30 to 150 percent of an employee's salary), the untold loss of time to absenteeism, and reduced productivity due to a distracted and stressed workforce. (According to a study by the American Management Association, employees spend about 25 percent of their time, or two hours a day, partaking of unproductive squabbles with colleagues.[6])

Workplace conflict and crises are not limited to the United States. In one study from the United Kingdom, 30 percent of employees surveyed reported interpersonal conflict with one another.[7] A Japanese survey of corporate counselors responsible for the emotional health of employees found that 81 percent of them "have seen or have been consulted over instances that can be regarded as workplace bullying."[8]

Why do tensions get so dialed up at work? There are a number of possible answers. The rise of communications technology at work might play a role by depersonalizing colleagues, muddling communications, and leaving individuals unsure and unpracticed at dealing with others. Commentators have also regarded the mass entrance of Gen Y into the workforce as a cause of conflict; after all, this is a cohort with styles and attitudes toward work that are radically different than its predecessors. And then there is society as a whole, which, with its road rage, celebrity feuds, and shoot-em-up video games seems more overtly violent and conflict ridden than ever before. Might not such influences be bleeding into our workplaces? Or maybe we've just become more sensitive to conflict. We do compete in a service economy, where relationships matter above all else. It makes sense that businesses would notice tension in all its forms more keenly than before.

Each of these explanations holds some value, yet systems thinking offers a simpler, more cohesive, and thus more satisfying interpretation: **conflict runs rampant in the workplace because of our *natural and universal* tendency to bring our families with us to work.**

Such situational factors as the generational composition of an office or changes in communication habits play a role, but they don't get to the heart of the matter. As human beings, we are practically guaranteed to bump up against one another because we each possess our own patterned ways of reacting. Unaware of our patterns and the anxiety at their core, we are prevented from dealing healthily and deliberately with the challenges and inherent stressors that face us. Constant conflict is the inevitable and costly result.

I wish I could cite quantitative data showing the frequency with which workplace flare-ups resolve down to family patterns. The studies simply have not been done, primarily because business researchers are not as aware as they should be of the home-work connection. For now we need to trust our intuition and personal experience about what happens at work. We know that professional relationships are filled with emotional tensions, just as are relationships at home. We strive to be wise, philosophical, and mature in our professional dealings. Much of the time we're successful, but then that guy over there tells a story that sets your teeth on edge because it reminds you of how your older brother used to mock you, or someone makes a mess in the community kitchen and you get angry when you find yourself cleaning up again, just as you always used to do as a child. Suddenly you are in conflict, without even knowing why.

This reality, played out again and again in endlessly different detail, is what the statistics about the prevalence of workplace conflict are ultimately about. It's a reality made up not so much of dramatic acts of violence, but of incidents of covert conflict— mundane slights, condescending tones, unanswered calls, and other provocations that make our offices such complex places in which to work. Our hurt feelings are real, yet they often seem over the top in comparison with the situations that triggered them. "Everybody gets so frustrated," one colleague said to me. "And it boils down to petty things that grown-ups should be able to resolve on their own, things like being excluded from a birthday lunch." Seen from a family systems viewpoint, however, these "petty things" mask far deeper emotional struggles that have carried over from when we were small—struggles relating to our families' anxiety to keep the tensions and stressors underground. It might *seem* as if a conflict between two coworkers is about exclusion from a birthday lunch, but for one of them, the situation might evoke associations with a stern and unloving father, and for the other, a memory of parents who could not even enter a restaurant because of race. Our past experiences pop up to haunt us in a thousand small ways and according to a logic that most of us don't perceive or appreciate.

Recent advances in biology help us understand the neurological basis for why such potent memory traces persist so long and give rise so often to behavior patterns in workplace settings. Eric Kandel, winner of the 2000 Nobel Prize in medicine, has shown that when specific behaviors are repeated over and over again, the involved brain cells are stimulated to grow dendrites (extensions) to connect with each other.[9] Hebb's law states that "neurons that fire together, wire together." With enough repetitions, the behavior becomes an ingrained pattern, and when something happens in the present that recalls past experience, the entire network of dendrites is activated.[10] Our patterned behavior is replicated even in a situation that is very different, superficially at least, from the original one.

There has always been workplace conflict—well before information technology, the service economy, Gen Y, and the coarsening of society had a chance to influence our workplace environments. Depictions of workplace tensions are common in literature—for example, in Shakespeare's *Richard III*, Dickens's *A Christmas Carol*, and Melville's *Moby-Dick*. Could it be, then, that a deeper human dimension is at play? As social psychology teaches us, conflict situations can be understood only when viewed through the filter of a vast array of personal variables, including family values, gender, culture, past crises, and daily experiences. Responses to conditions in the workplace are determined by ideas and feelings that include both present experience and experiences from our histories. The origin of much conflict is thus *not in the workplace,* as all the other previously mentioned explanations of workplace conflict assume, but outside it. All of us, on a daily basis, transfer our old, outdated behavior roles from our original familial systems to our work systems, where they no longer serve us well. Because all family systems assign invisible roles to their members and because so few of us deal openly with these roles and the psychic wounds that accompany them, it's easy to see how conflict at work becomes routine. In fact, it would be surprising if it *weren't* routine.

In Chapter Four, I'll teach you how to recognize patterns that emerge in the workplace and the behaviors associated with them. I invite you to study your own workplace with these patterns in mind; you'll discover for yourself that family patterns are in fact omnipresent, lurking in the corners, giving rise every day to conflict situations both big and small.

IMMEDIATE CONFLICT

Why does conflict seem to arise almost immediately in work relationships, before colleagues have even gotten a chance to know one another?

Although interpersonal conflict can take months or years to break out into overt crisis, the seeds of conflict usually form almost immediately. In his book *Blink,* Malcolm Gladwell reports on studies that indicate our overwhelming predisposition for "instant knowing."[11] People make snap decisions about whether they like each other or not, often without realizing it. The scenario looks like this. You walk into a room to meet your new boss, and before you've even shaken hands with him you decide you don't like him. Something about him rubs you the wrong way. Two months later, you and your boss have survived a number of meetings together, yet the tension between you persists. Nothing happens until one day an event, even a seemingly minor one, triggers a flare-up of emotion, and what had been a simmering dislike escalates rapidly into shouting matches, HR interventions, even job transfers, dismissals, or lawsuits.

Isn't it strange that we decide so quickly, so instinctively, about our feelings for other people when we first meet them? After all, we don't even know them. We might not even remember their names. It's all so irrational, as if some weird system of judgment were grinding away in our heads without our consent. It turns out that this is exactly what's happening. **Because of our family experiences and the roles we are used to playing and seeing our relatives play, we come into new situations at work with unconscious expectations of how the person we are meeting is supposed to look, sound, and act.** When our colleagues and bosses don't match our expectations, we realize this in a matter of seconds, and just like that, the seeds of conflict are sown.

Suppose you grew up in a home where your mother was the dominant figure, and she played the role of the perfect parent, always in control and on time, always managing new challenges with ease. Now suppose you walk in to meet your new boss and find that she's running twenty minutes late and her desk is a holy mess. It just rubs you the wrong way, grates on you. Not too hard to imagine that there might be conflict between the two of you a few weeks or months down the road, as your boss begins to make demands and as her apparent disorganization seems to hold you back. This is a scenario I've encountered again and again over the years. Different people, different details, different companies—same problem or, as bumper sticker philosophy states: same shit, different day!

CEOs I work with are often startled to discover just how much their employees' family backgrounds shape the gut opinions employees have of the CEO's leadership style. As one CEO told me,

> People find my management style pretty strong. It's one of the first things they notice. For a while I wondered why, because I see myself as a mild-mannered guy. And then I started listening. I can't tell you how often people say their parents weren't strong, so they expect strength from me. It's what they want, so it's what they see. And that's not all. Other folks believe their parents always said one thing and did another. So even though I'm a clear communicator and follow through on what they've asked for, they don't give me credit. It's like I can't win no matter what. They don't really see me; they see the image of ghosts of the past. Once I realized that as CEO I cast a bigger shadow than just my own, I began to understand the subtle parameters of my job, and it became more doable.

Now let's consider this issue of expectations from the subordinate's standpoint. Cynthia hated reporting to Emilio from the moment she met him. She felt angry, even violated in his presence. It was strange, because Emilio was known as a pleasant, well-intentioned professional. Fortunately for Cynthia, Emilio was soon promoted. Her new boss, Rose, seemed great during their first meeting, but Cynthia quickly realized that it was the same old song. She soon found that she hated Rose's voice and that she felt insecure, as if nothing she did were good enough. So Cynthia made a lateral move. Life settled down, but a few months later she felt the old anxiety and anger bubbling up.

Was this a company of bully bosses? Was Cynthia inadequate? Could it be something from Cynthia's family, her original organization? This last possibility seemed unlikely, as she had grown up in a loving home where there were music lessons, sports, and vacations.

With some soul searching, Cynthia realized that this privileged background was itself the problem. There had been many choices for her as a child, but also great pressure to succeed. This expectation had never been spoken aloud, however; instead it was an amorphous request that had hung in the air like perfume. Cynthia was programmed as a super-achiever, with the unspoken threat that failure would mean a loss of her parents' love. Cynthia had fallen back instinctively on her striving mentality, playing out a drama of insecurity and anger with her bosses—the same drama that had been muted but still active with her parents. As a result, she was primed to view her bosses as inherently threatening people who wouldn't hesitate to inflict severe emotional damage on her.

We assign unconscious expectations to our peers as well. The scenarios are endless. People who suffered through combative relationships with their siblings while growing up tend to come to work looking for this behavior in their peers; these are the ones who a few months later express resentment that such-and-such a coworker is getting more time off, more money, a lightened load. Some men in the workplace grew up in families where women were meek and played a subordinate role; these are the guys who chafe at their first contact with an assertive female coworker.

In many cases, it's possible to trace acrimonious and destructive relationships between peers directly back to a single point in time. At one business I've worked with, the CEO hired a new

CFO, Joel, who had grown up in a family that liked to engage in very spirited debates around the dinner table. Not surprisingly, Joel had developed an argumentative style in his dealings with colleagues. In Joel's second week on the job, the CEO convened a meeting with Joel and Milt, the VP of manufacturing, to discuss a new company-wide computer system that the CEO wanted to implement. Milt was in the habit of never projecting a hint of fallibility, having grown up with a father who had done the same. "Within the first few minutes of this meeting," the CEO remembers, "a dynamic took root in which Joel harshly critiqued Milt's ideas and Milt took affront, lashing back at Joel. I mean, you could see it in their facial expressions. These guys were uncomfortable. They didn't like each other. It was the start of open warfare that's still running and still dragging us all down. And I am ready for the nonsense to stop!"

This type of invisible pattern repetition occurs in all relationships we enter, personal and professional. Shaped by our family experiences, we bring preconceived notions about others into our interactions and make snap decisions on that basis. Before we even know it, the seeds of hostile relationships have been sown.

CRISIS FLARE-UPS

Why do interpersonal crises seem to flare up with no warning, and at the very worst of times?

Family systems theory offers an especially clear and intuitive answer to this question. Crises flares up unexpectedly at unfortunate times because family patterns come to the surface most powerfully when we are overworked, tired, and under pressure to perform. During stressful periods, the most ancient, fight-or-flight part of our brain (called the amygdala) kicks in, and we become hyperfocused on the task at hand. Our mission becomes survival, and to achieve that we either run instinctively away from the threat or move instinctively to save someone else from it. The rational side of us, which had formerly managed to keep subterranean conflicts contained, falls away. Confronted by some provocation, even a seemingly minor one, we fall back on our most primitive, ingrained ways of reacting—the roles we were taught since before we could speak.

Rochelle and Kent are a perfect example. They had been friends for years and were both accomplished clothing designers with a great sense of runway flair. When Rochelle became Kent's boss, he was disappointed; he thought he was more creative than Rochelle and should have gotten the job. Although he accepted the situation, trouble was brewing beneath the surface. Rochelle's demands were suffocating him. Although he had hardly been aware of it, he unconsciously equated Rochelle's behavior with that of his overbearing father. When Kent was small, his father had micromanaged his life, telling him how to behave at school, whom to befriend, what sports to play. To cope, Kent had learned to remain quiet, "keep his cool," and let his father have his way, all the while nursing secret resentments.

Kent's patterns and their affiliated frustrations burst through one sweltering and exceptionally hectic day in Manhattan. The company was launching a major spring-to-summer campaign, and Rochelle had called maybe ten times from Los Angeles to check in with Kent. He finally told his assistant to say he was not there. Minutes later, when his assistant handed him the phone with an "I have already taken five calls and she demands to talk to you" look, he grabbed the phone. In a voice that sounded like a clenched fist, he said, "You are behaving like a neurotic parent, and if you call again I'm outta here."

The entire team suddenly went quiet. Even though he didn't really raise his voice, Kent's obvious anger rocked the room. He handed the phone back to his assistant. When it rang again, he grabbed it from the assistant's hand and heaved it; everyone watched it smash through an entry door. Then there was a funny sizzling sound as the air conditioner suddenly groaned to a halt.

Kent went out to compose himself. One of his team members found him in the hallway. "You know," Kent said haltingly, looking sad and exhausted, "I can understand that Rochelle is nervous about this launch. Yet every time she calls, all I sense is that she doesn't trust me and won't let me make any decisions." He wiped his now sweating face. "And when I threw that phone I was beginning to lose confidence in myself. She's so overbearing I really don't think I can continue to work for her." In the months ahead, Kent moved to a new job, and his long-time friendship with Rochelle came to an end.

When confronted by outbursts like Kent's, we tend to write off the episodes as stress induced and leave it at that. Take a day off, we think, ratchet down the stress level, and everything will be back to normal. Everyone will be fine. Yet stress alone doesn't explain people's behavior; the underlying family patterns triggered by stress do. As evidence, we need only observe that the circumstances that prompt reversion to family patterns aren't always objectively stressful; even relatively mild conditions can be enough to trigger an amygdala response if they are *perceived* as stressful by the person in question. And what determines whether or not something is perceived as stressful? That's right: family history and the roles one has grown accustomed to acting out.

Nancy, a senior executive in a magazine publishing company, was known for her amazing insights and quick wit. She was elegant both in her dress and in her speech. Her manner was calm and comforting. No one, and I mean no one, would have guessed that she had grown up in a family where there had been sexual abuse. Nancy had spent years in therapy to make sense of her awful childhood, where secrets and betrayals were the norm. Yet she never thought about how her childhood experiences would affect her work life—until one day when she thought she was left out of the loop on a project. She was seething with anger. Her trusted colleague, a skilled and creative woman, had taken Nancy's draft and put the finishing touches on it without asking Nancy's permission or approval. As Nancy put it,

> I guess it was just too familiar, not being asked what mattered to me, taking what was mine with total disregard. By the time I got to her office I was almost out of control. And as I spewed forth my rage I was also listening to my words. I told her over and over that she had crossed boundaries that were inappropriate. How dare she not consider me and my feelings? And then I went limp, the way I would when my father would leave my bedroom. There it was right in front of me. And then I found out I was mistaken. She had not "abused" me; I just didn't have all the facts. After that I was much more cognizant about how I still needed to harness my childhood emotions on the job.

Individuals who perform regularly under conditions of extreme pressure often find their family patterns triggered by stressors that seem remarkably inconsequential. I once coached a secret service agent whose job it was to run next to the presidential car when there was a parade through cities around the world. When I asked the agent, a strapping man named Richard, how he handled the stress, he said it was easy; he had learned how to compartmentalize his thinking when he was a kid and had watched his parents fight. He would go into his room and turn the music up so that he could ignore the threats and accusations.

Yet Richard did eventually crack, experiencing an awful anxiety attack that left him scared and confused. But it wasn't an assassination attempt or other incident of extreme danger that did it.

Richard was in South America preparing for the presidential visit when he noticed a young couple holding hands. The man began to yell at the woman and then raised his arm, seemingly ready to strike her. Without thinking, Richard ran over to protect the woman. The man looked up, annoyed at this intrusion into their private lives. Richard shrugged his shoulders and nodded to them as if he were just checking around. He continued with his duties, but before the president arrived at the airport, he realized that he was too upset to function. Finding a replacement, he went straight to his room. As he sat alone wondering what in the world had happened, he looked at the couple in his mind's eye and realized that with their dark hair and long, lean bodies they resembled his parents. When he saw that man raise his arm, Richard became once again the small kid who wanted to protect his mother.

When crises erupt, they catch us by surprise, and we tend to think that they are created out of thin air. Even though we have "blinks" of remembrances, interpersonal crises at work usually develop slowly and progressively. For this reason, they are eminently *preventable* problems. Organizations have it in their power to address and help us manage the substance of our emotional responses—our patterns—long before these patterns have a chance to trigger an unwanted outburst. In almost all cases that I've seen where interpersonal conflict has careened out of control, ample opportunity existed to preempt the problem, if only management had known where to look.

Learn to read warning signs that invisible patterns are in play. Pay attention to subtle messages you can detect through language and actions. Family patterns are, first of all, *patterns;* when destructive behavior of any kind occurs in repetitive ways, that's a sign that hidden family patterns might be brewing trouble. Look for behaviors that allow people to avoid honest discussion of themselves, their feelings and behavior. Gossip, for instance, allows an individual to talk about others, thus deflecting attention from his or her own behavior. Others fall back on a "sky is falling" syndrome, worrying about their boss's health, the air quality in the office, the weather—everything but their own feelings. Still others strive to present themselves as protectors in the office, hiding the mistakes of others—and their own emotions—and playing the "Is everybody happy?" game. And then there is the ever-popular "huh" approach, whereby colleagues make it known that they just come to work, mind their own business, and never get involved in office politics. Of course, they never talk about themselves, either. In all these cases, the people involved are effectively masking emotions, seeking at all costs to prevent others from engaging with their inner worlds. And when that happens, watch out—there could be trouble afoot!

Besides keeping alert to specific personnel problems waiting to happen, firms need to adopt a structural orientation, creating office environments in which invisible patterns don't get much room to grow. Until recently, most companies have frowned on the public expression of emotions, especially negative ones; there is simply no room for anger, jealousy, disappointment, fear, frustration, rejection, or sadness. "Don't bring it to work" is the mantra; anything negative just gets in the way of getting the job done.

However, if we are shut down expressing ourselves in an adult way, stress builds and emotions get buried in deeper, more primal parts of our nervous systems until, like a latent volcano, they begin to bubble and finally erupt. Here are a few suggestions for nipping these old patterns in the bud and thus averting a poisonous office environment:

- *Create balanced workplaces.* When office environments are structured too rigidly, with excessive emphasis placed on rules and boundaries, creativity is shut down and employees tend to operate in rote, sleepwalking fashion. They are free to fall back again and again on what is most familiar—their patterns. The other side of too rigid is too flexible, where there are no rules and procedures, a three-ring circus with no rhyme or reason. Here the patterns show up as a way of limiting anxiety by helping the individual return to what is familiar.

In a balanced workplace, there is a heightened requirement to check out assumptions and ask lots of open-ended questions for verification and validation. No one is brushed aside as being "annoying" for wanting to get to "the heart of the matter." Employees are rewarded with acknowledgment for being accountable even when being accountable has a tinge of embarrassment connected to it.

• *Encourage the safe expression of emotions.* All too often, people don't feel comfortable talking about disappointments for fear of being misunderstood. At times, everyone is discouraged or displeased with what happens at work. Often fear of speaking personal truth shows in our actions, yet we are seen as "wimpy" if we actually "tell it like it is." Just think *Jerry Maguire* and the character's famous speech that eventually got him fired for telling his truth. (Granted, he was young and impulsive and had not spent the time to gain buy-in before he spoke; a lot can be learned from that film about "right place, right time.")

In "stiff upper lip" workplaces, everyone is expected to put on a happy face or simply pretend there are no problems at all. Invisible patterns are never brought to the surface, not even a little bit. Conflicts are left to simmer on the stove until it's too late. And when there is a mass exodus of employees, there is shock and surprise. Then there are the see-all, tell-all workplaces where conflicts never simmer; they just keep going and going like the Energizer bunny. In these workplaces, drama is like a virus run amok, and the activities of the gossip mill replace any real work getting done.

When there is room to talk truly about how we feel, and we develop the skills to express ourselves honestly, there is a healthy capacity to "see it, say it, and let it go," so issues neither simmer nor boil, and the work of the company can get done in a timely fashion.

• *Remove sources of undue and unnecessary stress.* Although stress is subjective, firms could do a lot more to remove the triggers that bring patterns to the fore for most people. Performance evaluations, for instance, inspire a tremendous amount of dread. Although honest feedback is both healthy and helpful, evaluations are usually structured such that the person being evaluated hears too much criticism or none at all. We still need a great deal of research in this area to find healthy ways of providing the feedback that people need to perform at their best.

Also, during tough economic times, fear of "the wolf at the door" looms large. This is when major anxieties surface, and people can become incredibly irritable and often irrational. Companies that offer some guidance about financial concerns are ahead of the game. Although firms cannot take away the fear, they can help people feel more prepared by making sure that economic issues are at least discussed. Half-day programs or "brown bag lunch" lectures can do wonders to minimize anxiety. Although downsizing may be a necessity, keeping lines of communication open can help those who leave do so without unbridled anger or a desire for retribution and can limit the "survivor guilt" of those who do keep their jobs. Many organizations are wise enough to add wellness programs, which include stress management, nutritional seminars, or exercise areas that encourage better methods of handling anxiety and are excellent ways to create "pattern interrupts" in our repetitive, conditioned lives.

- *Incorporate structured forms of communication.* Perhaps the most important general step an organization can take to avert interpersonal crises is to put mechanisms in place to get people talking on a regular basis. If employees have the opportunity to discuss their patterned reactions and how those patterns shape their impressions of others, invisible patterns would have far less opportunity to cause mischief. Education is the key. A series of workshops to create pattern awareness could help intact teams as well as the company as a whole. These could include workplace relationship seminars that would give employees at all levels of the company an opportunity to increase emotional intelligence, become pattern aware, and learn the skills to communicate more effectively, handle conflict more elegantly, and collaborate more efficiently.

- *Restrict personal explorations to one-to-one contacts.* No one should ever be in a position where personal concerns are forced to be aired in front of a group. However, teams do need mechanisms for constant open feedback about patterns so that those patterns can be exorcised or exercised to best advantage. In every company willing to offer individuals and teams an opportunity to seek new ways of working together, there is a "lightness of being" that shows up. Individuals begin to seek out others, whether peers, bosses, or human resource representatives, to query them about how to improve behavioral interactions. Rather than feel that they are being called on the carpet and being judged, individuals become proactive and request information about how to increase their emotional intelligence and ability to be pattern aware.

In his book *Emotional Intelligence,* Daniel Goleman called upon leaders to understand not merely the financial nuts and bolts of a business but also the behavior and communication patterns of those they lead. The most successful leaders, he suggested, learn to create safe environments where individuals are able to acknowledge and appreciate each other while also expressing upsets and discomforts.[12] Workplaces that are truly learning organizations, places where employees excel at acquiring and transferring knowledge, are the way of the future. The *Harvard Business Review* article "Is Yours a Learning Organization?" offers an online tool to assess the depth of learning in a company, suggesting that firms which foster open discussions and think holistically are the ones more able to adapt to the unpredictable than are their competitors.[13] The organizations that create healthy definitions of collaboration and community are the ones that will be on every "best place to work" list.

The more that business can become enlightened about the invisible world behind behavior, and can translate this enlightenment into actual policies, the more often needless crises and disasters will be averted. The more that every organization—for profit, not for profit, religious, educational, and government—can connect the behaviors from the past with reactions in the present moment and observe the self-fulfilling prophecies that keep us stuck in the same-old, same-old, the more we can help each other be more accountable for our actions and find new, more responsible solutions that ultimately increase employee and customer loyalty, as well as profitability.

Festering Conflict

Why does conflict so often fester and worsen rather than burn itself out on its own?

As any HR manager will tell you, workplace conflict often gets worse over time. From a family systems standpoint, it's easy to see why. **The invisible role playing that causes workplace conflict doesn't go away. It sticks around, continuing to cause trouble until either it is dealt with or the workplace system is changed.** Again, interpersonal tension isn't fundamentally the result of economic circumstances or specific people or a particular business challenge. It's the result of forces outside the workplace—family and cultural dynamics and old hurts that have made their way into the workplace. As long as these patterns remain invisible and still potent, the strife will persist.

I've already told the story of Cynthia, the woman who found herself immediately angry at boss after boss, for no apparent reason. In another case I know of, destructive conflict persisted for a full twelve years, spanning a series of promotions and even a company restructuring, all because the family patterns behind it were never addressed. Byron and Jason were high-level marketing executives who butted heads because they both followed patterns of constantly striving for recognition and a feeling of success. In Jason's case, the need to achieve had evolved because his father had required that Jason constantly prove how good he was in order to win his father's love. Byron's quest for achievement, by contrast, reflected a classic survivor's mentality; Byron's father had died suddenly in a car accident when he was thirteen, his mother of cancer two years later. He had always felt that he needed to succeed in order to justify his happiness in the face of their death. What neither colleague was able to do was confront his respective past, acknowledge his invisible pattern, and show compassion for the other. As a result, what had once been healthy, if somewhat strained, competition turned into backbiting and ill will. All collaboration between the two eventually came to a halt, and a schism formed at the firm, with colleagues openly taking one side or the other. The conflict was never really resolved, and it ended only when Byron got promoted and Jason, seeing the writing on the wall, left the company. They never talked again.

Clear examples of family patterns persisting and ruining work relationships over long periods of time involve feuding members of family businesses. The Mondavi wine family has been stricken for decades by endless fighting, legal battles, betrayals, and interpersonal disappointments. The underlying issues were not dealt with, and as a result of the feud between the two brothers Robert and Peter, their legacy of bruised egos and bad decisions was passed down to Robert's sons, Michael and Timothy.[14] Consider, too, the famous story of the entire German town that became embroiled in a long-standing family feud between two brothers who had started rival shoe companies. Animosity between the brothers was so great that residents declared their loyalty by wearing only one brand or the other and often talking only to those wearing the "right" brand of sneaker. Again, the family patterns were never brought to the fore and neutralized. Left to fester, the conflict and nastiness rendered the two companies vulnerable to competition. Those two companies, by the way, were Adidas and Puma, and the competitor that profited from family patterns run amok was none other than Nike.[15]

Although we might wish it were otherwise, family patterns don't just spontaneously combust; they linger on and on across decades, even persisting across generations. Studies done with the children of Holocaust survivors have found that even when children are born in safety and freedom, the scars of the past live on in the present in the form of "survivors' guilt." In these families, bright, competent people will often sabotage their success, feeling that they have no right to the joys of life when family members have suffered unspeakably. Generation after generation remains crippled, often having no conscious understanding of the details, yet repeating the patterns of betrayal, abuse, or neglect. Patterns, then, remain potent long after they've slipped from the forefront of consciousness, and that's precisely why they can become so debilitating.

In many cases, it's even possible to trace our present-day handling of relationships to ancestors who died long before we were born. Fred was a highly successful lawyer in his fifties—a graduate of Harvard Law and an adviser to high-profile business leaders. On a plane traveling from Chicago to New York, he happened to meet a new business contact, who a few days later offered him a "dream job" at a Fortune 100 firm. Yet during the month of negotiations that followed, Fred found himself frozen. He knew what he was worth, yet he was afraid to go above the firm's low initial offer. He didn't want to anger his prospective employer, neglecting the fact that they were used to wheeling and dealing and that they wouldn't look down on him for asking. Fred became so nervous and fearful that he was on the verge of convincing himself to stay in his old job and pass up the opportunity of a lifetime.

Days of anguish led Fred back to an event that had plagued his family for generations. Fred was part Cherokee Indian. In 1859, the Cherokee tribe had been driven from its land in what has been called "the Trail of Tears." Fred's great-grandparents had been so afraid that they had moved from place to place night after night so they would survive. One day, the great-grandfather did not come home to their newest hiding place. The story the family heard was that he had challenged a man in a general store who had tried to cheat him. The great-grandfather was shot and dragged to the edge of town, where he died. "Don't make them mad" became the family mantra, passed down from generation to generation. Harvard-educated Fred, brilliant and helpful, always challenging others to be risk takers, was not immune. He had long played it safe for himself, and here he was now, doing it again.

FAILURE OF HR INTERVENTIONS

Why do HR interventions fail to reduce the level of conflict in workplaces?

When conflict erupts at the office, managers run through a predictable series of steps. First, they research the situation and determine who is causing all the trouble. Then they sit that person down and put him or her on a performance improvement plan, often including regular meetings with HR, a small amount of coaching, and perhaps enrollment in a communications course. If the plan fails to bring about improvement in the offensive behavior, the powers that be then do one of three things: they push the whole thing under the carpet and leave the employee in place, transfer the employee to another department, or fire the employee altogether.

Despite the billions spent each year on conflict resolution, on remedial programs, on worker time spent in those programs, on moving or replacing "problem" workers—interpersonal conflict remains a fact of life in offices everywhere. By now, at least one reason why should be clear: **the standard intervention process stays on a superficial, symptomatic level; it doesn't even begin to touch on the systemic patterns that are the actual causes of workplace conflict.** When conflict erupts, a person is singled out and told to change his or her bad behavior, yet the emotional frame behind the bad behavior is left entirely intact. Invariably, the symptom will pop up again, disrupting team interactions and prompting various types of interventions to intercede again and again, until the employee is fired or the firm decides simply to live with it.

Conflict resolution processes that do not consider the larger system are not only ineffectual but also traumatic in their own right. There are many reasons organizations prefer to tackle conflict on the superficial symptomatic level. In the solutions-oriented cultures that dominate many workplaces, digging back into old upsets seems indulgent and does not belong in the workplace. Much easier to let bygones be bygones.

But bygones never really stay bygones. Nobody benefits from interventions that pass over the deeper causes of conflict. If organizations continue to attack conflict at the symptomatic level, they will continue to spend exorbitant amounts of money on programs that miss the mark and disappoint. More ominously, our unwillingness to tackle the invisible dimensions of workplace interactions leaves us with a workforce that is less productive, more protective, less fulfilled, more anxious, less creative, more stifled, less flexible, and more stagnant.

A second, related problem with the way firms typically respond to conflict today is **the tendency to single out a "problem" person and target interventions only at that person.** It's deceptively easy and reassuring to think that we can get a definitive handle on bad workplace interactions by attaching them to a single, recognizable face. Yet it doesn't work. When one or two "bad apples" are taken out of a workplace system, the problem isn't solved. Sure, everything seems to return to normal for a time; that is, until the next annoying person shows up. Then you've got the same destructive situation, and you have to waste time and resources all over again to deal with it in what is often an ineffectual manner.

As we've seen, individuals don't produce symptoms on their own; the whole system of the work team plays its part. It follows that the poisonous atmosphere of tension and discomfort that envelops a team won't dissipate until the whole team works together to accept responsibility and resolve the problem. Systems are like gravity; they exist whether you agree with the concept or not. If you happen to be standing in a spot where a ball thrown in the air will land, the ball will hit you on the head and not even apologize. Likewise, if your company is overflowing with interpersonal stress within the system, that stress will persist until you do something, despite the great confidence you have that the half-measures you are taking are working.

To reduce conflict and increase their competitiveness, firms need to become "systems prepared." When conflict rears its ugly head, firms should take a conscious look at their culture and structure. Leaders need to approach conflict solving with an awareness that everything is connected—our families and our work teams, our past and our present—and also a commitment to help contending parties spend time individually and collectively exploring the connections and working out their differences. Open and honest communication is critical: when addressing problems, leaders need to create safe spaces for entire teams to share freely what they do well together, what they do poorly, and what they can do differently.

A CEO I've worked with says it best: "Telling the truth isn't easy, and for that matter, neither is running a business. Yet businesses need folks who have learned the skills to handle conflict, not just run from it, who can be honest and then get on with the work. This sort of dialogue is always better to do sooner rather than later. Interpersonal problems rarely improve with time alone. Always deal with a problem now, if you can." Another CEO agreed, stating that "until recently all of the shifts for new ways of handling conflict at our company were 'forced shifts' and were crisis induced. Now we are becoming more proactive, moving to 'chosen shifts' that are consciously induced. We are permitting more freedom to express emotions, more willingness to address patterns, and more accountability for owning mixed messages."

I'd like to offer several practical guidelines for how to handle conflict better when dealing with multiple parties on a team. These guidelines will help you begin to do the hard work of slowing down, opening honest lines of communication, and facilitating a work team system as the team members get at the heart of a conflict. Follow these guidelines when dealing with frustrated and upset colleagues, and you will begin to move the company beyond the twin mistakes of obsessing over symptoms and scapegoating:

• *Stop downward spirals.* When you're helping people work out solutions to a conflict, remain open to the possibility that all parties can create a win-win out of the conflict. This is true even if someone has to admit that he or she was the "perpetrator." Win-win does not necessarily mean that the pie is evenly divided, but rather that everyone has been heard, that his or her issues have been duly noted, and that a solution has been hammered out to limit the same type of dispute in the future.

• *Remain open to the outcome.* Don't assume you have the answer. Let the group dynamic lead you to a solution. Follow the conflict with open eyes. Often your initial guess will be correct, but allowing the team to do its work might sometimes lead you to a far better conclusion than you ever expected.

• *Encourage team members to speak concisely.* Truth telling is an interaction, not a monologue. Sentences filled with truth are usually no more than ten words max. They are not run-on sentences. When people run on longer, stop them and ask them to clarify. One model that works is to have contending parties repeat the facts first, give an opinion, talk about how the situation makes them feel, and then state a possible beneficial outcome.

• *Encourage team members to breathe.* This might sound simplistic or obvious, but when we are in tense situations, we tend toward shallow breathing that inhibits our deeper thinking and also keeps us in a state of heightened alert. Taking time to breathe also slows down the process so that everyone can feel comfortable and the truth can come out.

• *Remember that solutions aren't Band-Aids.* Given the discomfort we feel at talking about invisible patterns with others, it's tempting to want to dispense with a conflict quickly. As the facilitator, you need to make sure the solution doesn't come too quickly. Really deep thinking takes time. It's always a good idea to revisit solutions after a break or to let people "sleep on it" before bringing a conflict to its final resolution.

Perhaps the most tragic part of a traditional conflict resolution process focused on symptoms and limited to the individual "troublemaker" are the lost opportunities. When you allow groups of people a chance to talk together and probe for better solutions, you open the way for lasting transformation. Team members don't need to engage in complex, continued exploration of their past in front of each other. In fact, I advise against this. It goes beyond the mandate of the workplace. Rather, they need to be aware that the patterns are activated and that anxiety is increased, and they need to notice how they can refrain from getting caught in the crossfire.

In the next chapter, we're going to look at the most common destructive workplace patterns. Understanding them will give you a shortcut for talking about conflicts and a way for individuals to be accountable for their part of a situation. The remainder of this book helps with what I referred to earlier as the way **OUT: observing, understanding, and transforming** the past patterns in the present time. Conflicts don't need to be seen as mere nuisances or disruptions; they can also be seen as gifts in disguise. Adopt a systems approach in your handling of conflicts, and your firm will become far more thoughtful and more inventive, not to mention a happier and more soulful place to work.

TAKEAWAYS

- The vast majority of twenty-first-century workplaces are rife with negativity, tension, and conflict, and the costs are huge, ranging from decreased productivity to lawsuits.
- Conflict runs rampant in the workplace because of our *natural and universal* tendency to bring our families with us to work. We are practically guaranteed to bump up against one another because of our patterned ways of reacting.
- Conflict and crises flare up most powerfully when we are overworked, tired, and under pressure to perform, due to our natural flight-or-flight instinct. Even seemingly inconsequential stresses can trigger family-based patterns of behavior.
- Conflict interventions that are superficial and symptom oriented and that fail to address the larger workplace system—such as by only singling out a "problem person"—are ineffectual and often cause more damage.
- Organizations benefit when they examine their entire culture to understand and address the source of dysfunction with an enlightened, compassionate approach.

PART TWO

THE WAY OUT

Observe, Understand, and Transform Your Patterns

CHAPTER FOUR

THE THIRTEEN MOST COMMON DESTRUCTIVE PATTERNS IN THE WORKPLACE

There are two kinds of people in the world: those who think there are two kinds of people, and those who know it's not that simple.
—ANONYMOUS

Now that we've accounted for the home-work connection and examined the pervasiveness and costliness of patterns in the workplace, it's time for you to do something about your own patterns. How do you prevent them from continuing to thwart your career success? How do you gain more freedom to reach your highest potential both at work and at home? Patterns are destructive because they are invisible—they inform your responses to events without your even realizing it. The first step to overcoming these patterns, therefore, is to *become aware of them.* Once you identify which specific patterns define your behavior, you can understand how they arose and then take specific actions to transform them.

Becoming aware of our patterns is more easily said than done. Pushed by the flow of life, we rarely take the opportunity to stop, take a deep breath, and notice our behavior. The best thing we can do for ourselves, for our families, for our coworkers, and for future generations is to take ourselves off autopilot and begin our own redesign process. This chapter helps you find the hidden patterns of habitual office behavior, focusing on the **thirteen most common patterns in the workplace.** Please note that you will resonate with maybe only three or four as your key drivers. Yet gaining an understanding of all the patterns is helpful for all your relationships, personal and professional.

Pattern awareness is an important skill of emotionally and socially intelligent leaders and puts you in a strong position to guide your team and your company. Your ability to discern patterns shortens the amount of time you have to spend resolving conflicts and helps limit the depth of upset that occurs.

Spend time on these exercises, really commit to working with them, and you will gain a whole new perspective on yourself and your behavior at work. As you become better acquainted with your invisible tendencies, you can observe yourself in action and understand how and to what extent they thwart your professional relationships.

CHARTING THE MOST COMMON PATTERNS

All relationships are based on the ebb and flow of interaction; by becoming aware of these major thirteen patterns, you'll possess a much deeper understanding of how you and your colleagues react unconsciously and counterproductively to everyday pressures.

The list of thirteen most common patterns in the workplace is the product of my decades of experience coaching executives and teams. I see a wide variety of people express these behaviors again and again in as many contexts as you can imagine. We all have a predilection toward two or three patterns that have become ingrained, although most of us can relate to all of them at one time or another. To bring the patterns to life, I present them here in a personified form, as a collection of characters that will be familiar to anyone who has ever worked in an office:

1. Super-Achiever
2. Rebel
3. Procrastinator
4. Clown
5. Persecutor
6. Victim

  7. Rescuer
  8. Drama Queen or King
  9. Martyr
 10. Pleaser
 11. Avoider
 12. Denier
 13. Splitter

The mere mention of some of these words might call to mind specific behaviors you've seen in your coworkers. When I conduct one-day programs to familiarize folks with these patterns, there is a common theme. At the lunch break, everyone talks about a boss, coworker, direct report, mother-in-law, spouse, partner, child, or neighbor who fits perfectly in the pattern mold. There is a sense of humor and relief. Then in the afternoon comes the hard work of the game we call "owning your pattern." A little bit more uncomfortable, yet people leave still with a sense of humor and a lot of humility. They have experienced the beginning of a new way to communicate, and it is highly rewarding to watch the change in direction that even one day can bring. We all know people who procrastinate, people who clown around. But who are these annoying characters exactly? How do they drag down a work team? Let's take a look.

PATTERN 1: THE SUPER-ACHIEVER

Super-achievers must **excel at everything they do**—to the point of obnoxiousness. Not only do they achieve every conventional measure of career success; their families, although in the background, must look picture-perfect. Partners are trophy worthy, and the kids—well, whatever the best school in the area is, that is where you will find them. "Happy" is not a word used by super-achievers; the **only word that matters is "successful."** How can you spot a super-achiever at the beach? He seems to be talking to himself, but nope, it's just the Bluetooth. There will be a pile of books in the sand. Usually you will find the *Harvard Business Review,* the latest best-selling novel, and a how-to book about the fad of the moment. If family members are there, they rarely bother this very busy, overscheduled person.

At work, **super-achievers see themselves as special,** and they want to be treated as such. They continually inflate themselves, often at the expense of others. Super-achievers **hate criticism** or being critiqued in any form. They are **conditioned to defend, explain, or justify,** needing to prove that they are right and others are wrong. Super-achievers are also **very calculating in making decisions** that will give them an advantage. If a super-achiever is a peer, no matter how competent you are, you will walk away from an encounter needing to shake off an uncomfortable sense of incompetence. If you report to a super-achiever, one of two things is bound to happen. Either you will sit at the feet of the star and be hypnotized into thinking that whatever he or she says is better than anything you could ever come up with or, if you have an idea of your own, you will fight for the right to be heard and then be told your idea is second rank. If you oversee a super-achiever, expect some competition and often some underhanded maneuvers to get you out of the prime office spot that he or she covets.

The super-achiever's antics are destructive because they **breed fear and resentment** within a team. Trust is minimal; everyone begins to guard ideas, and an uncomfortable sense of paranoia creeps in. Initially, a super-achiever will **charm certain individuals who look as if they can be the best stepping-stones to the super-achiever's success.** This creates a "class war" in the work environment between the "in crowd" and the rest of the world. Over time, super-achievers show their limited depth of caring, and a slew of bruised egos accumulate around the office. But by the time the rest of the team realizes what has happened, the super-achiever has been promoted.

Pattern 2: The Rebel

The rebel is a **born fighter,** yet this fighting is almost always *against* something—authority figures, social protocols, company rules and regulations. Rebels come in wearing jeans on a Tuesday when casual day is Friday. They miss deadlines or arrive late to work just to prove they don't have to follow the rules. Rebels do these things because they **thrive on negative attention,** seeing it as the only way to get noticed.

Rebels **don't like to be judged;** for them, the best defense is a good offense. Rebels often strike colleagues as **emotionally**

closed and distrustful, hypervigilant about making sure they and others are not being taken advantage of. Rebels claim to strive for change, yet they have not done their deeper homework and will take on a cause without really understanding the implications of their actions. If you have a classic rebel on your hands, watch out: about the only thing he or she loves more than throwing gasoline on a smoldering fire is getting others to do the same. The moment rebels hear of discontent, they will go to great lengths to convince others that they should go to HR or get legal advice. I've seen this happen again and again, sometimes with serious consequences.

Most companies cannot tolerate rebels for very long, which is why rebels often end up on performance improvement plans or are sent to communication or anger management programs. Rebels also get fired or quit their jobs, leaving with a tremendous amount of fanfare. It is when anger and righteousness get out of hand and revenge takes over that the rebel's willingness to prove a point regardless of consequences can bring down communities, teams, and companies.

Pattern 3: The Procrastinator

Procrastinators are **hard to trust.** They almost always say yes to deadlines and intend to deliver on time, yet usually they **fail to follow through** and then become **indignant when held responsible.** As deadlines approach, procrastinators cannot be found by cell phone, e-mail, or carrier pigeon. They hate to be in the limelight, because they perceive visibility as unsafe. When the work is finally handed in, procrastinators often go on multiple minivacations to "recuperate from the stress of all the deadlines."

Why do people procrastinate? **Perfectionism plays a role,** but although some procrastinators are perfectionists, this is not always the case. The perfectionist is much more prone to find a way to get the work done and then complain that it is not good enough, whereas procrastinators, well, procrastinate. A recent study at the University of Calgary has found that **procrastinators lack self-confidence** and are unsure whether they can actually complete a task. There also appears to be **a link between impulsiveness and procrastination;** impulsive people tend to value living in the moment and thus attribute no real meaning to deadlines.[1] Often this stems from **anxiety about choice**—the deep-seated fear that no matter which road is chosen, there could have been a better option. This type of thinking leads to a failure to act, what is often called "analysis paralysis."

For businesses, the cost of procrastination includes time spent counseling tardy employees, making sure the postponed work gets covered, managing disappointments, and handling the conflicts that are bound to erupt when many on a team are waiting for a solitary individual to produce his or her part of a project. Procrastination's full costs are hard to measure, as one can hardly plot out all the possible alternative scenarios and all the missed opportunities. Costs to the individual worker include missed opportunities related to job advancement as well as costs related to falling self-esteem.

If we look at history, we find that procrastination can have consequences in situations much more dire than just getting a report done on time. In November 1861, George McClellan was made commander in chief of the Union army. Frustrated by McClellan's unwillingness to attack, Abraham Lincoln recalled him to Washington, saying, "My dear McClellan: If you don't want to use the army I should like to borrow it for awhile."[2]

Pattern 4: The Clown

Office clowns are **extroverts who love to divert others** with their jokes and loud, witty banter. They know every detail about trivial issues and give their own two cents just to get a rise out of their colleagues. Often **the jokes are offensive,** insensitive, and downright embarrassing. Clowns goad folks into a contest of one-liners that may begin in good taste yet end up as HR nightmares. Even when clowns don't cross the line into blatantly inappropriate behavior, colleagues sense that these individuals possess **an underlying vulnerability,** and they grow frustrated that they can never push beyond the veneer of humor and really get to know office clowns as people. Colleagues find the constant humor distracting, to the point where they will purposely avoid working with office clowns.

As court jesters, clowns have historically served vital roles, using their humor to cut through to the heart of an issue or to show their royal masters the weaknesses of one who was not to be trusted.

Today, office clowns do display an uncanny ability to break open a tense situation with a joke. They can pick up the unsaid anger in the room and become heroes by **speaking the unspeakable.** More often, though, clownish behavior causes communication gaps that are at best wasteful and at worst the stuff of lawsuits. Organizations regard clowning as subversive, seeing it as giving rise to a shared negative critique of a team or boss. **Most firms write off jokesters** as pubescent employees who are not high-potential candidates. Bozos, jokers, smart-asses, motormouths—these are the names clowns are called.

Having a sense of humor is certainly not the same as being the office clown. Humor is healthy. Research indicates that laughing benefits the immune system and activates endorphins, the good stuff that makes us feel more contented. Although going for a jog also activates endorphins, a well-timed joke is faster, and you don't need to take a shower. Perhaps we should make more of a role for our office clowns—so long as their joking and banter don't get out of hand.

PATTERN 5: THE PERSECUTOR

Persecutors are bullies who love to control, micromanage, and display contempt for others, usually through verbal abuse and sheer exploitation. They constantly put others down with snide remarks or harsh, repetitive, and unfair criticism. Persecutors **see others as weak and sentimental,** and they only approve of and appreciate those who take power and bulldog their way to get what they want. You can spot a persecutor immediately because he or she rarely uses the words "I feel" in a sentence—unless, of course, it is to blame, as in "I feel that you don't listen to me."

Persecutors **need to feel important.** They tend to dominate conversations and want to be at the center of attention. They expect those who work with and for them to help maintain their "most important person" status at any meeting. That said, there are two types of persecutor. Loudmouth persecutors will **find fault with someone else's work** in front of a group and point out how much the person still needs to learn. Quiet persecutors are more subtle. They use the "red pen" technique, cutting up your work as deftly as if they were slicing your body with a sword. They act as if they fully intend to help you, yet you sense that they **delight in your potential failure.** Quiet persecutors will let you almost finish a project before they tell you that what you have done is not good enough and that they are pulling the work to give to someone else.

How are persecutors different from tough bosses? Tough bosses will give an individual or a team challenging goals to reach, along with timelines and clear consequences. **Persecutors give and withhold information as a means of exercising power;** often, he or she will insinuate that the work is not up to par, even though not all the knowledge to complete the tasks has been given. Persecutors are also **adept at playing the "cover your ass" game** of blaming others for mistakes or missed deadlines.

Unwillingness to speak out against the persecutor personality at work is a silent epidemic. There is no doubt that **persecutors are deadly for individuals and teams.** According to the Gallup Organization, bullying by immediate bosses is the single most important reason people quit their jobs.[3] Having a brutal boss or peer can cause depression, sleep disorders, ulcers, high blood pressure, lowered self-confidence, and a sense of inadequacy and isolation. Persecutors can turn an otherwise great job into an ongoing nightmare.

Pattern 6: The Victim

Victims are the **consummate complainers.** Pessimistic by nature, they never feel respected or trusted. They struggle with **feelings of inadequacy and fearfulness,** and as a result they tend to be quiet and to withdraw from any situations in which they risk being attacked or judged. They will also go out of their way to avoid folks at work who they think are highly competent; this allows them to push down their own internal feelings of incompetence. Yet **victims are not unsocial people.** They're always looking for someone to come to their rescue, and there is always an alliance to be formed with other victims who are also uncomfortable with conflict.

Taking what victims say at face value, coworkers sometimes think that these individuals care more about their work or their family than about themselves. Yet if difficulties come along, most victims will say they never had enough time to complete a project because of others' incessant demands. Complaining is much more appealing than going directly to the source, and most **victims make triangulation an art form.** They will take on another individual, usually a boss or a peer, or the organization, and if they are not getting enough attention, they will even take on aspects of society. The theme of the victim is "He did it, she did it, they did it, and it's not my fault."

Victims have difficulties in offices. They **hate to be micromanaged;** they hate having people look over their shoulders. In fact, if this happens, they tend to slow down, get sick, or ask to be given another task. Victims are also often **blind to solutions** and spend so much time focusing on problems that opportunities for real and lasting change pass them by. They believe that anything they do will only cause more problems and that the situation they find themselves in is basically hopeless. All too often, this becomes a self-fulfilling prophecy; victims often prove willing to stay in the same job in the same untenable situation for as long as they can. It often takes a structural change, such as a fire or hurricane or major illness, to get victims to move. Unfortunately, without doing some inner work to look at this deep pattern, victims will **re-create the same unhappy setting over and over again.**

The victim is so standard a pattern in our culture that we rarely pay attention to the fact that victims are responsible for their behavior. In the film *The Matrix,* there is a famous scene in which the victim protagonist, Mr. Anderson, comes in to work late on yet another day. He is called into his boss's office. While the boss chastises him in his best persecutory manner, window washers are cleaning the dirty windows so that Mr. Anderson can have a clear view of the possibility of a life that would obviously be much better outside the company. But why has Mr. Anderson come to work late in the first place? When I ask that question in our leadership seminars, I hear such responses as "He had a stomachache," "He partied late the night before," "He hates his job," and "It's the only way he can feel powerful." In the film, he never responds other than to acquiesce to his boss without really answering. That's a sign of a victim mind-set. Victims fear conflict so much that they convince themselves that they can never get their point across directly. There are lots of Mr. Andersons in every work setting around the globe.

Pattern 7: The Rescuer

Rescuers **live to save victims.** Whether it's women facing gender discrimination or minority employees who have not gotten promoted, rescuers will take up the cause and fix the problem. **Rescuers fawn over victims,** giving advice, hoping to win their attention and especially their gratitude. To burnish their image as saviors, rescuers have read all the latest self-help books and can get you the name of the best physician, lawyer, accountant, and hair stylist at a moment's notice. At home, **the rescuer will solve all problems,** in so doing keeping his or her partner and children feeling helpless and inadequate.

Rescuers are often the ones to start and maintain projects to help the less fortunate in the community near a workplace. They encourage coworkers to join in and will often make them feel guilty by noting how much time it takes away from their family yet how good it feels to do right by others. **Emotional by nature,** rescuers win acknowledgment for their capacity to drop anything to be there for you, so long as you have a problem. Until their cover is blown, **rescuers are seen as amazing people**—empathic, resourceful, and caring. Yet theirs ultimately turns out to be a **self-serving altruism.** Rescuers focus on others because they receive kudos and don't have to think about their own underlying inadequacies. Rescuers will go from person to person to make sure everyone is "happy," yet they are really only in their comfort zone when someone else is out of theirs.

If you have ever received help from a rescuer and no longer need his or her advice, you will find that the rescuer will quickly regard you as the enemy and attempt to convince you that you are making a mistake. When I supervise executive coaches, I am struck by those who resent clients that no longer need their advice. Rather than celebrate their successful intervention, these rescuers warn clients about striking out on their own too soon. I believe that this behavior is not so much about billable hours as the need to be needed. Like rescuers everywhere, these folks are uncomfortable when they have to look inward at their own requirement to be the savior. Little do they know that the person who really needs saving is themselves.

Pattern 8: The Drama Queen or King

This pattern in the workplace can be a lot of fun, yet most colleagues also find that it makes for some very high maintenance. The drama queen or king experiences **floods of emotions,** puts on major crying or yelling scenes, and may throw objects around the room, although the aim is not to cause pain as much as it is to make a noisy point. If one is not the target of the upset, watching a drama queen or king is often like watching good theater. The drama queen or king is **usually very intelligent** and possesses a vocabulary at once extensive, effective, and very colorful. Drama queens and kings **love gossip, rumors, personal traumas, and emotional breakdowns.** You never have to ask drama queens or kings how they are feeling; if it isn't written on their face in the form of either a scowl or a bright smile, they will tell you.

Drama queens and kings believe that their best work gets done when they are in a conflicted state. Although such people are resourceful and creative, they **waste a lot of time and energy** that could have been used more effectively if their **underlying craving for attention** could be tamed. In meetings, drama queens and kings offer stubborn, if clear, points of view. **They create polarization,** getting people to vote with them for whatever their idea is and making sure that everyone knows how wrongheaded the other side is. Drama queens and kings **love to stir things up.** If a conflict is settled and all parties are finally calm, the drama queen or king will often open up the next iteration with a "Yes, I know we all agree, *but . . .*" This is ultimately a play for attention; rarely is there enough drama to fill the empty space that exists in the hearts of those with this pattern.

There is a moment in the classic film *Gone with the Wind* when the drama queen heroine, Scarlett O'Hara, is having a spat with her lover, Rhett Butler. She goes on and on until the famous line from Rhett: "Frankly my dear, I don't give a damn." The response from the audience is one of cheers and hoots of approval; the drama queen has finally gotten her due. Certainly most coworkers would respond similarly if the drama queen or king in their midst were finally called on the carpet for her or his **entertaining but disruptive excesses.**

PATTERN 9: THE MARTYR

Martyrs are the **opposite of procrastinators.** Whereas procrastinators love to delegate, martyrs don't and won't. They will **do everyone's work,** bend over backwards, go above and beyond the call of duty. **Martyrs love details,** so much so that they will often compulsively go over lists and numbers three, four, even ten times to make sure that what they had calculated was correct. **They want to be the "special one"** in the office, the one whom everybody calls to discuss a problem, personal or professional. You will often hear a martyr say, "Well, I'm no psychologist, but I really helped Carol out of a tough spot," and then she will tell the story over and over for weeks on end until there is a new one to replace the old one.

Martyrs are great to have on your team, so long as you are immune to guilt feelings. Although **their work is usually quite good,** the refrain of "Look at all I did" gets old really quickly. **Martyrs love to suffer,** and they do it quite well. Although they claim they do not want any recognition, **they use guilt and silence** to get across how hard they are working. Ask a martyr how he feels about his job, and he will tell you many, many times that he is overworked, underpaid, and unrecognized. When martyrs feel underappreciated, they begin to talk behind your back. If ignored, they are often the most willing to find a lawyer and claim mental abuse and stress-related illnesses. It doesn't matter if you took away all the extra jobs they piled onto their work schedule. Even if you forbid them to take another project, they will claim you insisted they do the extra work. It becomes an ugly and impossible situation.

The martyr loves the role of caretaker and chief bottle washer because it gives her control. **Most martyrs are anxious people** who think that if they control a situation they will never be harmed. **Being a martyr does give the semblance of control** in the short run because you have lots of people coming to you for help. Over time, this starts to wear thin as people begin to see that the price they pay for the help is the requirement that they listen to the martyr's complaining. As time passes, fewer folks consent to the deal. Thus the martyr's paradox: the more you attempt to garner power by saying you don't want or have it, the less power you end up having. Although martyrs want attention and appreciation, their complaining drives colleagues away, and then the martyr begins to lash out with vindictive venom that can be quite deadly.

Pattern 10: The Pleaser

Pleasers, in essence, are people who **can't handle the truth.** Afraid that coming clean with honest emotions might offend someone, pleasers make sure to stay quiet. They **rarely offer opinions,** and they will do whatever it takes to avoid causing or being involved with conflict. Pleasers want to fit in, and this desire leads them to become **intensely self-conscious.** One pleaser I met had just gotten a tattoo on her ankle because it was "in" with her workmates. When she was told that the trend was really to have a tattoo on the back of the neck, she had the one on her ankle removed. It was around this time that one of our coaches began to work with her, and she admitted she hated tattoos altogether and just did it to be "one of the crowd."

Pleasers have a **hard time setting limits.** As important as it is to get others' approval, it is even more important not to arouse people's disapproval. If a coworker or boss makes a request, pleasers fill it on the spot. Yet full-blown pleasers are not the most popular people at work. They tend to apologize over and over. "I'm sorry" gets to be annoying, as pleasers apologize for everything from global warming to the distance from the coffee machine to your office door. Pleasers are **ineffective authority figures** and will change their position depending on who is in the room. This chameleon-like stance is a protective device allowing the pleaser to remain ahead in the popularity contest. The pleaser's mantra is "So long as you look good, you are safe." The pleaser talks a good game, yet **results often do not match words or intentions.**

Pleasers usually **love a micromanager as a boss.** That way they just salute and do what they are told. However, if the boss lets a pleaser make decisions on his or her own, the pleaser becomes upset and feels abandoned. When asked if anything is the matter, the usual reply is "Oh, nothing!" In general, pleasers tend to please until there is the proverbial straw that breaks their pleasing backs. At that point they express anger, and if the situation has been festering long enough, this anger can boil over into rage. The individual on the receiving end of the venom is often blindsided. The anger is real, yet the capacity to change whatever brought on the situation is vacuous. The pleaser has not learned how to take a positive and strong stand, and there is a sense of powerlessness in the rage.

PATTERN 11: THE AVOIDER

Avoiders frustrate coworkers because avoiders are **aware of problems yet won't talk about them.** If conflict is brewing, avoiders sense the tension and leave very quickly for "more important" settings. The avoider's **chief mantras are "Gotta go," "I'll get back to you," and "I have to think about it."** Avoiders hate to be blamed for anything, and they walk away rather than admit they were responsible for creating a problem. They will also "go down with the ship" rather than change course if it means they will be held accountable. Avoiders often **take calculated risks,** yet if the situation is more demanding than they expected, they will quickly relinquish control and slide into the background. If you challenge an avoider to complete the project he started, he'll give the "deer in the headlights" look and find an excuse for a fast exit.

One term defines avoiders: **passive-aggressive.** The avoider's instinct is protective, to keep peace by staying out of the line of fire. When stress becomes overwhelming, avoiders begin by passively getting out of the way. If this doesn't work, they aim aggressive, angry outbursts at their antagonists.

Avoiders usually **possess reserved personalities.** They won't admit to vulnerability, yet they will go out of the way to avoid any setting where someone could make negative remarks about them. When ticked off, avoiders employ subtle and tricky methods to register their unhappiness. They might come to work late and swear they called in, even though there is a call log in the office and they are not on it. They might turn off their cell phone after you specifically asked them to expect a call, then swear that you never told them. If you leave a paper trail, avoiders will insist they never got the message or that the wording was unclear. Unlike the rebel, who believes that the best defense is a good offense, the avoider's best defense is just that—a defense.

PATTERN 12: THE DENIER

Deniers **pretend that problems and uncomfortable situations don't exist.** They ignore the fact that work is not getting done, refuse to heed warnings that might upset the status quo, and keep poor-quality workers on the job, pretending that they are adequate. Deniers are the ones who would busily rearrange the deck chairs on the *Titanic* saying "It's a beautiful day," and they **especially resent truth tellers** who tell them otherwise. Fearful of looking at themselves too closely, deniers feel a **critical need for everything to look good** on the outside, and so long as others cannot see the dirty laundry—well, it just isn't there.

We all want to find ways to decrease stress so that we can handle what is in front of us. Sometimes we need to put traumatic situations away until we can handle their full impact. In her landmark studies of death and dying, psychiatrist Elizabeth Kübler-Ross theorizes that the first step toward coming to grips with one's own mortality or that of a loved one is to deny the truth, then to proceed to anger, bargaining, and, eventually, acceptance. Sometimes, though, people become trapped in one of these emotional stages. When that happens, the emotion in question begins to color their entire world.

Deniers become especially dangerous when they **hold up much-needed innovation.** Deniers do this because they feel threatened by information that could make them look at the world through new lenses. Global warming has been recognized for decades, yet there have always been scientists who argue that there is no such thing. As a result, we are playing a difficult game of catch-up, and our very existence is at stake. Morton Thompson shows the depth of denial in his classic book, *The Cry and the Covenant.* Ignaz Semmelweis was a Hungarian physician who, in the mid-1800s, found the cure for childbirth fever that was taking the lives of so many women. All the physician had to do was wash his hands before the procedure. Yet the medical community remained in such intense denial that Semmelweis was thrown out of the medical academy and died a pauper, ignored by his peers.[4] As his example illustrates, denial is one of the most pernicious patterns that we are required to address.

Pattern 13: The Splitter

Do you have splitters in your midst? If so, you probably aren't aware of them. Of all the characters considered here, **splitters are especially insidious** because they are so **difficult to spot.** They seem so congenial and helpful. They always want to be your best friend and watch your back. Like your own personal CIA, they often have private information that they share because they claim to want to help you climb the ladder of success. Almost always, this information concerns someone who is hell-bent on betraying you. But not to worry—the splitter will keep his ear to the ground and make sure you are going to get all the information you need to play the game for your own success.

Splitters are **masters of covert power games.** They use innuendo, emotional bribery, mixed messages, and gossip to get you to be their puppet. They play these games because they are **insecure, powerless, and unsure of their skills and talents. Corporate environments have been fertile ground for splitters,** because in most companies, emotional openness is considered either a sign of weakness or as potentially dangerous. Take the head of a department who held an e-mail over the waste basket and said to her direct report, "I can't decide if I should show this to you or not. As you can see, I don't agree with what the new HR business partner has to say about you, and yet, if you want to see it, here it is before I put it in the circular file." Of course the direct report was curious, and she spent several minutes studying the piece of paper that had terrible things to say about her. Then she had to hand it back to her boss, who threw it in the wastebasket and said, "Now this stays between us; don't let HR know I showed it to you."

As this example suggests, splitters **love to feel important,** and they also love to have control over you as well as the others who are "out to get you." Serious interpersonal problems arise because while you are busy creating tactical alliances, the splitter is also busy telling your adversary that *you* are out to get *her.* **Splitters do all the work up front, then sit back to watch the fireworks** as you and your adversary plot and plan and walk past each other in the hall with a deep sense of mistrust. If warring colleagues manage to make sense out of this ugly mess, splitters sit back and act shocked that such underhanded dealings were going on between such basically good people. They also offer to help heal the rift in any way possible. Quite often, these rifts cannot be healed; the relationships are permanently ruined. When healing is possible, it usually requires the investment of considerable time, energy, and attention on the parts of all parties. Either way, splitters are bad news for a company or a work team.

IDENTIFYING YOUR OWN PATTERNS

With this framework in place, let's now see how these patterns compare with your own work behaviors. I remind you, the intent here is not to analyze your behavior definitively, but rather to initiate you into a way of thinking—to begin a process that you continue elsewhere using other tools. I wouldn't dream of reducing all of your life experiences to one of these thirteen patterns. In some cases, we develop patterns that are idiosyncratic or unique to us, and it takes careful work, either on our own or with a coach, to uncover and name them.

Like any list intended to help sort out ideas, this one is both helpful and limiting. On one hand, the thirteen patterns can become like a straitjacket. They cut off our ability to think fluidly and expansively, just as a straitjacket restricts our ability to move freely. On the other hand, they give us a great shortcut for seeing how our behavior and that of others interface.

Completed honestly, thoughtfully, and slowly, the following exercises will reward you with some wonderful "Aha" moments as you make initial connections between seemingly unrelated incidents and behaviors in your professional life. You'll see your everyday experience from a whole new perspective and tease out meanings you never knew existed. Which of the top thirteen patterns apply to you? When do they come out to play, and in relationship to whom? Put your legs up and get comfortable: it's time to become acquainted with your shadow self that never went away and that continues to pop up again and again, especially during times of stress. It's time to think more closely and seriously than ever before about how you behave in relation to your colleagues.

Exercise One

Career History Inventory (CHI)

This exercise helps you look at the larger patterns in your life and determine the subtle ways that they that have had an impact on you across the whole span of your career.

Directions: On a horizontal axis, your time line, mark increments of ten years. On a perpendicular axis, go halfway up and draw a line across as the 50 percent point for job satisfaction—above the line for jobs you enjoyed and below for those you were glad to leave. Chart all jobs you have had since you were a kid and rate your satisfaction with each job. Think about how you might have displayed one or more of the thirteen patterns at each job, and also note the following:

- Did you like to work with others?
- Did you prefer to work alone?
- Were you a leader?
- Did you take direction well?

To give you a sense of how you might proceed with this exercise, let's follow a woman I'll call Sophia, senior vice president of HR at a large pharmaceutical company, as she fills out her Career History Inventory. Sophia is in her second marriage and has two grown, married daughters and three grandchildren. As a child, Sophia wanted to be an actress, but she grew up in a conservative suburban home where work options for girls were limited to teaching or nursing. Her chart is shown in the figure.

As Sophia does her CHI chart, she is surprised to find how, forty years later, thinking about her very first chance to earn money brings tears to her eyes. What a beautiful little girl she had been!

Sophia's Career History Inventory (CHI Chart)

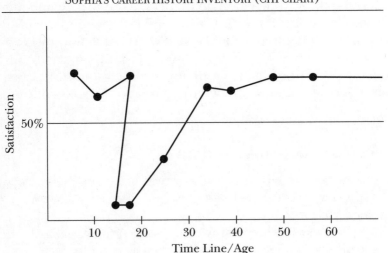

She was spunky and curious and filled with love of music and dance. She had taken tap dancing lessons with the neighborhood kids and had stood outside on the cement and practiced the dance they called "Shuffle Off to Buffalo."

One day, she got all the neighborhood kids together and enticed them to put on a variety show. They could dance, sing, read a poem, or tell a story. She convinced her mother to let her clear out the garage, and presto—instant theater. Sophia was nine and had never realized before that she had the entrepreneurial spirit in her. She just wanted to sing and dance that Buffalo shuffle. They charged one quarter for the entire show and convinced the neighbors that it was a great deal. When the applause had died down and they counted the proceeds, Sophia was able to keep three dollars. That was the very first money the little nine-year-old had ever made, and was she ever proud of herself!

What Sophia learned as she began to look at her patterns and her talents is that she had taken the drama queen personality that often showed itself when she threw a tantrum, and channeled it, along with her need to be the center of attention, into this fun show. By God, she even earned money for it! She smiles and says, "This is where I learned that work can be fun and easy and that you can earn good money. And all these years, that has been what has happened for me." Then she fell silent. "I wonder what would have happened if I also had been less of a pleaser and would have taken the risk to go into show biz."

She continued to consider the evolution of her work history. The chart's next part indicated that she thrived in jobs offering a great deal of social interaction and an opportunity to "help" people—such jobs as her summer high school position as a Macy's sales clerk and her stint as a waiter's assistant at a Catskill Mountains resort. She remembers feeling fascinated listening to the full-time employees complaining to each other about their bosses and about anyone who was not on duty at the time. "I guess that was where my interest in human resources began. Boy, there was so much 'He done me wrong' or 'Who does she think she is.' I remember saying simply, because it seemed so easy, 'Why don't you just go directly to the person?' and they all told me to shut up, that I didn't know what I was talking about, but some day I would."

Continuing to follow her chart through college, Sophia remembers that as an English major she had thought she would teach school, and she had had several after-class jobs to help with the tuition. Here she sees that she had been confronted with the realization that she would rather kill herself than take a job involving a lot of structure and routine. She still finds it curious that even in these benign jobs, filing folders for hours on end three afternoons a week, she would listen to the other clerks and find that they were doing the same type of complaining she had heard at the department store and the resort. It was always about bosses or other employees who were not around at the time.

After graduation, Sophia found that her options were limited and that teaching didn't really interest her. There was, however, an opening in pharmaceutical sales. Fortunately she had taken several biology courses, so she passed the initial tests with ease. Looking back on it, she realizes now that the job allowed her to use all her talents, especially her people skills. She found the work fun and well paid. Most interesting of all is her realization that all her jobs had something in common. She heard the same complaints about problem bosses and coworkers and realized that she wanted to be part of the solution. Just as she had gathered the neighborhood kids to put on the play in the garage, she began some after-work discussion groups to look at gender inequities and work-life balance. Looking back on it, she realizes that she had seen a chance to do something different, to take her patterns both as a pleaser and as a drama queen and turn them into positives.

Sophia was called in to the HR manager's office. She remembered feeling worried that the after-work discussion groups would get her in trouble. She knew her sales numbers were good and that she had a great relationship with her boss. As it turned out, the off-hour chats had taken on a life of their own. HR and her boss suggested that she become an approved HR provider. She gladly took their advice, and when she finished her schooling, she realized she was in her dream job. She could help people go directly to the source of their upsets at work and find creative solutions for all manner of people issues. She was able to begin myriad team-building initiatives, and her company's HR department began receiving award after award.

Exercise Two

POP Quiz (Pattern Observation Perspective)

Directions: For the questions that follow, circle the action you are most likely to choose. Don't ponder, just pick. Remember, there is no right or wrong answer. Go with the one that you think or feel is most like you. If you're not sure, picture yourself on a fence, note which way you would tend to lean, then let yourself "fall" in that direction. If you absolutely can't choose, leave that one blank and don't "angst" over it. This activity is intended to give you a broad-based view of yourself, not to paint yourself into a very small corner. When you are finished, go back and see which pattern or patterns show up the most. Are there more than one? How might these patterns relate to one another?

1. In a conflict situation, when someone expresses anger in a loud, defiant voice, do you:

    a. Get louder to prove your point?
    b. Lower your voice, look down, and feel defeated?
    c. Divert the situation by talking about your own, bigger problem?
    d. Walk away?
    e. Tell a joke or mimic the person's angry voice?

Answers: (a) persecutor; (b) victim; (c) martyr; (d) avoider; (e) clown

2. In a meeting, when two colleagues are in a debate that is taking all the airtime, do you:

    a. Jump in and make them "play nice"?
    b. Text-message a coworker across the room about whom you side with?
    c. Wait until the break and enlist others to go to HR with you and complain?
    d. Agree with both of them just to STOP the arguing?
    e. Quote research to prove that they are both wrong and that you know better?

Answers: (a) rescuer; (b) splitter; (c) rebel; (d) pleaser; (e) super-achiever

3. When you see a coworker taking home lots of office supplies, do you:

    a. Write an anonymous e-mail to his boss?
    b. Begin a petition about office policy?

c. Offer to help him put things in his car?
d. Complain to everyone that you never have enough paper clips?
e. Begin a monologue about your personal wants and needs?

Answers: (a) splitter; (b) rebel; (c) pleaser; (d) martyr; (e) drama queen or king

4. If someone tells you, "Thanks—you have gone the extra mile for me," do you:

a. Acknowledge what a privilege it is to help by using your VIP contacts to get a job done properly?
b. Let him know how glad you are that you could support her by telling her about the naysayers who were causing the trouble?
c. Thank her by putting on a Chinese accent and saying, "I'm just an old philosopher who turns every obstacle into opportunity"?
d. Admit that you stayed late for many weeks to help out and that you missed your kid's soccer games, but that that really doesn't matter, it was worth it?
e. Blow off the comment with, "I'm just doing my job, nothing more, nothing less"?

Answers: (a) super-achiever; (b) splitter; (c) clown; (d) martyr; (e) denier

5. You are at a required dinner with your boss, your team, and several important clients. People are looking at the menu and sharing thoughts about what to order. Do you:

a. Talk about the dangers and social implications of eating red meat?
b. Share your knowledge of how to decide which wine goes with which food and the best vineyards for the different selections?
c. Keep changing your mind about what to order and finally decide to eat whatever your boss chooses?
d. Keep telling the waiter to take someone else's order while you continue to contemplate what you want?
e. Tell a long, detailed story about the last time you ate at this restaurant and how the chef came out specifically to check if you liked your food because the time before that . . .?

Answers: (a) rebel; (b) super-achiever; (c) pleaser; (d) procrastinator; (e) drama queen or king

6. There has been an economic downturn, and there is a meeting to discuss the possibilities of future downsizing. Do you:

   a. Write a memo as soon as you get back to the office with sage advice about how to handle employees during difficult times?
   b. Cancel your planned vacation and let your family know they can go without you?
   c. Tell your key employees that you will keep them safe no matter what happens if there really is a downsizing?
   d. Gather a group to go to HR and make a strong statement that there is no reason for downsizing except corporate greed?
   e. Make an appointment to meet with your boss, give him your full support, and tell him you will do whatever he asks of you?

Answers: (a) super-achiever; (b) martyr; (c) rescuer; (d) rebel; (e) pleaser

7. Your company has just been cited for dumping toxic waste into the local river. As head of corporate communications, you are asked to appear on the local news. You call an emergency meeting of the executive committee, all of whose members claim that they had no idea this was happening. Do you:

   a. Suggest they set up a committee to look into the matter and provide answers for the media in one or two months' time?
   b. Talk about the unfairness of the situation and that given the firm's ethical standards, you know the allegations cannot be true?
   c. Redirect the problem to your competitors, who are upstream from you, arguing that just because you are the bigger company you get all the blame?
   d. Go on the offensive and blast the media for their weak, underhanded reporting tactics?
   e. Talk about all the good the company has done for the community, how little appreciation had been shown, and how disappointed you are in the lack of gratitude?

Answers: (a) procrastinator; (b) denier; (c) victim; (d) persecutor; (e) martyr

8. You worked late, and on your way out you see a coworker who is married with children making out with a single coworker. They both just happen to report to you. Do you:

   a. Say hi and tell them you were glad they were getting the report ready for the morning meeting?

b. Turn around and go back to your office to work for another hour, hoping that they will leave quickly so that you can pretend you never saw them?
c. Ask the married coworker to go back to your office with you and lecture him on family values?
d. Go back to your office and call the spouse of the married employee to tell her that you are worried about burnout and that perhaps she should have a talk when her husband gets home?
e. Tell them about your own mistakes in the past and how you are now divorced and regret what happened and how easy it is to be taken advantage of at work?

Answers: (a) denier; (b) avoider; (c) persecutor; (d) splitter; (e) victim

9. The VP of IT, to whom you report, has been coming to work dressed provocatively. She is the talk of the company. In a one-on-one meeting with you, she stops in the middle and asks if there have been people spreading rumors about her and the way she dresses. Do you:

a. Acknowledge her good taste in clothes and change the subject?
b. Tell her about a style consultant you know who is a very close friend and to whom you would love to introduce her? Tell her as well about the research you have done on the way to dress for success in the contemporary business world?
c. Make a joke of it by telling her the latest gossip about Paris Hilton and Hollywood trends?
d. Share with her how upset you felt when you heard two other colleagues making negative remarks about her and that you would be more than willing to tell her who they are?
e. Tell her you are tired of all the drama at work and that you are prepared to take a stand with her to get the jealous and calculating folks to stop, while also mentioning that the gossip at your last place of employment nearly caused the company to fold?

Answers: (a) avoider; (b) super-achiever; (c) clown; (d) splitter; (e) drama queen or king

10. You have an office mate who comes to work disheveled and bleary-eyed. This has been going on for weeks. Do you:

a. Bring her a cup of coffee and tell her you would be pleased to bring a salad from the cafeteria for lunch, yet never say you are concerned about the way she looks?

b. Go to your boss or HR and complain about the drug and alcohol policy and ask whether employees who are questionable are being talked with?

c. Stop at her desk and tell a joke about the rabbi, priest, and monk who had a hangover?

d. Tell her that you can see she is having a rough day and that you would be pleased to finish her urgent work for her?

e. Sit down and ask her why she looks so worn out and then admonish her for the poor example she is setting, especially for the younger employees?

Answers: (a) pleaser; (b) rebel; (c) clown; (d) martyr; (e) persecutor

11. There has been a lot of staff turnover, with many folks taking early retirement. The firm's environment has changed. Although you are not planning to retire, you are hearing that some of your thinking is old-fashioned. Do you:

a. Complain to HR about age discrimination?

b. Ignore the "kids" and talk only to the seasoned veterans?

c. Let everyone know that it's no fun getting older?

d. Request time to have a discussion about generational perspectives and leave a bunch of handouts for your colleagues to read for a follow-up meeting?

e. Take every opportunity to point out the ringleaders of the "youth brigade" to senior management?

Answers: (a) rebel; (b) avoider; (c) victim; (d) super-achiever; (e) splitter

12. You received a well-earned promotion and hired your replacement from outside the company. Although all your coworkers are glad about your new job, they hate the person who replaced you. Do you:

a. Call a meeting and chastise the group for not welcoming the new boss in a friendly manner?

b. Call the new boss in and tell her who to watch out for?

c. Decide to take over the group for now until they can acclimate to the new situation, even though you really don't have the time?

d. Have your assistant tell the team you are too busy to take their calls?

e. Take your group out to dinner and tell them that their comments are affecting your health and that you may end up on high blood pressure medicine if they keep up the negativity?

Answers: (a) persecutor; (b) splitter; (c) martyr; (d) avoider; (e) drama queen or king

13. When it looks as if a project won't meet deadline, do you:

   a. Give excuses about how "the dog ate the research"?
   b. Ask "What deadline?" and mean it?
   c. Offer to pull an all-nighter to get it done?
   d. Delegate in a strong "I dare you to challenge me on this" voice?
   e. Defend the project manager who is "always given too much to do"?

Answers: (a) procrastinator; (b) denier; (c) pleaser; (d) persecutor; (e) rescuer

Exercise Three

Our Inner Voices

Whereas the questions in Exercise Two focused on things that you do, this set of questions is geared to help you become more adept at listening to things that you think—the self-talk that you hear in your head all the time. (Right now, for instance, you're probably saying, "I don't talk to myself"—it's that voice I'm talking about!). This voice is usually repetitive in nature and sends the same message over and over, whether it fits the situation or not. Just as we change our clothes every day, we need to be conscious of changing our thinking so that it feels appropriate to the situation at hand. Once we are able to observe our ways of responding to situations, we can limit what has been called "monkey mind chatter"—that is, thinking the same things over and over.

   Directions: Choose the sentence that best expresses what you would think to yourself when encountering the following situations. Again, don't ponder, just pick. When you are all finished, go back and see which patterns show up the most.

1. Your boss asked you to speak at a national meeting in two weeks because she is suddenly unavailable. You think:

   a. It will put me in a power position.
   b. Maybe I can get out of it by getting the flu.
   c. I'm always the one they all turn to, and it's not fair.
   d. I'll go to her boss and complain.
   e. I'll get someone else to write the speech; I'm always so swamped.

Answers: (a) super-achiever; (b) avoider; (c) martyr; (d) splitter; (e) procrastinator

2. During your performance review, you are told that some of your colleagues are complaining about the quality of your reports. You think:

   a. I'll get back at them somehow.
   b. They're the ones who do crappy reports, not me.
   c. I don't know what they're talking about.
   d. I'll take a writing class and show them I'm better than they are.
   e. My lawyer will hear about this.

Answers: (a) persecutor; (b) avoider; (c) denier; (d) super-achiever; (e) rebel

3. You used to be one of the carefree and popular coworkers. You were recently promoted to a senior position, and now see your new direct reports as frivolous and wasting time. You think:

   a. I have to whip them into shape before they give the department a bad name.
   b. I'll have to spend my evenings and weekends developing policies and procedures so that we have some order here. I can't believe this was not handled before now.
   c. I know they are good people, so I'll just hang back and hope they start to buckle down.
   d. I'll set up classes and teach them how to be a team. It's a good thing I have my MBA.
   e. I don't believe they will really listen to me. I was just one of them, and I really have no power with them.

Answers: (a) persecutor; (b) martyr; (c) procrastinator; (d) super-achiever; (e) victim

4. You have recently joined an organization that sends a mixed message. The major theme is "We want your innovative ideas developed, so long as they don't disrupt the status quo." You think:

   a. It's a good thing I joined this company. I can help them see their convoluted thinking and free up everyone's creative energy.
   b. I have to bring some banners into the place that say, "The emperor is naked." Then maybe we can begin to tell the truth.
   c. I will just come in and do my job. I never get heard anyway.
   d. I'll just play the game and pretend I love this job. No one will ever know that I think they're all nuts.

e. I'll do some research on double-blind messages and then go to my boss with the results so that we can set up some communication classes.

Answers: (a) rescuer; (b) drama queen or king; (c) victim; (d) pleaser; (e) super-achiever

5. You work with three others whom you think of as "cowboys." They shoot from the hip and never coordinate with anyone. Working with them is like living in constant chaos. You think:

a. I can only work with them by dividing and conquering. I will get the weakest as my ally and then the next weakest and then we can take on the big gun.
b. I don't need their cooperation. I can get my job done with no problems and let them worry about themselves.
c. I can win them over by telling them how good their work is and how much I can learn from them.
d. Every time I go by one of them, I will say, "Yee-haw" and talk like a cowboy. They'll get the point.
e. I have every right to sit them down and tell them how disgraceful their behavior is and how I won't stand for this level of chaos.

Answers: (a) splitter; (b) denier; (c) pleaser; (d) clown; (e) persecutor

6. You tend to be uncomfortable when major projects are heading to deadline and the stress level increases exponentially. You think:

a. My colleagues have all the help they need, and no one has come to ask me for anything, so I guess I'm not really needed.
b. I have to tie up loose ends from the old project, so I can't get involved with this one.
c. They expect us to stay late, and that is not fair. I will put in only the allotted time, and if they want more time, they have to pay me.
d. Some people are cut out for excessive stress. I'm not one of them, so I'll just claim I have chronic headaches.
e. I guess that means no home life for the next six weeks. What else is new? I always do the dirty work.

Answers: (a) denier; (b) procrastinator; (c) rebel; (d) victim; (e) martyr

7. You recently received a poor performance review and are worried you may be asked to leave the company. You think:

   a. I never really liked working here. It's not creative enough for me, and I'll be glad to get out of here.
   b. I'll meet with my boss and convince him that they can't replace me. I'll also promise to work harder.
   c. I was never given any chance to improve myself. Why am I always the last to know?
   d. If I lose this job, my family will not survive. I may as well kill myself; at least they'll get insurance money.
   e. This can't be happening to me. I'm the most competent person on the team, with the best degrees from major universities. I'll use my influence with the big bosses.

Answers: (a) avoider; (b) pleaser; (c) victim; (d) drama queen or king; (e) super-achiever

8. You just found out that you were not invited to two senior meetings in the past month. You think:

   a. That's exactly what they mean by micro-inequities. I'm calling a lawyer.
   b. I was out of town and didn't expect to be invited, so it's no big deal.
   c. After all the nights I have spent completing those complex charts for the annual meeting, I can't believe I'm so unappreciated. It doesn't pay to go the extra mile.
   d. I know it was just an oversight, and I will take some coffee and go into the boss's office and tell him I understand that he was too busy to remember to invite everyone.
   e. I'll just wait and see who gets invited to the next few meetings before I even think about saying anything.

Answers: (a) rebel; (b) denier; (c) martyr; (d) pleaser; (e) procrastinator

9. You have taken the initiative to develop some team-building programs for your business unit and have been told to leave the "soft stuff" to HR. You think:

   a. I'll never do anything extra for this company again. After all I've given, I just get pushed aside.

b. I'll go to HR and give them my help. I've put so much into what I created; I want this to continue, and I know it won't without me.

c. I don't really care; I just did it to fill some time.

d. I'll do what I want with my team and just not let them know what I'm doing.

e. They can't tell me what to do with my team. It's not soft stuff, and I'll take this to the executive committee.

Answers: (a) martyr; (b) rescuer; (c) denier; (d) splitter; (e) rebel

10. You have become the unadvertised counselor for your small company. People seek you out and ask for private time so that they can vent their frustrations. This is taking too much time from your other work. You think:

a. I am doing a great service to the company. I hope they appreciate it.

b. I can't keep doing this; my work isn't getting done. But if I don't, whom will they have to talk to, and how will they feel safe?

c. I'm glad I went to all those conferences. They helped me become so proficient with personnel issues. I'm probably better than most of the coaches the company hires.

d. I love doing this. I get to hear all the dirt, and I have already bought stock in Kleenex, so bring it on!

e. I don't know how this happened. It's taking so much time, and I go home drained and depressed.

Answers: (a) rescuer; (b) martyr; (c) super-achiever; (d) clown; (e) victim

11. You are in a tense meeting where two colleagues are in a battle of wills and no one is saying anything. It is uncomfortable, yet the meeting facilitator is simply staring into space. You think:

a. I've been there; the facilitator is an arrogant bastard, and I'd cut his head off.

b. The leader is doing the best job possible. It's better just to let them handle it themselves.

c. I will probably have to intervene, since no one else seems to know what to do. It's frustrating that I'm always the one to do what has to be done.

d. If they don't settle this soon, I'm simply going to stand up and leave. If they ask where I'm going, I'll tell them that the manure is too much to inhale.

e. I am going to talk some sense into them and help them see that they are both right if they start to play nice and listen to each other.

Answers: (a) persecutor; (b) pleaser; (c) super-achiever; (d) drama queen or king; (e) rescuer

12. You're in the break room, and one of your colleagues just announced he is getting the promotion you wanted. You think:

   a. It's never my turn; life is so unfair.
   b. After all I've done for him! I work myself to the bone for all these jerks.
   c. I really didn't want that job anyway.
   d. He got that job because of favoritism. I'll complain to HR about that.
   e. That makes me think of the joke about the two guys in a rowboat.

Answers: (a) victim; (b) martyr; (c) denier; (d) rebel; (e) clown

13. You lent money to a colleague to help him pay his doctor's bill. He has not paid you back, yet he came in wearing an expensive new sweater that he is showing off to the troops. You think:

   a. I always buy the "sob story" and get left holding the bag.
   b. Wait until he asks me for something again; I'll let him have it between the eyes.
   c. I'm glad he's feeling well enough to buy himself something nice.
   d. I'll tell them all how he took money I needed for my poor, starving kids.
   e. I was going to ask for the money back, and I got busy; I'll do it tomorrow.

Answers: (a) victim; (b) persecutor; (c) rescuer; (d) drama queen or king; (e) procrastinator

Exercise Four

Pattern Recognition Questionnaire

Each of the following questions helps you see more clearly who you are, where you find comfort and solace during difficult times, how you interact with others, and the self-fulfilling prophecies that your inner voice is telling you when you feel backed into a corner.

One of the most important reasons to take time with these exercises is that they are designed to help you gain awareness of the degree to which stress affects you. Armed with this awareness, you can handle the stress before there is a big explosion or meltdown. Answer the following questions in open-ended sentences, or write a long ramble if you prefer. We have created such a culture of sound bites and yes-or-no responses that we rarely go further and think about what is beneath the obvious. As a result, we often settle for mediocrity. Probing the essence of how our thoughts became long-standing patterns, we can connect with the core themes of our lives. It is then and only then that we can make corrective choices. These exercises, then, are not about quitting your job to find Nirvana; they simply give you a chance to look deeply into what best supports your long-term hopes, dreams, and growth.

None of these questions has a single right answer. Your responses are not right or wrong; they are simply expressions of you. So please take a deep breath and open your memory banks; let the wonder of who you are bubble up from the invisible world. Soon you'll be in a position to decide which behaviors in your life to keep and which to discard.

1. How does my work environment support my personal growth and development?
2. Whom do I go to when the stresses of the job are building up?
3. What is my self-talk when I feel unappreciated for my work contributions?
4. Who at work do I need to recognize and appreciate me?
5. What happens when I speak out at work?
6. What happens if there are difficult situations and I remain silent?
7. How do I respond to people in positions of authority?
8. What role did I play in confronting the authority figures in my family?
9. In what work situations do I feel guilty?
10. What mixed messages come from my workplace?

TAKEAWAYS

- Doing a CHI chart helps you gain a perspective on underlying patterns, which you can then choose to see as an opportunity for change.
- Listening to your inner voice gives you power over repeating thoughts. Once you become comfortable with this part of yourself, you can begin to ask yourself different kinds of

questions, breakthrough questions that will lead to new and innovative "Aha" ideas. And that is where the fun and delight of life is.

- As you become more adept at pointing out your own patterns and more sensitive to those of others, new and more appropriate behavior choices will reveal themselves.
- Being open to learning about yourself at work can increase your overall skill base as well as your creativity.
- Pattern awareness is a key indicator of high-level emotional intelligence.

CHAPTER FIVE

GOING DEEP
Exploring the History of Your Family Patterns

*The further back you can look, the farther forward
you are likely to see.*
—WINSTON CHURCHILL

Allowing our workplaces to become our teachers means examining our careers and work lives. As we saw in Chapter Four, the first step toward changing our patterns is to identify and observe them. The second is to understand them—to determine where they came from and how they relate to the totality of our lives. And this leads us inexorably out of the workplace and back to our families.

Remember the emotional underbelly that every family has, the places of caring and creativity as well as that secret netherworld of hurt feelings, mixed messages, shame, blame, and much else that gives rise to our invisible roles? Well, if our transformation is to be truly profound and lasting, we need to open this underbelly and bring its contents to the surface. Difficult as it may be, we need to become conscious of our complicity in our family's shadow drama, acknowledging the hidden roles that we've adopted in relation to our relatives, the hidden roles that they've adopted toward us, and how all this makes us feel. We need to consider objectively the secret behavioral legacies that we've inherited from our families, legacies that in many cases span the generations, and realize how they've shaped who we've become. Our pasts so often thwart us, and in ways we don't even realize; by reconnecting with these stubborn adversaries as adults, we lay the groundwork for turning them into our friends.

This chapter presents exercises designed to identify patterns from your childhood behavior and from the interactions of family members and ancestors. After explaining why an historical approach is so essential, I'll introduce you to a proprietary coaching process I have developed called Sankofa Mapping, in which you graphically explore and organize relationships in your family system and then apply the results to your work life. Creation of a Sankofa Map allows you to discover surprising and powerful connections between unresolved family conflicts and the behavior patterns you exhibit in the workplace. To supplement Sankofa, I also include an exercise to help you hone in on key moments of family conflict and tension. By noting how you and your relatives responded to family crises, you'll be able to understand even more deeply how patterned behavior emerged in your family context, and how family experiences continue to shape your workplace behavior today. I close the chapter with two extended case studies illustrating just how critical exploring the past can be when one is trying to change behavior at work.

THE IMPORTANCE OF HISTORICAL EXPLORATION

Many business, coaching, and personal growth books instruct readers on how to change behavior, but few (if any) emphasize the importance of investigating the personal and familial roots of work behavior. This isn't surprising; most of us in business aren't oriented toward looking at the past, much less our *own* pasts. Think of how much time and effort you spend each year hoping to stay on top of future trends and divining what "the next big thing" will be in your industry. Think of how much attention you devote to developing strategic plans and ensuring that the infrastructure will be in place to serve your anticipated needs. By contrast, how much time do you spend wanting to understand the history of your company, your career, or your family? If you're like most people, the Career History Inventory in Chapter Four was the first time you looked methodically at your previous jobs and tried to discern patterns. As for the history of our families, most of us see that as yesterday's news and would rather just push our deep, dark family conflicts into a corner and forget about them.

If you're like many of my clients, you're probably wondering why delving into your past is helpful or necessary to your future success. It's a valid question, yet in asking it you might also shift the focus a bit and consider whether you are not actually experiencing an internal *resistance* to revisiting your childhood traumas and hardships. Warren Bennis and Joan Goldsmith note, "It is in our families that we have the least examined and most determining experiences. Because our family life was so powerful in influencing our views of leadership and because we often maintain an unconscious barrier to recognizing its impact, it is difficult to uncover the lessons we learned and the messages we received."[1] I've certainly seen my own clients put up unconscious barriers to exploring their family's impact. Bringing your family's emotional underbelly to the surface might well be the most difficult thing this book asks of you. Many a reader will exhaust a box of tissues when working through the exercises in this chapter, and let me say this loud and clear: that's okay!

So why *should* we bother to explore our pasts? Even if we acknowledge that family patterns determine so much of our current behavior, couldn't we achieve profound personal transformation simply by trying to modify our own behavior going forward?

Most of us believe that we make decisions based on conscious deliberation. But a new study has found that, in fact, our unconscious brains are engineering our decisions milliseconds before our conscious brains can get around to them. German brain scientist John-Dylan Hayes states, "Our brains make decisions based on emotional and rational assessments that we're not aware of; only later, after the decision is actually made, do we explain our decisions and actions to ourselves."[2]

Studying your family history also helps by allowing you to normalize your patterns and realize that you are not somehow strange or blameworthy for taking them on. When we assess the relationships between life patterns and family history, we find that specific patterns correspond to certain kinds of family experiences. Avoiders often come from families where traumas or pain has not been discussed, where emotional connection between family members is weak, and where there is a lot of argument and sarcastic judging. Victims tend to be the product of families where one or both parents are judgmental and critical, and nothing is accepted as "good enough." In these families, failure and shame become the overriding themes, and blame is always placed elsewhere. Rebels often come from families whose members were seen as second-class citizens in their countries of origin or adopted countries. They also come from families where doing things differently was seen as having a positive outcome, whether for the family members or even for distant ancestors. In all these cases, an individual's life patterns can be understood as a logical and even predictable outcome of systemic conditions beyond the individual's control.

The actor Marlon Brando was a classic avoider whose famous "mumble" both enhanced his acting talent and allowed him to keep people at a distance. Another tactic Brando used to avoid contact with others was maintenance of a weight problem. So how can we understand Brando's life pattern? Just look at his family history. Born in 1924 in Omaha, Nebraska, Brando was a lonely child of alcoholic parents. His father was a distant, highly judgmental man who worked as a traveling salesman. His mother was an alcoholic whom an adolescent Brando would often have to pick up after she had spent a night in the "drunk tank" at the county jail. Actor Anthony Quinn once commented about Brando, "I admire Marlon's talent, but I don't envy the pain that had created it."[3] Brando himself was quoted as saying, "The more sensitive you are, the more likely you are to be brutalized, develop scabs and never evolve. Never allow yourself to feel anything because you always feel too much."[4] Such a statement illustrates quite well how painful it can be to exist in a family with strong avoider tendencies. In such families, the pain is too intense to bear, and family members conclude that it is better to ignore the pain than to confront it head on.

The great poet Emily Dickinson came from another classic avoider family marked by emotional distance and repression. When Dickinson was fourteen, both her cousin and a close friend died of typhus, and she grew so despondent that she was sent away to live with a family in Boston. Before then, she had struggled to deal with a mother who was seemingly cold and unloving. In those days, children wouldn't think of confronting a parent, so the safest thing to do was back away, push down the feelings, and try to forget about them. In at least one of Dickinson's poems, written in 1862, you can glimpse the sense of disconnection and solitude many avoiders feel:

They shut me up in Prose—
As when a little Girl

They put me in the Closet—
Because they liked me "still"
Still! Could themselves have peeped—
And seen my Brain—go round—
They might as wise have lodged a Bird
For Treason—in the Pound—[5]

Dickinson's parents liked her "still"; she had apparently enjoyed little permission to "be herself," and presumably little freedom to bring up unpleasant topics in a healthy way. Brando had acting and eating; Dickinson's solution as an adult was to withdraw from relationships and construct around her a private world of poetry. By the age of forty, she was staying in her home and beginning to talk to visitors from the other side of the door rather than face-to-face.

If you are an avoider, you can look to such figures as Brando and Dickinson and realize that you are not alone or idiosyncratic in your behavior. For readers with other patterns, please consult the following chart; it offers a summary description of the kinds of family experiences that tend to be associated with the thirteen most common life patterns visible in the workplace, as well as the names of some famous people whose own histories bear these patterns out. Not everyone with a given pattern will have a family experience exactly such as I describe here, yet I invite you to scan for your own patterns and see if at least some elements in my descriptions ring true. Realize that no matter what your upbringing, you have nothing to be ashamed of in embracing one or more of these patterns; everybody adopts patterns, and a great many people with family situations very similar to yours have wound up adopting one exactly like yours.

Workplace Pattern	Typical Family Experience	Famous Examples
Super-Achiever	There is financial or emotional bankruptcy in past generations, a history of failures or losses that instill shame.	Richard Nixon William Clinton Jerry Lewis

Workplace Pattern	Typical Family Experience	Famous Examples
Rebel	Family members are seen as second-class citizens, not respected in their countries of origin or adopted countries; child does things differently to make up for "inadequate" parent.	Che Guevara Evelyn Waugh Madonna
Procrastinator	Mistakes are seen as deadly; it is better to stay under the radar. Poor decisions lead to ridicule.	Samuel Coleridge Neville Chamberlain Agatha Christie
Clown	There is chronic illness or early death, and a need to do whatever it takes to bring levity into a depressed household.	Gene Wilder Harry Houdini Chi Chi Rodriguez
Persecutor	There has been abuse or neglect that has often remained a family secret or the source of unresolved shame.	Hitler Stalin Idi Amin
Victim	One or both parents are judgmental, and nothing is accepted as good enough; blame is always on "the other."	Tatum O'Neal Vincent Van Gogh Floyd Landis
Rescuer	One parent is usually dominant and tyrannical, and there is a perceived need to save others from neglect or abuse.	Steve Biko Sister Helen Prejean Oscar Schindler
Drama Queen or King	One parent is upset with the other, and the child "acts out," deflecting attention humorously or angrily; the aim is to get the family to pay attention to the imbalance.	Britney Spears John McEnroe Dennis Rodman

Workplace Pattern	Typical Family Experience	Famous Examples
Martyr	Parents could not fulfill their dreams or gave up their dreams to help their child, and the child takes on the burdens.	Martin Luther King, Jr. Joan of Arc Malcolm X
Pleaser	One or many members behave inappropriately, and the child represents the good in the family; abandonment, foster care, or adoption is often present.	Laura Bush Marilyn Monroe Doris Day
Avoider	Pain or traumas are not discussed, emotional connection between family members is weak, and there are arguments and sarcastic judging.	Marlon Brando Emily Dickinson Alice Walker
Denier	Fear of facing unpleasant emotions is so great that everyone agrees to ignore the truth at any cost.	Eugene O'Neill George W. Bush Barry Bonds
Splitter	Children have to choose between parents, because pleasing one means displeasing the other; child is used as a peacemaker in a no-win situation, and mixed messages are the norm.	Joseph McCarthy J. Edgar Hoover Larry Ellison

More than merely helping us comprehend and accept our patterns better, exploration of our personal and family histories implies a whole new perspective on our behavior and indeed our lives. I'm certain you've all had the experience of looking in the mirror and suddenly recognizing that you have your father's chin or your grandmother's smiling eyes. As we delve into our pasts, we discover that we've inherited our ancestors' ways of thinking and behaving as well. This leads in turn to a deep understanding that our decisions are less "ours" than they are formed by the collective energy of many, often long-dead ancestors. We are not merely individuals, but expressions of something much bigger, something both wonderful and burdensome—a lineage, a heritage, a tradition.

Throughout the world, cultures talk about an individual life being a thread woven into the family or tribal tapestry. Each generation retains a responsibility to preserve life's flow. All too often, this reality is lost to us in the competitive and analytical world of business; delving into our own past allows us to reconnect with it.

Recognition of our connectedness also alerts us to the possibility of real change. Digging up the legacies and loyalties that shaped who we are, we realize that we have the ability to consciously accept or reject the values, traditions, and habits of thought that have been passed down from generation to generation. We discover how ancient conflicts and crises continue to drive our actions, and with this understanding we become free to choose another way. Gaining clarity, we are able to respond to all challenges at work, at home, in our community. Without an understanding of the ancient conflicts and crises, we just end up behaving instinctively over and over again. As one leadership expert has observed, "there is power in becoming one's own personal historian."

So far we've focused on the intellectual benefits of acquainting ourselves with our personal and family histories. Understanding our patterns has an *emotional* impact as well, in that it allows us to heal old hurts, some of which we might not even be aware of. Books about emotions in the workplace have become quite popular in the last ten years. These books help us consider our feelings as motivations for how we behave. Emotions, like gravity, were there all the time, yet it is refreshing to discuss them.

Thanks to advances in neuroscience, we now know that our unconscious emotions occupy a different region of the brain from our conscious perceptions, often exerting a more powerful influence on our preferences and actions. Daniel Siegel's book *The Developing Mind* synthesizes information to explore the idea that "the mind emerges at the interface of interpersonal experience and the structure and function of the brain."[6] Research has also shown that we can reshape our brains as we get older, creating new neurological connections. Telling the story of our life patterns either orally or in writing helps connect the limbic system of our brains (where we feel pain) with the neocortex (where we analyze and make sense of it). Thus, by telling our own story, we make sense of our own lives. As we bring the power of the neocortex to bear on experience contained in the more ancient part of the brain, our brains physically alter, and this in turn allows us to express ourselves more fully and authentically in our work environments as well as in our personal relationships. Real change, then, doesn't come from merely isolating our patterns and trying to depart from them; rather, it requires coming to grips with the past and *clearing* the emotions that gave rise to our patterns in the first place.

Through personal research to find out about ourselves and through narrative, either writing down or talking about our biographies, we can alter our view of the past, and as author Tom Robbins has said, "It is never too late to have a happy childhood."[7] This is not meant to be a flippant statement; it means that by viewing ourselves through a larger lens, we can begin to put the past to rest, to complete it so that we don't have to repeat it.

If we don't heal the wounds of our past, they continue to haunt us, affecting our behavior and state of mind in the present. Three men who understand this well are authors George Jenkins, Sampson Davis, and Rameck Hunt. In their book, *The Bond: Three Young Men Learn to Forgive and Reconnect with Their Fathers,* the three, who left inner-city Newark to become doctors, recount their attempts to come to terms with troubled fathers who had abandoned them to lives of poverty. "I had buried [bitter feelings] about my dad," one of the authors relates, "feelings that eat at you and can eat you up." Another acknowledges the necessity of healing old wounds, explaining, "Sometimes a son has to take it upon himself to bridge the gap when a father can't."[8] All three display an emotional maturity and a new sense of well-being borne of tackling head-on the painful legacies of their families. You too can achieve new fulfillment in your career and at home. Be brave, go deep into yourself and your past—you'll be taking an essential step toward controlling the life patterns that have long bedeviled you.

THE WORLD OF SANKOFA

Let's now turn to the task of exploring your patterns' familial roots. To make this complex and unwieldy task more manageable, I've developed a process called Sankofa Mapping. *Sankofa* is a word from Ghana that means "heal the past to free the present"; the term reflects a basic theme of the chapter and this book: that you can go home again to rebalance, to rectify, to repair, and to reconcile. Sankofa Mapping, the creation of a chart that depicts one's family relationships, is an outgrowth of this theme. The chart, also known as a genogram, has been used in the field of family therapy for decades.[9] It's a shorthand representation of the family and cultural influences that determined how you became who you are. Going beyond a traditional family tree, the genogram allows you to visualize hereditary and psychological factors that color relationships, including repetitive patterns of behavior. A genogram will not only tell you that your uncle Randy and his wife, Betty, have three kids, but also that their youngest child was sent to boarding school, that their middle child was always indifferent to her mother, and that the oldest son has cancer. It will tell you that Uncle Randy is depressed, that Aunt Betty has not spoken to her mother for years and has a history of moving from job to job, and so forth.

My version of the genogram—the Sankofa Map—emphasizes the patterns and tendencies that help determine our behavior in the workplace. In addition, it asks you to consider the gifts as well as the challenges that have been handed through the generations. In every family and in every life, there are positive moments as well as struggle, suffering, and conflict. It is the complex whole that makes us who we are. I want to help you become not only more observant and less reactive to the anxiety and stress life offers but also more attuned to the strengths in even the most difficult family environments.

CREATING YOUR MAP

A Sankofa Map is a very personal, expressive thing, like a drawing or a letter written by hand. It is both a representation of your family history and an artistic expression of the person you are right now. In this section, I provide all the tools and ideas you need to explore visually the history of your patterns. All you need to bring is your creativity. Follow my guidelines, but not too closely. Let your personality come out so that you can discover insights about yourself and your past—the buried treasure that will lead to your future growth.

The first step is to map the basic structure of your family. Take out a blank piece of paper and a pencil. Starting in the middle of the page, draw a square for your father and a circle for your mother. Above the symbols, put their names. Below the symbols, write the dates of birth and, if needed, the dates of death. An X through the circle or square can serve as a quick visual representation of the deaths in your family. Also, below the name, or on a separate piece of paper, place anything you know that may be significant about births, health issues, divorces, and causes of death.

When you've got your parents down, add their siblings (your aunts and uncles), as they range in age from oldest to youngest. If your parents are still alive and you feel comfortable with it, you may want to ask them for information.

Go back one generation and fill in as much information as you can about both sets of grandparents, following the same process you used for your parents and their siblings. And go back further if you can. One man in our leadership program was able to map his family back to Sir William Wallace, known as *Braveheart,* a twelfth-century resistance leader during the wars of Scottish independence, whereas another only had information about his parents, who were both raised in orphanages. Each map was equally informative.

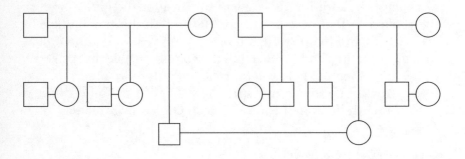

Now add you and your generation, your siblings, and their partners and spouses. Finally, add the next generations, your children, your siblings' children, and any grandchildren. For all these relatives, follow the same process outlined for your parents. Don't be discouraged if you lack all the information. You can fill in the gaps as you learn more from the appropriate family members or family friends. In any case, you'll quickly learn that gaps can often be as informative as facts.

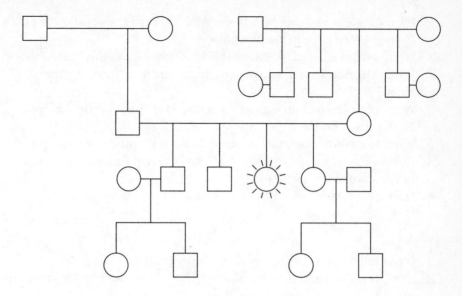

Now that the outline of your family relationships is in place, it's time to go deeper and probe into the hard stuff—the experiences that formed you, your parents, and other relatives. Consider the emotional content of relationships in your family, and the underlying values that persisted around such subjects as money, religion, and work. Here it is beneficial to interview family members and friends to the extent that you can. Sankofa Mapping can be fun, but it is also hard work. Probing for the traumas, emotions, and values that have determined who we are is always difficult, because we all have positive and negative legacies from our families. Here we learn about and confront these legacies head-on.

Think about the gifts and challenges, the courage and betrayals, the joy and the hurt in your family, and as you ask others about them, you might want to use the following questions to guide your inquiry and lead you to recurring themes and patterns:

Health
1. Is there a pattern of illness through the generations? Consider types of illness, age at onset of illness, and sudden deaths (heart attacks, accidents, suicides, and so on).

2. Who took care of sick family members? Were they cared for at home? Were they institutionalized?
3. What stories were passed down about how illness was handled? Were illnesses denied, or was time spent obsessing about them?
4. Were people courageous as patients? Did they see themselves as victims? Did they give up?
5. What verbal messages were passed about blame? For example, did a parent or sibling say, "It's your own fault you got sick because of your bad habits?"
6. Is there a history of addiction? How did that play out?

Wealth

1. What role has money played in your family?
2. Are there stories of heroes or victims who used or misused money?
3. How important is financial security? Do you yourself save or spend?
4. Do you need financial help? Do you offer financial help to others?
5. Are you comfortable talking about money in your primary relationship?
6. How healthy is your credit? Is it maxed out? Are there bankruptcy issues?

Relationships

1. Is there a pattern of either enmeshment (overly close family) or disengagement (distanced family)? How did it develop, and how do you respond to your family of origin today?
2. What messages were you given about how men and women treat each other?
3. How did guilt, fear, denial, and shame play out in your family of origin, and how do they play out in your family now?
4. What are the family secrets that are still affecting you and your family relationships?
5. How true are you to your cultural history?

6. How are children encouraged or discouraged from fulfilling their potential?

Work
1. How was accomplishment rewarded through the generations?
2. What did people do to gain attention?
3. How have your patterns of success and failure shown themselves at work?
4. Who at work plays similar roles to those in your family?
5. What messages were you given about the role of work in your life?
6. How has work been seen as fun, creative, or burdensome?

Spirituality
1. How did you develop a relationship with "the mystery"—that is, a higher power, God, religion, spirituality?
2. How important was religious practice or affiliation?
3. How have religious beliefs affected marriage, parenting, self-esteem, sexuality, and familial responsibilities or loyalties?
4. How does your family observe rituals of celebration as well as rituals of connection (meals, rituals around coming and going, couple rituals)?
5. Who in your family was especially spiritual, and how did it show in their way of life?
6. What positive or negative messages did you receive about spiritual beliefs and practices?

As you go through the process of posing and answering these questions, you can note answers directly on the Sankofa Map (for example, writing "not religious" under the symbol for Aunt Sheila). You can also put the information on a different piece of paper or in a journal. You can use some of the symbols in the following legends (pp. 116–119), or even create legends of your own. For instance, if religious observance played a special role in your family, and if there was considerable variation in observance, you might improvise a legend that expresses these differences.

EMOTIONAL RELATIONSHIPS LEGEND

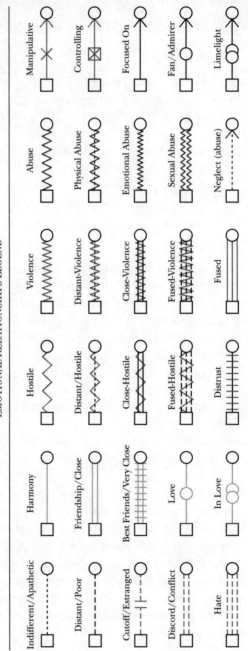

FAMILY RELATIONSHIPS LEGEND

Marriage

Separation in fact

Legal separation

Divorce

Engagement

Engagement and cohabitation

Engagement and separation

Nullity

Legal cohabitation

Legal cohabitation and separation in fact

Legal cohabitation and official (legal) separation

Committed (long-term) relationship

Cohabitation

Cohabitation and separation

Non-sentimental cohabitation

Non-sentimental cohabitation and separation

Casual relationship or dating (short-term)

Casual relationship and separation

Temporary relation/One night stand

Love affair

GENOGRAM SYMBOLS

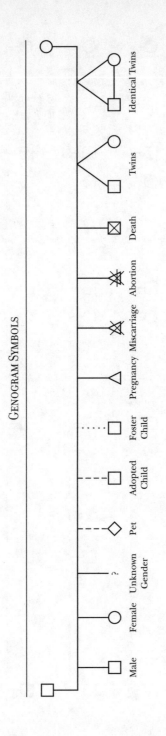

Male Female Unknown Gender Pet Adopted Child Foster Child Pregnancy Miscarriage Abortion Death Twins Identical Twins

MEDICAL GENOGRAM SYMBOLS

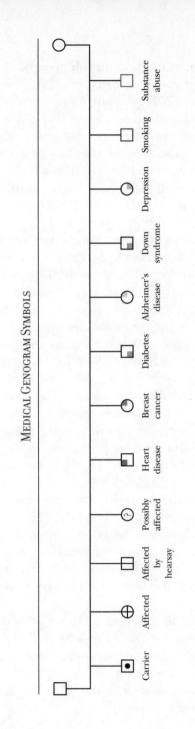

Carrier

Affected

Affected by hearsay

Possibly affected

Heart disease

Breast cancer

Diabetes

Alzheimer's disease

Down syndrome

Depression

Smoking

Substance abuse

ANALYZING YOUR SANKOFA MAP

The point of Sankofa is not merely to create a nice little chart documenting your family history, but rather to use the chart as a tool for discovering important connections between elements of your family background—such as past crises or role playing by relatives—and your own patterns. As you gather information to fill in the chart, you will quite naturally begin to relate your own behavior, thoughts, and values to those of other family members. When the chart is complete, spend some additional time scanning it, looking for examples of function and dysfunction, and assessing the roles each relative played (or is likely to have played) within the family system, and consider how all of this might have affected you. Think about the patterns you manifest as well as those of your family members, and if you wish, note these on the Sankofa Map. You might also want to talk through your map with a friend or spouse, introducing him or her to your family, and thinking about any patterns that he or she might discern.

To give you a sense of how a Sankofa analysis might run, I have created and analyzed a Sankofa Map for the great American writer Ernest Hemingway. Hemingway's literary works indicate a pattern of asserting his masculinity, both in his writing and in the rest of his life. What relationship does this have to Hemingway's family background? We begin by mapping out the basic family relationships that defined the Hemingway family. In the following Sankofa Map, I've included entries for Hemingway's father, mother, siblings, children, and grandchildren.

As you'll see in the following list, I've also included side notes with important information about the family, up to and including his grandchildren's generation. These notes, along with the simple circles and squares of the Sankofa Map, become markers of an individual's place in the ebb and flow of human connections and turn them into "the legacy of a life once lived":

- There were five suicides in the Hemingway family (Clarence, Ernest, Ursula, Leicester, and Margaux). Various members suffered from depression, alcoholism, and drug dependency.
- Hemingway killed himself in the same way his father had— with a shotgun to the head.

HEMINGWAY FAMILY

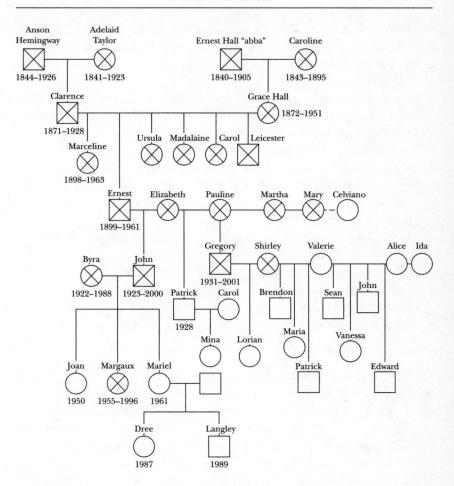

- Hemingway's father was a strict, quick-tempered disciplinarian; his mother was domineering and religious. Although Hemingway's father was a doctor, he earned less than Hemingway's mother did from the voice and music lessons she gave.
- Hemingway's father was the physician attending to his future wife's mother when she died.
- Hemingway's mother had wanted twins, and she would dress Ernest and his sister Marceline in similar clothes with similar hairstyles. In one surviving picture, we see a nine-month-old

Ernest wearing a pink dress and hat decorated with flowers, the caption beneath the photograph reading "summer girl."

- I also noted Hemingway's attitudes toward his parents. He once claimed that his "first big psychic wound was discovering his father was a coward," and he once called his mother the "All American Bitch."
- Hemingway was married four times, each relationship ending when Hemingway joined up with the next wife through an affair.
- Hemingway's father taught him to love the outdoors, and Hemingway's sons carried on this tradition. Jack Hemingway became an avid conservationist, outdoorsman, and author; Patrick lived in East Africa for most of his adult life, running a safari firm and teaching game conservation for the United Nations.
- Hemingway's son Gregory was a physician like his grandfather and a writer like his father. He became a cross-dresser, eventually had a sex change operation, and took the name Gloria.
- Hemingway's granddaughter Margaux (Jack's daughter) committed suicide through a drug overdose.
- His grandchildren who are authors include Lorean, Patrick, John, Edward, and Mariel.

There is much more one could say about this colorful family. Putting together what we have, we can see the power of emotional patterns flowing across generations. Suicide and alcoholism are comprehensible as family legacies. It becomes clear that all families have unspoken ways for members to live out legacies and that a legacy of doom hovered over the Hemingway clan. As for Hemingway's hypermasculinity, it seems quite possible that this stemmed from unarticulated doubts about his own and his father's masculinity, doubts that may have originated in a perceived power imbalance between Hemingway's parents. It is startling to discover a parallel between Hemingway's enforced childhood cross-dressing and his son's chosen proclivity for that behavior. Versions of Hemingway's hypermasculinity also carried over in his sons Jack and Patrick's love of the outdoors. Finally, it is worth noting that certain members of Hemingway's family have taken positive steps to break old family patterns. His granddaughter Mariel, for instance, had bouts with eating disorders (another form of addiction akin to alcoholism), yet she is now a yoga practitioner and teacher of holistic living. In addition, she has authored two books of her own: *Finding My Balance: My Memoir* and *Healthy Living from the Inside Out*.

It is not necessary to allow your family patterns to sink you, as Ernest Hemingway regrettably did. Understanding the relationships of cause and effect among traumas, conflicts, and life patterns, you will begin to comprehend many of the choices you have made. This understanding will in turn provide you with guidelines for making more appropriate decisions in the present.

The following exercise is designed to help you focus in on key moments of conflict and tension you experienced in your immediate family while growing up. By noting how you and your relatives responded to family crises, you should be able to understand how patterned behavior emerged in your family context, and how family experiences continue to shape your workplace behavior today.

Family Relationship Charting Exercise

Directions: On a piece of paper, create a chart with four columns and as many rows as there are members of your family. Using the examples here as models, enter the information that describes your relationship and reactive pattern for each family member. Notice how you and other family members interact when confronted by the patterns of other family members. Who aligns with whom, and in opposition to whom?

When filling in your chart, choose from the following list of behavior patterns:

Attacking	Bribing	Intimidating
Smothering	Withdrawing	Bullying
Blaming	Protecting	Humoring
Shaming	Manipulating	Slapping
Placating	Avoiding	Ignoring
Abusing	Demanding	Controlling
Babying	Threatening	Rescuing
Sympathizing	Gossiping	Defending

EXAMPLE ONE

Family Member	Ways Family Member Relates to Me	Ways I Relate to Family Member	Pattern
Mother	Babying	Humoring	Clown
Father	Attacking	Avoiding	Victim
David (oldest brother)	Intimidating	Avoiding	Victim
Neil (second oldest brother)	Rescuing	Sympathizing	Rescuer

Key insight: "My father and David are very similar, and I feel like a victim in their presence. I become a clown and use humor to lighten my mother's sadness, and I align with Neil and protect him—we are mutual rescuers."

EXAMPLE TWO

Family Member	Ways Family Member Relates to Me	Ways I Relate to Family Member	Pattern
Father	Avoiding	Attacking	Persecutor
Ellen (older sister)	Demanding	Avoiding	Avoider
Diane (younger sister)	Manipulating	Shaming	Persecutor

Key insight: "I attack my father to get his attention, and Ellen's demanding behavior makes me avoid her. I behave with her like our dad does with me. Diane and I are locked in a 'gotcha game' of one-upmanship."

CAREER EPIPHANIES THROUGH SANKOFA

Sankofa's great power lies in its ability to help you gain an entirely new perspective on destructive behavior that has befuddled you for years in your career. Sankofa may seem like a diversion from workplace concerns, yet it is eminently practical. One woman I worked with, Lila, had been passed over for a promotion because she was too soft spoken and not willing to participate in conflict. She possessed all the IT skills necessary for a higher-level job, yet she was dismissed as a pleaser and an introvert who would collapse back into silence and smiles when confronted. As she presented her San-kofa Map, she began describing her mother's story, unknown to her until she specifically asked about her mother's childhood in Italy. She stopped in midsentence, breathless. When I asked her what was wrong, she replied,

> My mother had never talked about this to me, never, ever. Yet when I asked one of the key questions about defining moments in her childhood, she sat quietly, sighed, and said, "I guess I owe it to you to tell you. I never could before because I thought it was too sad and I didn't want to burden you. But here goes: When I was almost four years old, old enough to remember things, World War II was raging, and we were taken from our town in Italy, a whole group of little kids. They brought us to the countryside, away from the bombs and shooting. It was night, and we were gagged so we wouldn't cry out—only in that way would we be safe. I learned then, I suppose, that the only way to be safe was to be quiet."
>
> And look, that's it: she learned that safety came from keeping your mouth shut, and here I am, decades later, a pleaser. It was passed on to me, and I didn't realize it until this very moment! The whole time I was growing up, my mother would get upset when my sister and I got rambunctious. She was always saying, "Be quiet, you're too noisy, if you don't be quiet I will have to gag you." As a result of this, my sister and I became scared and shut up. And now as an adult, I'm still afraid I'll get in trouble if I talk.

As you'll find, studying your Sankofa Map will move you beyond a one-dimensional perspective of parent-child relation-ships, the notion that "I did (didn't) like them" or "They did (didn't) take care of me." Like Lila, you'll discover your parents as people with their own wounds and struggles, and you'll realize how your parents' attempts to cope and survive were passed on to you, contributing to your own patterned behavior at work.

I offer two extended narratives of people I've worked with who experienced epiphanies from Sankofa and who were empowered to make career-enhancing changes as a result. Read these carefully and let them inspire you as you embark on this complex and rewarding process of discovery.

Emma's Story

Emma, a brilliant scientist at a large research company, was always getting herself into trouble. She hated being on teams because she was sure everyone was "an idiot" who would take forever to understand the implications of a research proposal. On some occasions, she would go to her department head and plead to be left alone with an assistant and a small laboratory. Emma chided her colleagues for pursuing lives outside of work. "Who cares if your family wants you to be home for dinner," she would taunt them. "What we're doing is much more important." She would stay late, ruminating on "all this team bullshit" and dreaming of the day when she alone would get the Nobel Prize for medicine. Her most dreadful habit involved taking other people's great ideas and reshaping them as fully her own. If the people with the great ideas protested, Emma would stare blankly and say, "I have no recollection of that. I only remember you went home early and I stayed and figured out this part of the project."

Her boss saw the discord Emma was sowing, and to help remedy the situation, she suggested myriad ways to "play nice." Nothing worked.

After Emma's midyear performance review, she was put on a performance improvement plan. Then she was called in to HR and asked if she would accept coaching. Ambivalent yet feeling backed against the wall, she agreed. We met for lunch; it was clear that Emma couldn't wait for our time to be over so that she could get back to the lab. We met regularly during the next few weeks, and Emma began to observe her behavior closely for the first time. When I asked her about her deepest dreams, all she could talk about was one focused area. "Are you kidding?" she said, without hesitation. "All I want to do is win the Nobel Prize for medicine."

We began to explore her Sankofa Map, which she regarded as a waste of time, more bullshit to keep her away from her work. Yet we plunged onward. With a few circles and squares on a piece of paper, Emma and I began to probe into the forces that helped form her obsession to be the best. She began to see that her whole life had been about living the super-achiever pattern, about proving that she and her family were the best.

Where did this pattern come from? Delving into her childhood history, we made some interesting connections. Emma grew up in Poland under the Communists. Her parents, both physicians, were assured of good jobs. However, her mother began to question authority and was replaced at her high-level research job. Emma's paternal grandmother, who had always lived with them, berated her daughter-in-law for making waves and thus making life uncomfortable for the family.

Although such chronic mother-in-law–daughter-in-law wrangling had been in the house ever since Emma could remember, it was getting progressively worse. The grandmother would turn to Emma and tell her that she had better learn to be like her father and not like her stupid mother. Emma was constantly defending her mother to her father and grandmother. Sometimes she felt that she was drowning in the shame of it all. She would show the world that her mother was smart and brilliant because, after all, she had birthed a courageous and brilliant daughter.

Recognizing her pattern and discovering its roots, Emma found herself adrift in a sea of conflicting emotions. Did she pursue achievement because she was brilliant and wanted to give something back to the world, or was it all just an attempt to prove that her grandmother had been wrong about her mother? One thing was certain: as Emma struggled to redefine herself and reframe her pattern of super-achieving, she became less abrasive at work. She realized that she had never really looked at or talked with her colleagues as live human beings who had their own hopes and dreams. Her career as a cardiologist and scientist began to take on a whole new meaning, and she started to treat people more kindly. Her boss noticed the change, and so did her colleagues. There was still a long road to travel and serious resentments among her colleagues to overcome, but Emma was on her way.

Brett's Story

Brett, a senior technical project manager, was widely regarded as a "really, really nice guy." He was well mannered, soft spoken, and above all a great listener. He was the one everyone sought out when there were personal disputes.

One day, two coworkers who had been good friends fell into an unpleasant dispute about working from home. Each thought the other had gotten preferential treatment. When they met in the cafeteria, they greeted each other with an icy "hello." Finally, the braver of the two said, "Hey, this is stupid; we really need to sort out our own problems." They sat together for maybe forty-five minutes and took turns talking about the advice each had gotten from Brett. By the time they were finished, not only was the ice gone; it had turned into steaming anger on both sides—not at each other, but at Brett. Apparently, Brett had told each one that the other had gotten special treatment.

The two went to their vice president to sort things out. There was quite a bit of innuendo and uncertainty about who had said what to Brett. Within less than an hour, the VP and these two competent employees were once again on an even keel. All three decided to let the situation be forgotten, and Brett was never consulted. When Brett called the coworkers for another one-on-one, they refused. He was confused and concerned. He called the VP to insist that these two keep their appointments; after all, how could he help if they were not there to be counseled? The boss, who wanted nothing more than to avoid conflict, simply said, "Thanks; it's all handled. We'll get back to you if we need to." Brett was furious. He predicted to those around him that without his expert help, all the troubles would probably start up again.

Over time, others around the company began to ignore Brett. There was a saying, "Talk to Brett and get mad at everyone else."

Brett was, as you might have guessed, a splitter. Splitters can cause a great deal of harm to a company, but not indefinitely; there is only so much a firm can take. Brett was great with the tactical part of his job, yet the interpersonal polarities he created were limiting the quality of his work with his team. I was asked to help sort out the mess.

As I conducted some preliminary phone interviews, I began to think, *It's like carbon monoxide. You can't see it, you can't smell it, yet it can kill you.* It was that funny, disquieting feeling that a splitter was at work.

Brett was willing to consider executive coaching, and over the next few weeks, we sat down to do his Sankofa Map. It took a bit of time, but Brett finally began to see the connection between his ostensibly helpful remarks and the role he had played as an inter-mediary between warring parents. Throughout his childhood, he had tried to protect his parents from each other. Brett hadn't liked being the go-between with his parents, yet he really had loved the power. And here he was, playing all this out again at work. It was a real shocker.

With his colleagues on to this charade, Brett had a great opportunity to reframe this truly deadly pattern and become a peacemaker rather than a relationship destroyer. And in the months that followed, that's exactly what happened. Brett concentrated on really helping others to be the best they could be. Little by little, the senior leadership started to trust him again, and the conflict in the company began to subside. Brett reported being much happier. The weight had been lifted, and although the sense of power was gone as well, Brett was enjoying the new personal power that came with mastering his feelings, his past, and his behavior.

TAKEAWAYS

- The family is the most basic, intense, powerful system in the world. Our only ticket onto this planet is through the two people who constitute our original family.
- We may call our relatives by their first names; we might call them "identity unknown." What we cannot do is "ex" them out, as in "ex-neighbor," or "ex-boss," or even "ex-spouse."
- The best, most fruitful thing we can do is tackle our past head-on, grapple with it, and finally accept it.
- Only by accepting and thereby clearing the past can we hope to freely choose our behavior as adults and reach our true potential in our work environment.
- As the writer Isak Dinesen remarked, "All sorrows can be borne, if you put them into a story or tell a story about them."

PART THREE

A New Me, a New You, a New Organization

CHAPTER SIX

DEFINING A MORE AUTHENTIC YOU AT WORK

The key to being a good manager is keeping the people who hate me away from those who are still undecided.
—CASEY STENGEL, MANAGER OF THE NEW YORK YANKEES

Now that you have taken steps to identify and understand the life patterns that contribute to your workplace behavior, the next step is to *transform those patterns.* It would be an exercise in futility and, from my point of view, a waste of time if all you could do is see your patterns and then have to live with them as they are. No, this is much more exciting! You have the opportunity to reframe relationships so that you won't have to worry about keeping friends, enemies, and "undecideds" away from each other—you'll be too busy creating a "kick-ass team"!

In this chapter, the first of three on transformation, I examine what happens in the workplace when we begin to take action to deal with patterns and our unresolved family conflicts. I begin the chapter by briefly discussing the nature of change and the specific results that people with the thirteen most common patterns can expect. Then I help you transform your behavior by showing you how to take those ever-elusive steps toward your enhanced, more authentic self. I end the chapter with an extended case study that reveals the workplace to be not only a teacher, as suggested earlier, but a safe haven for practicing the transformation of your patterns. As part of a process triggered by workplace demands, you can simultaneously tackle the task of responding in new and improved ways at home.

Personal Growth: Becoming What You Already Are

Personal development books in the leadership field often inadvertently portray change as an abrupt break with the past. When you reach your goal, they suggest, the "old you" will have somehow been banished, and a new nirvana of success and fulfillment will await you. In truth, personal growth does not magically change you into someone else. Rather, it helps you become a better, more developed, more fulfilled version of the person you already are. Deep, lasting, meaningful change can most profitably be thought of as a metamorphosis that involves both stasis and transformation. When a caterpillar turns into a butterfly, it is still a caterpillar, albeit in a new state. When a lobster molts, its old shell comes off and it begins to grow a new one, yet the lobster remains the same organism, albeit at a different point in its life stage. When we humans reach puberty, we grow hair in new places and our sexual capacities flower, changes that suggest we can no longer live the life of a child and that we need to rethink our roles in order to meet the responsibilities of reproducing humans. The essence of our beings remains intact, yet we take on new characteristics and leave behind some of the characteristics we had as children.

As you transform your patterns, don't expect to break entirely with your old behaviors. Rather, you will metamorphose your patterns, allowing them to take on a different and fuller expression. Consider the ancient Chinese saying, "The bigger the front, the bigger the back." What this means is that we all already have everything within us—the good and the bad, the sublime and the ridiculous. The more potential for bad we have, the more potential for good is also there. We've seen this play out in the last decade as many high-flying business leaders have been disgraced for lying, and politicians preaching family values have ended up on a prostitute's client list printed in national magazines. But we have also seen condemned murderers who become beacons of light in their prison communities and drug dealers who turn their lives around to help street kids find a better way. The tools in this chapter offer you the opportunity to realize more fully the positive potential that has for so long gone untapped. What we are really doing in addressing our patterns is taking one tendency in our personalities and turning it to its healthier, more effective, more productive opposite. And as one person in the system begins to change, opportunities for profound changes in others open up.

According to the Swiss psychiatrist Carl Jung, the human psyche contains a "shadow side" that is composed of the unknown parts of the personality, the parts that are repressed.[1] If as a child you chose to be quiet and shy, then the shadow part of you would be loud and extroverted. As Jungian analyst Robert Johnson has said, the shadow self is "our psychic twin that follows us like a mirror." It is critical to understand that this psychic twin contains both good and bad elements. Johnson notes that "there is gold in the shadow," and that "this gold is related to our higher calling." In his book *Owning Your Own Shadow,* Johnson claims that it is by embracing our shadow selves that we can live most authentically; "to own one's shadow is whole making."[2]

In workplace settings, the untapped potential or "gold" of our shadow selves translates into very specific kinds of behavior. Just as we described the thirteen most common patterns in the workplace in terms of readily recognizable office characters, so too is it helpful to represent as characters the transformed patterns of our shadow selves. Those who once reacted to conflict by avoiding it, for instance, become initiators of new solutions for the entire team; those who had reacted by rebelling become community builders; and so on. The full list is as follows:

1. From Super-Achiever to Creative Collaborator
2. From Rebel to Community Builder
3. From Procrastinator to Realizer
4. From Clown to Humorist
5. From Persecutor to Visionary
6. From Victim to Explorer
7. From Rescuer to Mentor
8. From Drama Queen or King to Storyteller
9. From Martyr to Integrator
10. From Pleaser to Truth Teller

11. From Avoider to Initiator
12. From Denier to Trust Builder
13. From Splitter to Peacemaker

In what follows, I expound on each of the desirable or "golden" office characters in more detail. I hope you will take my comments as a general description of the goal or end state of the transformation process outlined in this book. Remember at all times that these more desirable patterns of behavior are not new patterns, but merely the old ones turned in a happier direction—caterpillars flying away as resplendent butterflies. I have given examples of people who exemplify the healthy, robust patterns we all wish to achieve. I do not claim that those who are examples of the healthy patterns necessarily changed from the less desirable ones as I have outlined; I only know that these are people who are role models of the better way. It is with that acknowledgment that I respectfully include individuals, some well known, some not well known, who can be guides to finding our own next levels of positive responding.

TRANSFORMATION 1: FROM SUPER-ACHIEVER TO CREATIVE COLLABORATOR

As we saw, super-achievers were often called by their family systems to make up for a family shame or tragedy. Super-achievers change when they begin to realize that success doesn't have to entail only individual accomplishment, that it can be more rewarding when it includes working together and collaborating. With this new awareness, super-achievers can stop their habitual judgment of others and rethink the essence of that emotionally packed word *success*. The attainment of wealth, position, and fame are included, yet they are no longer the only purpose for defining what really matters in designing one's life.

Creative collaboration is consistent with even the greatest individual accomplishment. Many people don't know this, but the renowned artists Vincent van Gogh and Paul Gauguin worked together for a period of nine weeks, painting side by side, and each claimed he learned a great deal from the other.[3] In her Pulitzer Prize–winning book, *A Team of Rivals*, Doris Kearns Goodwin shows how Abraham Lincoln, one of the greatest individual leaders in American political history, formed his cabinet by taking a group of individual super-achievers, each convinced of his own personal superiority, and helped them begin the complex task of working together in harmony.[4]

When super-achievers come together in support of a larger vision for the common good, amazing things can happen. In 1993, British filmmakers Bill Leeson and David Wilson formed a group called War Child to bring aid and comfort to children living in war-torn areas of the former Yugoslavia. Famous classical opera star Luciano Pavarotti joined the cause by putting on concerts in Italy. Rather than give himself over to super-achiever egotism, Pavarotti took the long view and invited all types of popular singing stars to join with him. As a result, War Child has the finances to sponsor psychosocial workshops and other measures designed to "take the war out of the child."

In the business world, the demand for creative collaborators is greater than ever. As Warren Bennis and Patricia Ward Biederman note in their important book *Organizing Genius: The Secrets of Creative Collaboration,* the time-sensitive nature of work in a globalized society demands that collaboration become the way we work together. This century will demonstrate that only very rarely can one person alone produce what we need. We must remember that greatness comes from a group effort.[5]

Super-achievers who tackle the need to be "the one," when they learn to include, to work together, to collaborate, gain entrance into a more rewarding world of heightened creativity where it is easier to achieve a state of intense focus and immediacy, what is commonly described as "flow."[6]

TRANSFORMATION 2: FROM REBEL TO COMMUNITY BUILDER

Some things are worth fighting for—even fighting "to the death." Yet most of the time, there is a better way. Whereas rebels thrive on the negative attention they receive from their opposition to almost anything, community builders are capable of transcending opposition when appropriate, respecting other viewpoints, and exploring areas of potential unity. They learn to embrace the notion that we are all connected and that no one wins unless we all do.

When we think about community and what it takes to build community, the concept of eating together comes to mind. In ancient cultures, there were rituals around mealtime and extending hospitality to strangers. One woman who has brought her skill as chef into the role of being a community builder is Alice Waters, whose Berkeley, California, restaurant, Chez Panisse, is considered one of the best in the country. She is using her talents to teach youngsters the important relationship of healthy food to their lives. She states, "Teaching kids how to feed themselves and how to live in a community responsibly is the center of an education." Her school programs are about more than just food. They are a way to teach children respect for each other and respect for the planet.

Judy Wicks, owner of the White Dog Café, a popular Philadelphia restaurant, is a creative entrepreneur and a community builder who believes "Business is beautiful when it's a vehicle for serving the common good." The restaurant is not only dedicated to natural food but also is a center for dialogue on political and other issues of local and national importance. Judy has created a place for the community to talk together, and there is always a vast array of people who gather there. Judy says she learned from Gandhi that "Noncooperation with evil is as much a duty as cooperation with good." Her Eating with the Enemy program takes groups to emerging countries to help begin a dialogue around the needs of people in all areas of the world. When one person decides to make a difference and include others, individual lives and entire communities can make positive and speedy change.

Another excellent model for the turning of a rebel mind-set into a community-building one is Neve Shalom–Wahat as Salam, an unusual Israeli-Palestinian village located between Tel Aviv and Jerusalem. The name of the town means "oasis of peace," and if you visit there you will see Jews and Arabs living side by side, sharing both laughter and tears. Founded in 1970, the town was the vision of an Egyptian-born Dominican brother of Jewish origin named Bruno Hussar; as he states in his autobiography, he simply "set up his home there and waited for others to join him." In 2000, my husband, Herb, and I did exactly that, visiting the town with a group we had formed, the Center for Intercultural Dialogue.

We went to study the impact of open dialogue on conflict-ridden groups. It is an amazing and worthwhile place to visit.

One evening during our trip, I happened to meet a woman whose father had been a high-ranking German military officer during the Nazi era. He died when she was only two. During her teen years, she began to ask questions about her heritage and was met with stony silence. After some digging, she learned that her father had been instrumental in the deportation of thousands of Jews to Auschwitz. The shame deepened and the anger grew until she finally rejected her family and began traveling, searching for freedom. She roamed the world as a "hippie chick" and felt unworthy of close relationships. She never talked about her father to anyone, finding the shame too hard to handle. What she did was take her personal anger and put it into any situation that had an edge of injustice. She was against anything there was to rail against and marched in protest after protest.

As I've mentioned, you can't push your family heritage away; it will come back to haunt you until it is dealt with. In this woman's case, the void inside her kept getting larger and larger. After visiting the Anne Frank House in Amsterdam, her anger and sadness came crashing down, and she attempted suicide. After several days in the hospital, the floodgates opened, and she was finally able to cry. She cried for herself, her father, her country, for the waste of war and the tragedy of polarization. Subsequently, she learned about Neve Shalom–Wahat as Salam and made her first trip to Israel. In this complex yet peaceful setting, she learned new ways of talking together and healing the divide between people. Now she has attained an inner calm and spends her time teaching conflict resolution around the world. She returns periodically to the village for more training and personal comfort. It is, she told me, her own oasis of peace.

Like the village itself, this woman's life story suggests just how much good can flow when rebels clear old wounds and come to grips with their shadow side.

When rebels become community builders, they can tackle problems at a core level and accelerate change. Their focus on the basic wants and needs of the community and their desire to move from what exists now to what is possible can stimulate a groundswell of activity, as more and more people feel included and become activated to help. When the rebel pattern is transformed, societies can flourish in amazing ways.

The benefit of turning from rebel to community builder is that problems can be tackled at a core level and change can be accelerated. When there is a desire to consider basic wants and needs of a community and move from what is now to what is possible, there can be a groundswell of activity as more and more people feel included and become activated to help. When the rebel pattern is transformed, societies can flourish in amazing ways.

TRANSFORMATION 3: FROM PROCRASTINATOR TO REALIZER

What is it like when you are in the atmosphere of someone who really makes things happen? Most people report having a feeling of effervescence, as if they had just taken the first sip of a good champagne. Realizers help open doors that seemed nonexistent minutes before, and there is a sense that all things are possible. In contrast, working with a procrastinator can have the effect of a dull toothache that won't go away. Procrastinators are often afraid to complete a task because they don't want to cast a poor image on themselves or their family.

At work, procrastination causes havoc and dissention. Take Leonardo da Vinci, for example. He has been called a Renaissance man partly because he had so many interests. Yet he was known to be highly distractible. In fact, his painting *The Last Supper* was only finished after his patron threatened to cut off all funds. And that may be a clue as to how to handle a procrastinator: give timelines and keep payment from them!

When procrastinators can get in touch with their shadow sides, they are able to base their success on timelines, clear strategic plans, and, most of all, strong personal determination. For example, when John F. Kennedy proclaimed that there would be a man on the moon within ten years, he spoke with the conviction of a realizer who had his feet planted firmly on the ground and would do what it took to make things happen. Helen Keller could have sat and waited for others to take care of her. She didn't. With the determination of her helper, Annie Sullivan, and her own strong will, her capacity to say "I can do it" has been an inspiration not just to those with disabilities but to everyone who has ever faced a daunting challenge. Her saying "Life is either a daring adventure or nothing" gives courage to everyone who has ever wanted to wait life out on the sidelines.[7]

Realizers can get us to the moon, become examples of communicating when it seems impossible, and find the essence of hope in the haystack of adversity.

Amber Chand is an entrepreneur who knows how to make things happen. She was expelled from Uganda in 1973 when the dictator Idi Amin came to power. As she relates, "That period was very powerful for me. I lost my house, my country, and my father—he died that same year of a heart attack." Like Helen Keller, Amber faced a critical question: "Was I going to live my life in bitterness and anger, or use the experience as an opportunity to grow?" Amber's answer was to take life in her own hands and start a handicrafts company that supports women living in the shadows of war and deep, enduring poverty. She is making a difference and bringing hope where there is none. Moving from a "maybe tomorrow" attitude to a "can-do" mind-set almost always ensures success. When the energy that was stuck in the older procrastinator pattern of "maybe tomorrow" is transformed into the "yes I can" or, even better, "yes we can" attitude of overcoming obstacles and building for the future, individuals and businesses are in a strong position of being the leaders of innovation and can break through to new creative ideas.

Transformation 4: From Clown to Humorist

As children, clowns usually play the role of lightening things up when sadness and despair mount. In office settings, adult clowns annoy us because they tend to divert us from unpleasant or tense issues, preventing us from ever dealing with conflict. Humorists, in contrast, help us put discomfort in perspective so that we can laugh at ourselves or the situation and pause before tackling the difficulties ahead. Humorists don't push us to avoid conflict, but instead handle it in a balanced, healthy way.

An excellent example of a humorist is the great American writer Mark Twain. The sixth of seven children, Twain saw three of his siblings die by the time he was seven years old. His father died when Twain was eleven, and his younger brother died when the steamboat he was on exploded. Having encouraged his younger brother to join him as a steamboat pilot, Twain was guilt stricken and would hold himself responsible for the rest of his life. His only son died at nineteen months, and he outlived two of his daughters and also his wife. Twain dealt with all this heartache not by avoiding it through clownery, but by writing stories that contained both pathos and humor and that openly dealt with the harsh realities of violence, death, hatred, and racism. Twain's biting satire was entertaining even as it cast a clear eye on the foibles of humans in society.[8]

Several of today's most popular humorists continue in Twain's tradition. Jon Stewart has an ability to blend hilarity with a serious treatment of the day's top news stories. Night after night, he entertains us while asking hard questions about divisive issues, such as the economy and health care. He is both funny and well prepared, and it is interesting that so many people are getting their news from his show rather than from more traditional stations. Stewart's colleague Stephen Colbert, like Stewart a critic of the narcissistic personalities that inhabit the traditional media, is also noteworthy for his ability to lampoon these puffed-up egos even as he casts a new perspective on the unpleasant challenges we all face.

Such organizations as General Electric and Kodak are starting to recognize the value of humor, even hiring comedians as "humor consultants" to help lighten things up. Monty Python's John Cleese has served as one such humor consultant in many organizations. Stu Robertshaw, a professor at the University of Wisconsin, cites a study indicating that having a chance to express some silliness at work led to a 38 percent decrease in Friday absenteeism.[9]

When office clowns can diminish the anxiety that is at the core of the sometimes funny, sometimes not-so-funny jokes and refine the sense of timing required for humor to be appropriate, there is the possibility of making a significant contribution at work. We all know that laughter is good for our health, and someone who has the skill to put a great joke in at the right time can help reduce office stress and build camaraderie among the staff. This is a valuable and much-needed service in today's fast-paced and tense work environment, where employees often say they are "functioning on fumes."

TRANSFORMATION 5: FROM PERSECUTOR TO VISIONARY

Have you ever seen a persecutor point his or her index finger at you in an accusatory manner? It points with the precision of a knife ready to plunge into your chest. When that same finger moves two inches and points at the sky, you catch a glimmer of the visionary that resides behind the venom and the angst.

Most kids who are labeled bullies learned early in their lives that they had little alternative than to fight to be heard, and they took this need to be recognized into the realm of intimidating others. Peel away the tough façade, and there is an individual who yearns for harmony and has an uncanny sense of a world where there is cooperation and respect. Persecutors are often afraid that if they show their "soft side" they will be annihilated, yet once this fear is contained, they can use their leadership capacities to help create a kinder world.

Visionary leaders have learned the art and craft of conflict transformation, and their core aim is to unite rather than divide people. Visionaries who used to be persecutors as children prove especially responsive to the real needs of others. They have internalized the feeling of what it is like to be judged and told that one is wrong, and out of that comes an ability to listen to others and imagine a better future. Anwar Sadat overcame immense hatred and the claims that he was a traitor to extend his hand in peace to the Israelis. As he related, he remained steady during the grueling Camp David talks by remembering a vision he had in which the prophet Mohammed told him to make peace.

In business, visionaries are in short supply, yet wherever they reside, their visions involve a profound respect and appreciation for others. Herb Kelleher made Southwest one of America's premier airlines by running the company according to the Golden Rule; customers are treated with the same respect as the employees who serve them. Jeffrey Swartz of Timberland Shoes reinforces the firm's success by paying employees to volunteer in the community.[10] Eileen Fisher helped make a name for her eponymous clothing line by giving her Asian suppliers a short and fair period of time to provide break rooms and properly ventilated work areas for their employees, or risk losing their contracts.[11]

"When I despair," Gandhi once said, "I remember that all through history the ways of truth and love have always won. There have been tyrants and murderers and for a time they can seem invincible, but in the end they always fall."[12] Enlightened persecutors don't fall; they look inward, redefine their shadow selves, and reinvent themselves as path breakers. The next time you feel angry at a persecutor, remember that even these most difficult of office characters have something to offer, if only they can overcome the underlying wounds that gave rise to their patterns. A persecutor's behavior may have been terribly unjust, yet once they transform, we can applaud when they take a leadership role to help us envision a more just workplace, a more compassionate world. In these contemporary times, we have to look far to find the visionaries who can make a real impact. There is too much rhetoric without the follow-through. Think about the visionaries you respect and would be willing to follow. When the persecutor becomes the visionary, he or she becomes the one who can point to that place we know is the better place to go and give us the courage to take the steps to get there.

Transformation 6: From Victim to Explorer

When a victim transforms into an explorer, they have a lust for life that can leave spectators breathless. Whereas the victim is fearful and barely moves either physically or emotionally, the explorer is curious and adventurous. The victim sees limitations and is prone to blame, judge, and hide behind others, even enjoying their mistakes and mishaps. The explorer thinks not of dead ends but in terms of possibilities, mobility, and adaptability.

An explorer plays full out. They read books, surf the Net, go to lectures, talk to just about everyone, ask for information, and take interest in a vast array of subjects. There is willingness, optimism, and a daring that is infectious.

At work, explorers volunteer for projects and love to collaborate. The one thing they dread is ambiguity. They will challenge all who seem unsure and hold them accountable for their words and actions. Explorers want to conquer the world and hate to be held back by illness and limitations.

One legendary explorer who had every reason to see himself as a victim is Earnest Shackleton. While on his famous voyage to Antarctica, Shackleton and his crew of twenty-seven survived nearly two years on the wind-swept ice. His ship sank, yet he never allowed his group to become discouraged, even when it seemed impossible that they would ever survive. He realized the explorer's true reward: to live life to the fullest, never fearing the consequences.[13]

Explorers can be both amazing businesspeople as well as make an impact on the planet. Richard Branson has ballooned across the Atlantic, has been knighted by the Queen of England, and has over 360 companies under his Virgin brand. And if you too are an explorer, you can join him in one of his newest adventures: Virgin Galactic is going into the "thermosphere" in 2009, with tickets at $200,000. He is also passionate about the environment and has offered large prizes for solutions to the problems of global warming as well as pledged vast amounts for development of renewable alternatives to carbon fuels. Explorers live life with a special zest you can feel in Branson's statement, "Sometimes I do wake up in the mornings and feel like I've just had the most incredible dream. I've just dreamt my life."[14] It would be great if we could all get that kind of kick out of life!

It takes hard work to explore our vast inner realms and untie the "nots" (as in *am not, cannot, should not*) to create an exciting life. One victim-turned-explorer I worked with, Jeanne, had been sickly as a child and for years was the weakest link in the family insurance business. She became angry when she finally understood that because she had been born months after her older sister died of the flu, her parents had hovered over her out of their own fear. She played the invalid in her family's drama, a role she had never wanted. Jeanne and her mother eventually had several tearful confrontations, and slowly but surely things changed.

Jeanne started behaving rebelliously. Everyone was aghast when she drove to work on a Honda motorcycle, even more so when she countered with such comments as, "This is nothing— just training wheels to prepare me for my Harley." Small steps like these helped Jeanne build the courage necessary to ask her mother, the firm's CEO, for more challenging work, and she started to interact with key customers. The change took some getting used to, and personality clashes occurred, especially with her mother, yet Jeanne pushed on.

One day a favored client invited Jeanne to go with a group to the Ice Hotel in northern Sweden. She was thrilled and told her worried mother, "If I get lost in the Arctic you can send Shackleton to find me." Jeanne eventually became the CEO, and to reward her staff for a job well done, she takes them on challenging and fun adventures around the world. Perhaps they will join Branson in the thermosphere. It's simply magical to see Jeanne and other victims-turned-explorers reach their true potential and live life to the fullest.

Businesses gain a great deal from having explorers as part of the staff. They are excellent collaborators and are willing to do the legwork to get new projects going. Say to an explorer, "I wonder what would happen if . . . " and watch his or her eyes light up. They are team players who will help and guide and neither hog the limelight nor shrink away from it. Explorers have a great sense of timing and can withstand holding back on a project until the kinks have been worked out; they are always willing to be part of the first tests to make sure that the project will succeed.

Transformation 7: From Rescuer to Mentor

Good mentors know how to listen and give good advice at just the right time. They know how to stand in the background and applaud without needing credit, and they are willing to let you go when you are competent to make excellent decisions without them. But the best mentors are not those who have sailed through life without setbacks; rather, they are those who have had to go through their own intense training and overcome obstacles and challenges. Rescuers who have performed the exhausting work of helping ease difficulties in their own families have a special ability to become master mentors. When their anxious and fearful rescuer energy has been transformed into something more patient and focused, they can also become amazing leaders.

Leon Fleisher is a pianist, conductor, and teacher who by the age of sixteen was singled out as one of the most gifted keyboard artists of the century. Then he was diagnosed with a rare neurological disease that cost him the use of his right hand. He subsequently moved from playing concerts to becoming an inspirational teacher and coach and an inspired conductor. At the 2007 Kennedy Center for the Performing Arts celebration, one of his students played the piano before a vast audience. I was particularly struck watching the way Leon and his student acknowledged each other after the performance. Their shared nod of appreciation lasted for just a fraction of a second, but its meaning and power were clear. What a world it would be if every student had a Leon Fleisher to help him find the best in himself.

Another mentor with a tragic but inspirational story is financial adviser Azim Khamisa. In 1995 his only son, Tariq, a twenty-year-old college student, was shot and killed while delivering pizzas in San Diego. During the trial, the elder Khamisa identified with the pain and sadness felt by the murderer's grandfather Ples Felix, and also realized the tragedy that would ensue if the young man who had pulled the trigger were allowed to rot in prison for years. Khamisa approached the grandfather with a plan: together the grandfather and he would go to San Diego–area schools, talk about the racism dividing the community, and encourage teens to take a moment and think before committing a violent act. The program, called Violence Impact Forum, was so successful that it is now being replicated across the country.[15]

The world of work is certainly an important place for large-scale mentoring. Kevin Roberts, international CEO of Saatchi and Saatchi, one of the world's leading creative organizations, mentors on multiple levels. In his adopted homeland of New Zealand, his mentoring helps youngsters transform negativism into positive action through the Turn Your Life Around program. His books, including *Lovemarks,* teach businesspeople to consider the importance of infusing products with mystery and intimacy to win loyalty and, most important, to consider the foundational role of business in making the world a better place. In the workplace, there is great power in mentoring programs. I have seen the power of both outside coaches and internal mentoring programs. Often it is good to "mix it up" by pairing people of diverse backgrounds. The more we can learn about each other and ask open-ended questions to begin authentic dialogues, the more we will move toward creating workplaces where there is a common ground of shared perspective.

Transformation 8: From Drama Queen or King to Storyteller

Although a good drama can be entertaining during your off hours, we've seen that it can be a real problem when it takes place at work. Drama queens and kings won't stop until every last thread of the drama has been teased out—for them, that is; the heck with you.

Yet when drama queens and kings learn that they no longer need to start drama to diffuse a tense situation, they become storytellers who help those around them unite, collaborate, and create.

Storytelling has played a fundamental role in all societies to help human beings make sense of their world. Storytellers the world over establish a sense of credibility, authenticity, and wholeness in their communities. Rather than shrinking from conflict, storytellers help communities precisely by sustaining the space of tension so that complex problems can be dealt with and real solutions found. In a business context, storytellers transmit company values, share important business knowledge, and help limit office politics. They take a firm's agenda and communicate it to all stakeholders, helping them feel comfortable and motivated even in periods of wrenching change. With their spiritual depth, storytellers move teams to places that PowerPoint presentations alone cannot take them, places of true meaning and connection. In this respect, the wise words of a good storyteller help make up for the distance that voice mail, e-mails, and other forms of modern communication create between us.

Anita Roddick, founder of the retail chain the Body Shop, had an uncanny way of telling a story. Whether she was talking about business matters or broader social and environmental change, she always had an inspirational tale to tell about the countries she had visited or the people she had met. Anita died several years ago, leaving behind thousands of inspired employees and customers as well as a powerful legacy of doing business for the right reasons. As she has said, "I want to tell—and hear—stories that lift our spirits, that celebrate how glorious our planet is. Outrage and celebration—let's run this gamut together."

The best use of media is in storytelling, and one of the major storytellers of our time is Steven Spielberg. He has probed into the invisible corners of his own life to help us shine light on our own darkness. After completing *Schindler's List* to understand the legacy of the Holocaust, he brought *Saving Private Ryan* to the screen for us to understand the unspoken terrors the "silent generation" brought back from World War II. This was his way of paying tribute to his father, from whom he had been distanced after his parent's divorce.

Another firm in which storytelling plays an important role is Ritz-Carlton. Known for their world-class service, the hotel helps keep employee commitment strong by incorporating storytelling into morning meetings. Each day, someone reads aloud a "Wow Story" of the day about a staff member who went above and beyond in providing guest service. Without even realizing it, the company is reinforcing the healthy opposite of the drama queen or king pattern, teaching employees that there is a better way to be noticed or to handle the tensions and stresses that arise during a typical workday. As a reformed drama queen myself, I can only say, Way to go!

Although it is rather easy to tell a story, it is more difficult to be a great storyteller. What matters most is that the storyteller is clear that he or she is telling the story to teach something that matters on a higher level. That is what Aesop did. Although he lived in ancient Greece and his characters were usually animals, his fables still pack a moral and ethical punch today. "The Boy Who Cried Wolf" and "The Tortoise and the Hare," for example, are modern tales for the world of business.

TRANSFORMATION 9: FROM MARTYR TO INTEGRATOR

At some point in our lives, most of us have to decide if we will do something for others and then demand that they pay us back for our help, or if we will forgo payment in the interests of getting everyone to work together. Martyrs are unable to forgo the payment; they do good deeds and then use them as justification for endless complaining. Martyrs have as their healthy opposite the ability to gather a group together and find ways they can work together. In other words, they can *integrate* people in a profound way.

Integrators base their success on their ability to see all sides of a situation and allow conflicting parties to be not only heard but acknowledged. A great practitioner of this art is Nelson Mandela, one of the most beloved leaders of our time. It has been said that South Africa under apartheid was ripe for a bloodbath and that Mandela's "integrative" leadership played a major role in stemming the terror. Transforming racial division and oppression into open democracy, Mandela was able to help others take the longer view and honor all sides as capable of being part of the solution.[16]

Another man who could have wallowed in the martyr's endless bitterness is Thich Nhat Hanh, the respected Zen master, poet, and peace and human rights activist. Exiled from his native Vietnam in 1966 and only recently allowed to return, Nhat Hanh has led meditation retreats for Vietnam veterans at which these veterans had a chance to meet with Vietnamese people who were part of that war's tragedy. He has also worked with prison populations to listen and help alleviate suffering.[17] I had the honor of spending time with Thay (which means "teacher" in Vietnamese) both at Plum Village, his wonderful Buddhist center in France, and as part of a group of 180 people from around the world who accompanied him in 1999 on the first trip ever made by a Buddhist monk to Communist China. It was an emotional and mesmerizing time as I watched this master teacher bring together all types of people and help envision a better world. His words are so needed at this time: "The practice of peace and reconciliation is one of the most vital and artistic of human actions."[18]

In the workplace, transformed martyrs can help a company move ahead at warp speed. One nonprofit I recently worked with had a team filled with pleasers, victims, procrastinators, and rescuers. The head of the agency was a bona fide martyr. Working around the clock, he would complain about his "aching back" yet do nothing about it. Everyone was in awe of his work ethic while resenting his constant talk about how hard he worked—as if they were slackers who sat around simply smelling the coffee. When team members finally had a chance to voice their concerns, he was somewhat surprised—actually, shocked. Meanwhile, they had to admit their own culpability: they had listened to his complaints and made snide comments behind his back, yet never confronted him directly. Well, it did not take more than one month for major changes to occur. The head of the agency began to ask others for help so that he could leave work at a reasonable hour. Soon you could see a group of vibrant colleagues who would laugh together and who became a smoothly functioning team, helping each other without any one person carrying too much of the workload.

Integrators work wonders in organizations. They are the ones who can help change the silo mentality to one of real cooperation. They have learned to break down the opposition of the interest groups who only want to make sure their budgets are safe; they help people learn to share. These integrators have an uncanny way of slicing the pie: although every piece may not be identical, all the recipients feel content, sensing that they are being treated with fairness and respect.

Transformation 10: From Pleaser to Truth Teller

Pleasers want you to feel good; they don't want to offend you or rock the boat. And that's why they're unhelpful—because, like avoiders, they prevent you from ever dealing with the hard issues that need to be dealt with. Truth tellers are the opposite. While they certainly care about the consequences, they tell it like it is—simply, powerfully, without lecturing or grandstanding. They will not change their minds just to pacify someone, although they are not averse to adjusting their opinions if that will enable a conflict to push toward resolution. Truth tellers have a firm grasp of what they want to say and have given deep thought as to the possible outcomes of their discourse. As a result, they do not beat around the bush, and people in their audiences generally listen.

In the business world, truth tellers are wonderful people to work with. They give colleagues and subordinates a tremendous amount of room to explore and learn. They are eager for people to ask their opinion, yet they feel no great attachment to their ideas and also no great need to be worshipped. With truth tellers, you always know where you stand. You are treated as an adult, and even though what is said can get uncomfortable, you know that a truth teller is not out to embarrass or ridicule you. Finally, truth tellers are flexible, yet they will not bend to others who are manipulating.

Truth tellers are not a populous species, yet they pack quite a punch when they do appear. Erin Brockovich, subject of the film by the same name, risked everything in her stand against big corporate interests because she felt that the truth alone was worth fighting for. Farmer, activist, and author John Mohawk spoke out with clarity and conviction about the fundamental differences in worldview between indigenous cultures and those of the industrialized West. Mohawk was a keen observer of natural patterns, and he questioned in an honest and open manner the impact of technologies that modern cultures adopt without a second thought. Truth tellers bear out a statement made by Bill Moyers in a recent speech: "Truth tellers, without a license, remind us that the most important credential of all is a conscience that cannot be purchased or silenced."[19]

Having grown up in Philadelphia, I was thrilled when Ed Rendell became mayor. The city was in a sorry state with a major inferiority complex, coming up short against neighboring New York, Washington, and Boston. What Rendell did was show the power of truth telling and taking hard stands. In the early 1990s, Rendell gave Philadelphia the truth it needed. He commented to the *New York Times*, "I was determined to tell people what I planned to do. If they didn't want it, I was reconciled to not winning."[20] By telling the truth, he was able to balance the budget and dramatically improve services to the neighborhoods. The *New York Times* called Rendell's job as mayor "the most stunning turnaround in recent urban history."

Let me end this section by confessing that I myself played the role of the pleaser for many years, allowing my creative energies to languish in dark corners while I focused (excessively) on raising my young family. I would say yes when I meant no and then steam about it for days. I would give superficial and flimsy feedback rather than hurt anyone's feelings. After doing my Sankofa Map, I realized that the unfettered giver in me ultimately stemmed from a long-forgotten family tragedy—the loss of my great-grandmother during my grandmother's birth. That set the stage for family members to play "nice" so that no one would feel such wrenching pain in the future. After much hard work and some difficult if insightful conversations with my mother, also a mega-pleaser, I managed to turn my energies in a healthier direction. I created appropriate boundaries and took more time for myself, an unheard of selfishness for women in my family. I took on the roles of truth teller—taking my career in new directions and even starting to envision this book. And as I grew and changed, miracle of miracles, so did my mom!

In the workplace, truth tellers are both feared and loved in equal measure. People are not used to hearing concisely stated truths that are offered in an unvarnished, uncensored, and undistilled manner. It can be challenging to work with a truth teller when there is a need to reveal injustice, corruption, lies, or hypocrisy. Yet when we are in the presence of the truth, we also feel comforted, energized, and nourished.

TRANSFORMATION 11: FROM AVOIDER TO INITIATOR

Avoiders hurt a firm's bottom line by pushing conflict underground; colleagues become paralyzed by their fear of saying something that will disturb the avoider and touch off a "Gotta go" response. Initiators reflect the healthy opposite of the "Gotta go" syndrome, showing resourcefulness and endurance while taking challenges on directly. Initiators aren't pushovers who go along with situations with which they are not happy. Instead they take charge and become full participants. All the pent-up energy that had formerly been directed into a fear of being judged now is freed up to fuel the initiator's activities as a positive collaborator.

In situations where creativity is especially important, the initiator's talents become essential. The initiator is the one who can hold the space for the conflicts that inevitably show up when the creative process comes into full boom. Instead of issuing a stream of sarcastic, passive-aggressive commentary that tends to shut down attempts at innovation, the initiator takes joy in the creative process and shows a willingness to let in all who wish to be included. Initiators take a chance and stay in the thick of arguments, allowing them to be resolved more quickly and the creative process to move forward once again. As reformed avoiders, initiators can withstand conflict because they have come to see life as a grand experiment. With no test to pass and no judging to withstand, the initiator can see the day's events as a series of amazing things from which to learn. Initiators thus have the ability to step out of the box and see how ideas can connect in a new way.

Initiators think big thoughts—actually, "monster" thoughts. That's what Jeff Taylor did, in the shower to be exact, when he came up with the idea of monster.com, the ever-popular job posting Web site. He was there in the beginning, when the Web was still an infant. And when that brand took off, Jeff again went into uncharted territory, creating eons.com, a social networking site to help boomers live "the biggest life possible." Always on the cutting edge, Jeff has the capacity to look into the future and bring it into the present.

Jim Collins, author of the acclaimed book *Good to Great,* is a researcher and scholar. He helped countless businesspeople become initiators through his concept of BEHAG (Big Hairy Audacious Goals). He encourages business thinkers at all levels to question the status quo and helps steer leaders into innovative thinking about what really matters in business. He suggests that we go beyond the "rock star" leader and look for deeper meaning in what constitutes exemplary leadership; he challenges us all to initiate new, more effective and inclusive ways to do business as Level 5 leaders, those who "blend extreme personal humility with intense personal will" as we go from good to great.[21]

An initiator is one who steps out of the box and is able to see how seemingly unconnected ideas can come together to develop something brand new. That is what Richard Saul Wurman did when he created the Technology, Entertainment and Design (TED) Conference and coined the term "information architect." During the early 1980s, he foresaw isolation and loneliness as two unintended consequences of the computer revolution and attempted to mitigate them. TED, acquired by the Sapling Foundation in 2001, continues to foster the spread of great ideas and effect beneficial change. The essence of TED is similar to the overriding theme of this book: it's about patterns and how patterns connect. TED is a beacon of light for innovators and initiators to meet, exchange ideas, and change the direction of the world.

At work, initiators are a bonus to the bottom line. They have an amazing ability to create an inclusive environment and are uniquely sympathetic to those who are fearful of confrontation—after all, they spent their lives running away and now know the benefits of staying until the "bitter gets better."

TRANSFORMATION 12: FROM DENIER TO TRUST BUILDER

In the 1996 film *The War at Home,* starring Kathy Bates, Emilio Estevez, and Martin Sheen, there is an intense scene that portrays a family's painful first dinner together after the son has returned from the Vietnam War, physically intact yet emotionally destroyed. The family plays "Let's pretend," and the mother, oblivious to any anguish, talks about how wonderful it is to have the happy family together. Emotions finally explode, and the mother is seemingly "shell shocked," unable to grasp what is really going on. It's a scene that will ring true to members of denier families everywhere.

How do you build trust? It isn't easy. You need to peel away defenses that have built over lifetimes, and the truth, when it emerges, usually comes in the form of a volcanic eruption. The good news about such eruptions is that despite the short-term pain they cause, they create a foundation on which to build deep, long-standing trust. Deniers, the very people whose role it was to push problems away, turn out to possess the skills and insight vital for forging powerful relationship bonds between otherwise skeptical and defensive individuals.

Denial's destructive face is readily obvious in business. How is it possible for a company like Enron to go from a market capitalization of $65 billion to bankruptcy in four weeks? How is it possible that Enron's thousands of employees suddenly found themselves abandoned and their retirement funds vaporized, while the top executives left the sinking ship with hundreds of millions? Watch the documentary *Enron: The Smartest Guys in the Room,* and you realize that a culture of denial produced Enron's implosion. Ironically, Enron's slogan was "Ask why." Not enough people did that.

My daughter, Mikayla Lev, has always been one to ask why. She has spent many years researching the complex components of trust building required in areas of the world where conflict is rife. Presently filming her documentary *Without Walls* at the Mexican-American border, she is again asking why. She spent many years focused on how the expressive arts can be a creative force in the quest for truth; in filming *Living in Conflict,* she followed Palestinian and Israeli artists as they searched for peaceful coexistence and trustworthy relating.

In the workplace, leaders build trust by considering all aspects of the business, from a successful bottom line to creative and engaged employees. Yvon Chouinard, founder of Patagonia, has spent his career as a trust builder. His concern for his employees was expressed clearly when his company became the first in the United States to provide onsite day care, maternity and paternity leave, and flextime. The Patagonia catalogue has been used to speak out about environmental concerns, and Chouinard's intention is to prove that "business can make a profit without losing its soul." That is a core value in trust building!

Deniers in the workplace transform into trust builders when they begin to ask questions and then, if not satisfied, ask again. The only way to build trust is through honest dialogues with colleagues, bosses, and subordinates; in this respect, reformed deniers ease office politics by becoming clear mirrors for those around them. A word of caution: telling the truth is not the same as spilling your guts. Truth telling is a high art form. Please consider that the time and place are as important as the words, and one's intention underpins the entire dynamic. Happily, people who grew up in families where denial reigned are far more sensitive to the corruptions in the name of truth. This is the true gold of their shadow side.

TRANSFORMATION 13: FROM SPLITTER TO PEACEMAKER

As we've seen, the splitter's world is polluted with innuendo and whispers that pit otherwise well disposed people against one another. Splitters do their destructive work because they crave the sense of reassurance that comes from being well liked relative to the alleged enemy. They also crave the power that comes with serving as the shoulder on which everyone else can cry. How different is the peacemaker's sense of connectedness and compassion. When transformed splitters get in touch with their shadow side, they unleash a unique capacity to believe in the dignity of humankind and to stay calm in the face of dissention. Peacemakers are not people who can be swayed to side with or against a particular person or group; what they care about—and what they'll fight to preserve—is the integrity of the *whole* system.

One peacemaker whom I have had the privilege of hearing speak was the Dalai Lama, who has an amazing capacity for calm and compassionate dialogue. The Dalai Lama is now well into his seventies, and he has continued to bear the burden of leading a people brutally stripped of their ancestral homeland. His capacity to pray for all of humankind and not focus on winners and losers is stunning. Although the Chinese have behaved unjustly toward the Tibetan people, he is still able to transcend animosity by saying, as he did in an interview with Deepak Chopra, "I don't dislike the Chinese, only their actions."[22] The Dalai Lama teaches us that peace is a state of mind, and that it is still possible to be happy in the midst of turmoil and chaos.

Another individual who exemplifies the pattern of the peacemaker is Rosa Parks. On that fateful day when she refused to give up her seat on a bus to a white man, she was strong, determined, and emotionally exhausted by the treatment that African Americans were receiving under segregation and the Jim Crow laws. It would have been so easy for her to adopt the splitter's habit of engendering bitterness. In the years that followed, she focused her energies on encouraging people to find better ways of relating. Even after a young robber attacked her in her home, she wrote, "I pray for this young man and the conditions in our country that have made him this way. Despite the violence and crime in our society, we should not let fear overwhelm us. We must remain strong."[23]

The feeling behind this view is so different from the energy of the splitter pattern. In the world of work, this is the hardest pattern to observe and the hardest to change. Splitters are everybody's friend, and when they gossip, rest assured, they are only doing it for benign purposes, or so they say. The sense of power that a splitter feels is utterly opposite to the sense of connectedness and compassion felt by peacemakers.

We are at a point in world history where we cannot suffer the splitter's divisive mentality any more than our environment can suffer old-fashioned, unfettered industrial expansion. We need more peacemakers to come forward and say, "It will stop with me." And when there are more peacemakers in our organizations, there will be diminished workplace violence and little need for myriad lawsuits that are the result of misunderstandings and grievances caused by excluding and judging each other.

Beginning Your Transformation

Now that we've explored the end state of the growth process outlined in this book, it's time to take the next steps. Going down any new road can be difficult, so I'll say it again: it's not enough to identify and understand your patterns; you also have to commit to pushing beyond your comfort zone and taking positive action in the present. Action is key, but *interaction* is actually more to the point. As the noted anthropologist Gregory Bateson has stated, we are not merely individuals, but "individuals-in-interaction."[24] Change comes about when we *interact* with the important others in our lives. As we talk and listen and respond and listen some more, the "knots" of our lives are untied, and we are freer to find more wholesome, appropriate ways of being.

To make starting this dialogue with others a bit easier, I advise that you take the time to practice, practice, practice before going further. One way to do this is through a very powerful exercise that I use in my Total Leadership Connections retreat, called **PEPtalk** (Pattern Encounter Process). You begin PEPtalk by thinking about a pattern you wish to change, then letting your memory take you to a difficult or conflict-laden work situation where the pattern is pronounced. Find a friend or several friends who would be willing to role-play with you, with you playing yourself. Give your helpers a full description of the other person, including physical characteristics, the person's job responsibilities, how the person communicates, and how the person tends to react emotionally. As you role-play the scene, remember that a common trap is our tendency to tell the other person in the PEPtalk about *her*—how we want *that person* to change and what upsets us about *her,* rather than focusing on and taking responsibility for *ourselves.* Speak clearly, concisely, and directly. You will usually need about five or more takes of this scene to really get it right, but when you nail it, you'll feel something click deep within you. (Note: If you would prefer to do this alone, write it out and then speak your role out loud. Hearing your own voice creates a "pattern interrupt" that often stimulates both the connection to the earlier patterns and the courage to take action.)

Sample PEPtalk 1

One of my clients was a CEO who needed to transform his troubled relationship with his CFO. The CEO scanned to find the pattern he wished to transform. Avoider came out loud and clear. The CEO hated to confront others and saw the CFO as a procrastinator who was always late with his financials. During the first five role-play rehearsals of his PEPtalk, the CEO failed to imagine a truly transformed encounter and wound up berating the CFO as a procrastinator, never claiming his own avoider pattern. This was to be expected—by continuing to talk about the other guy, he could avoid his own discomfort. On the sixth attempt, he finally turned it around, and this is what his initial approach sounded like:

> Elliot, you are a very competent CFO, and I trust the quality of your work. Yet it is never done in a timely fashion and my tendency, as an avoider, is to shrug my shoulders and not say anything. The problem is that tension builds within me, and I find myself looking for reasons to stay away from you and send others to you to get the information I need. All this inhibits progress in the company, especially now that we are in acquisition mode. I want to change my avoider behavior to become an initiator. So, I'm not going away and I'm not sending others to do my bidding. I want to sit with you and develop a plan that will work for both of us.

As the CEO finished the role play, he said, "Oh my God, I finally get it: Elliot is just like my stepfather. The man was a powerful force in my life and held the purse strings, yet I never felt I could talk with him directly, and I used to send my younger brothers to him when I needed money for something. Wow! Who would have thought that I avoid Elliot just like I did my stepfather?"

By the time the CEO had his actual PEPtalk with Elliot, it had lost the ragged edge of challenge. The conversation was not an unfinished dialogue between stepson and stepfather, but rather a polished and productive business exchange between CEO and CFO.

Sample PEPtalk 2

In this case, a COO, Javier, wanted to tackle his pattern as a denier. He had ignored cues from the CEO about the reporting processes in their very large company, and as a result was leaving gaping holes in the international structures, especially as regarded the procurement process. The tension between him and the CEO was becoming obvious. The HR representative had intervened, and the COO was finally coming to grips with his tendency to deny anything unpleasant, especially if it meant he was at fault. In his initial PEPtalk rehearsals, he maintained his focus on the CEO as a persecutor who was demanding and unforgiving. After half a dozen aborted attempts, he began to claim his own behavior, using a friend to play the CEO. It went like this:

> Andrea, you have every right to ask for quality reporting, and I pride myself on being a stellar performer. However, when I am put on the spot and told that my work is not meeting your standards, I have a tendency to turn it back on you and say, "You're too demanding and don't really understand the process and there's no problem over here, everything is working just fine." I refuse to see the elephants in the room and I dig my heels in. Not good. Denying is a form of self-protection and it really can destroy an infrastructure. Just admitting my pattern as a denier is horribly uncomfortable, yet paradoxically it is a relief, and it actually gives me a sense of comfort. In telling you this, I am making myself vulnerable, and yet in not doing so I would be setting myself up for

failure. So I have to put a team in place to rethink our procedures, and I will get back to you in two weeks with a clear plan. My hope is that by admitting my tendency to deny I am opening the route for building real trust and honesty in our working relationship.

And with that final bit of role play, Javier experienced a realization that changed this behavior forever. His father and grandfather had lost money, lots of money, because of bad business decisions, and the stories he had heard were always about "the economy" or the "shoddy partner" or "the bad luck of lousy weather." As Javier related after his PEPtalk, he had become yet another male family member denying any part in his difficulties. In fact, he could already see his teenage sons playing the "he did it, she did it, they did it" game. "My pledge," he said, "is that this unproductive pattern of denial stops with me."

Creating an Action Plan

Once you have put in some practice, it's time to get real and frame a **formal action plan** for your transformation. You need to give yourself goals and deadlines and take the time to strategize the best way forward. The initial step in developing an action plan is to decide which person at work you want to speak with first. He or she may or may not be the person you used for your PEPtalk. It is best to begin with someone with whom communicating would be the easiest. You want some early wins to gain confidence. Think of it as like strength training; you work with the lesser weights as you build up to the heavier ones. Also remember that as you take your pattern that no longer works and change it to its healthy opposite, flexibility is key. You are embarking on a growth process, an adventure whose exact course you can't predict.

How long does this process take? Research indicates that basic habits require six weeks to "unlock," so **your initial action plan covers six consecutive weeks.** There is no hard-and-fast rule; just stay committed to the process. Make a list of your proposed actions in the order in which they will occur. Paste a replica of this action plan in one or many places—on your refrigerator, on your bathroom mirror, in a computer file—and keep a copy in your wallet next to your credit cards.

Before you begin constructing your six-week plan, answer the following questions about the key issues you want to address:

- What specific patterns of mine cause conflict with my boss, peers, and direct reports?
- When did I first become aware of the conflict my patterned reactions cause?
- What are three possible changes that may come about when I tackle the conflict?
- What are the possible consequences of my implementing each of the three changes?

With answers to these questions firmly in hand, next commit to a six-week plan by writing a sentence or two about what actions you intend to take; as the weeks go on, you will reassess and make any necessary changes. The following is an example:

Week 1

Action	Immediate Changes	Desired Long-Term Outcome
Commit to speaking with my boss about my martyr pattern of taking on too much work. I will reassure him that I intend to continue to do a great job in a new way. I want him to know I am experimenting with different ways of using my time so that I don't burn out and then feel resentful, and that I am ready to find more satisfying ways of responding to my coworkers.	Make adjustments to go home from work at a reasonable hour—no later than 6:30 PM every evening for the next six weeks. Plan to observe how this behavior affects the rest of the team; they are used to dumping work on my desk. I know there will be pushback, and I am committed to staying the course.	I am willing to change from a martyr to an integrator who is able to lead the team in developing a best-case scenario for sharing the project loads more equally.

WEEK 2

Action	Immediate Changes	Desired Long-Term Outcome
Have coffee with my admin and share my strategy for changing the martyr pattern. Ask for her support. When she hears me talking about how "swamped" I am and how I "never have time," she has permission to tell me to stop.	Make changes by observing my language patterns and changing the words that have become my trademark—so that "swamped" becomes "energized," "never have time" becomes "all is possible," and so on.	My language will reflect my new perspective that I am not alone in the world and do not have to carry all the burdens.

WEEK 3

Action	Immediate Changes	Desired Long-Term Outcome
Have lunch with John and Sandi, the two colleagues who have been the most willing to help in all projects. Tell them about my "pattern busting" experiment and ask for feedback now and in three weeks.	Help the team gain clarity on my behavior changes and forge an alliance with the two easiest folks who will most likely be encouraging and accepting.	I will take a more active role in discussions about workload and shared responsibility.

WEEK 4

Action	Immediate Changes	Desired Long-Term Outcome
Tell my immediate family about the changes I am accomplishing and let them ask questions. I am not yet ready to directly take on the conversations	Prepare my family for changes they can be sure to expect once I have the work schedule handled. I am willing to listen to their concerns without having to cushion the path. I will just listen and observe.	I will become an initiator at home and find a fairer balance in who does what, to share the load. I will not jump in and do someone else's share of the work just to make it seem harmonious.

Week 4 (*continued*)

Action	Immediate Changes	Desired Long-Term Outcome
necessary with my husband and teenage sons to let them know I expect changes from them also.		

Week 5

Action	Immediate Changes	Desired Long-Term Outcome
Ask Dan and Kate for separate meetings and tell them about my commitments. Offer them insights into my patterned reactions and explain how Sankofa Mapping helped me see the martyr pattern that was leading me toward burnout.	Have Dan and Kate stop complaining that I am not fulfilling my promises and help them get a handle on how a healthy work system is balanced between individual needs and team responsibilities.	The whole team will become more accountable about the "push and pull" of everyone's patterns. I want them to understand how a highly functional team is both flexible and honest about the balance of skills and what needs to be done.

Week 6

Action	Immediate Changes	Desired Long-Term Outcome
Check in with boss to get feedback. Check in with admin to get feedback. Check in with John and Sandi to get feedback. Check in with my family to get feedback. Check in with Dan and Kate to get feedback.	Engage in new, more healthy dialogue using language that (1) keeps the "inner martyr" from becoming strong and (2) helps me as an initiator manage the old guilt and concerns that have plagued me for so long.	I will stay strong and responsive to this new way of sharing the load and taking more time for myself; now that I have it, I will use it to do things that will enhance me personally and professionally.

Tom's Story

To give you a sense of how an action plan can work to put you on a path toward real and lasting change, I end the chapter with a story from my practice. Tom was a highly talented sales representative in the computer industry; he had risen up through the ranks and was now being offered the job of VP of global sales. This was a huge deal, the promotion of a lifetime. It meant a big raise and a chance to work as an equal with the company's top leadership. There was only one problem: Tom would have to uproot his family and move them to the other side of the country. The family had already relocated seven times for the sake of Tom's career. When they bought their present home in Virginia, they had all agreed that this would be the last time they would ever pack and go again. Tom's two high school–age daughters were happy in school, and his wife, Noreen, had a great job as a nurse in a top regional hospital. Moving again would be tough on everyone.

Tom didn't know what to do. He had hardly mentioned the possibility of a promotion at home and could feel the pressure building. He wasn't sleeping well and suffered from a continuous knot in his stomach. He had agreed to go through the formal interview process that was required for the new job. This was no big deal, as he had been with the company for a long time and knew the men and women he would work with. By the end of this process, Tom knew that he wanted this job, yet he felt torn and terribly anxious. His boss wasn't much help. Having recently gotten divorced, his boss had very little sympathy for what he termed "family bullshit." "Just tell them that things have changed and that they'll love California," his boss advised.

Tom asked if he could have an outside coach to help him make sense of this grand dilemma. That's where I came in. I found Tom to be a friendly, likable guy with an ingratiating Southern manner—the kind of person who exuded competence and caring so much that he instantly put you at ease. Tom stood six foot four, was at the pinnacle of his career, and was also the picture of health. He was the "apple of his father's eye" and had been the sports hero as well as the academic success that had his dad bragging to anyone who was within earshot. His mom would smile and quietly say she was proud of her son, but for his dad, Tom was somehow bigger than life size. It was an interesting paradox. Tom loved being the center of so much attention, yet he also felt burdened by always having to live up to inflated expectations. It was not until we began coaching and he reluctantly agreed to embark on the Sankofa Mapping process that some surprising truths came out.

Tom had been the victim of a shooting accident while he was training to be a Navy Seal, and as a result he continued to suffer an immense amount of physical discomfort on a daily basis. He harbored silent resentment against his old friend Jed, who had miscalculated his aim and shot in the wrong direction. As the consummate pleaser and avoider, Tom had managed to hide this pain from everyone around him; only his wife and his boss knew. Tom hated to think about the pain, had learned to avoid talking about it, and at times would even deny that it was real. The bullet he had taken had been fired so long ago that it was, as he liked to say, "Dead and buried."

After connecting the rest of the dots in his life, Tom was willing to put together an action plan and let the process help him make his decision about the promotion. For logistical reasons beyond his control, Tom knew that the six-week process would probably stretch out to about three months, and I told him that this was just fine. The steps were as follows:

Step 1: Have a conversation with his father.
Step 2: Write a letter to Jed.
Step 3: Meet with his boss to discuss the new promotion. Suggest an alternative arrangement that involved a flexible living situation with regular trips to the West Coast.
Step 4: Talk with Noreen about the promotion.
Step 5: Have a family meeting with Noreen and the girls in which they discuss the potential promotion and also, for the first time, Tom's searing physical pain.
Step 6: Meet with the firm's CEO to request the flexible living situation.

The first step was frightening to consider, yet Tom hunkered down and did it. He called his dad, described the avoider pattern he had carried his whole life, and asked if they could talk. For once, Tom and his dad spoke about more than sports scores or the price of gas. For the first time, the father told the son about how he had attempted to save a buddy and had been shot. The dialogue between the two men was quiet and strong. Like father, like son. Tom commented to me that he was amazed at the emotional release he experienced, and he thought that the clearing of old wounds seemed to make his physical pain more tolerable. In any case, it kicked off a process that built a new father-son foundation, a process that empowered Tom to carry through with the other steps of his plan.

Step 2 was more complex. Tom decided to write a letter to Jed talking about the accident and Jed's poor judgment, but also forgiving Jed. The last part proved too difficult at that time, and Tom put the letter in a drawer instead. Yet he was able to see Jed as a young college kid who must have spent many sleepless nights thinking about the friend he almost killed. Although Tom was not ready to contact him, the possibility was not as bleak as it had been even two weeks ago.

In comparison, step 3 was something of a breather. Tom had a strategy meeting with his boss, exploring the possibility of remaining in his home and arranging for a flexible schedule at the corporate headquarters in California. Tom was willing to keep an apartment in California and be there as needed. Until now, full-time presence at corporate headquarters had been strictly required of senior management, and no one had raised the possibility of doing things differently. Tom's boss said it was worth a try and that he'd support Tom when he brought the issue up before the firm's CEO.

Steps 4 and 5 were both big deals. Tom and Noreen talked—really *talked*—about the options and possibilities before them. Tom admitted his avoider pattern and took responsibility as well for behaving as the consummate pleaser with her. He told his wife that he could understand how hard it must be to watch him wince in pain and worry that he might end up in a wheelchair. At the family meeting that followed, Tom owned up to all the pain he felt and his tendency to go into "avoidance mode" when one of his daughters would ask, "Dad, what's the matter?" He had been an avoider, he told them, but he had only behaved that way because he had wanted them to feel safe. The girls burst into tears. Then they shocked Tom by telling him that finally knowing the truth made all the difference. All these years, they had sensed something was wrong, but they had guessed that their dad had been upset about something *they'd* done. With no way to check their intuition, they had come to doubt themselves. Now they could feel much better about themselves.

Step 6 was the graduation test. I had been asked to facilitate Tom's meeting with the CEO, and when I showed up I could tell that Tom was extremely nervous. We gathered in the CEO's office, and after the requisite handshakes, I described the purpose of the meeting and turned it over to Tom. Trembling slightly and wiping the sweat from his upper lip, he articulated his deep desire for the job. He admitted that as an avoider he had been reluctant even to have this meeting, but that he had gone through with it, eager to finally step up and initiate a new work policy. He then talked about the reasons he thought the flexible schedule would work not just for him but for others who loved the company yet were looking for greater work-life balance.

When Tom finished speaking, the room was quiet for several long minutes. Then the CEO looked at Tom and said, "Great idea. Let's make it work. Come back to me with a specific proposal and a timeline, and we'll hammer it out with HR." He clapped Tom on the shoulder. "Maybe some of you longtime guys will stick around and help us continue to grow the company."

Today, Tom is commuting regularly to his job on the West Coast. One daughter chose to go to college in California, and his younger daughter, soon to graduate from high school, thinks that looks right for her too. His wife has been exploring the possibility of an advanced nursing degree from a school down the road from Tom's West Coast office. Change is in the air.

Takeaways

- Pattern transformation entails taking action and talking to the important individuals in your life to do repair work.
- You become whole by owning the parts of yourself you would rather ignore.
- Pattern transformation takes effort and is worth the sweat.
- Once you claim the healthy opposite of your outmoded patterns, you can develop an action plan that is accurate and effective.
- Leadership really begins with an *A* and includes a personal commitment to authenticity, accountability, accuracy, action, and achievement.

CHAPTER SEVEN

TALKING TOGETHER

I don't want any "yes-men" around me. I want
everybody to tell the truth, even if it costs them their
jobs.
—SAMUEL GOLDWYN

Samuel Goldwyn seems to have created a traditional double bind: whether you agree or disagree, you lose! This no-win mentality is prevalent in many organizations and keeps people from being able to really talk together, to engage in honest dialogue. Dialogue, unlike casual conversation, fosters truthful and deep discussion and is seen as a high art form. It takes knowledge of human relationships, and mastery comes only with lots of practice. Once you have learned to consider your own patterns and how to transform them, you can begin to talk with others in a clearer, more expedient, and more effective manner. You become the trailblazer for authenticity. No more need to discuss your real feelings behind closed doors. No more need to acknowledge that everything is "just fine" as you sweep your truth under the rug. No more need to agree with "popular opinion" when it sticks in your craw. It is time to bring your understanding of the interactive aspects of patterned behavior into your workplace and be a change agent for more open, more real, and more beneficial communication. Dialogue requires you to go beyond anger, defensiveness, and posturing to the heart of the subject, and to search for what really matters.

In this chapter, you will learn about the complex yet vitally important role of dialogue at work. This is when you become acutely aware of how the puzzle pieces of communication fit together. This is when you begin to observe how a variety of individual thoughts and feelings blend together to create a symphony of either harmony or dissonance. Once you have mastered the concept of PEPtalk, you are in the enviable position of taking your own emotional and social intelligence into the realm of "talking together." In our Western culture, we have not spent adequate time learning how to listen effectively and respond appropriately. Our tendency is to "almost" listen and have our answers ready before the other has even completed the first sentence. The ability to engage in dialogue is critical for contemporary leaders and has the capacity to short-circuit disputes and increase creative communications. This may involve you and a direct report, you and one of your peers, you and your boss, or you and your team. In any case, there are four ground rules (discussed in the next section) for bringing the powerful process of dialogue into your work setting. Dialogue is neither debate nor conversation. It is a more challenging and more exciting way of relating than that.

In true dialogue, you and another, or many others, bring together each person's unique points of view, going back and forth taking aspects of each viewpoint, gathering bits of information until you can all come together with a newer, more vital perspective than could have been developed individually. Dialogue is systemic in nature, is the essence of collaboration, and, in our argumentative and debate-oriented culture, a vital force waiting to be harnessed.

By now, you have done enough study about the more obvious as well as some of the invisible forces found in behavior and communication to add the power of dialogue to your tool kit. Be vigilant by paying attention to the specific way you construct questions to your work colleagues. Stay alert to tonality and body language as you respond, and watch how others answer. Keep the dialogue going by seeing this as an adventure to find the hidden treasure underneath the obvious. Actually think the words "open-ended" in your mind as you begin your sentence. Choose from *What, Where, How, When,* or *Why* as your first word. Beginning this way makes it impossible to answer with a simple yes or no. Give this method a shot. You will be pleasantly surprised to find responses that have more depth and leave more room for innovative next thoughts. There are fewer tendencies to become battle ready and to defend a position. Pay attention to the type of information you gather as you ask and listen differently. It is most often kinder, more helpful, and more useful.

As you continue with this chapter, you will become more proficient in asking depth questions rather than merely accepting the first answer given to you, and you will learn how to continue to ask probing questions without being intrusive. Then you will be helped to go to the heart of empathic listening and learn what cues to listen for and how certain words or expressions are pattern indicators and what to do with them. I offer some "sound bites" of typical conversations so that you can get comfortable with listening in a new way. I then complete this chapter with a list of ten guidelines, your "PAL list" to help you as you continue on the road of becoming a pattern-aware leader.

FOUR GROUND RULES

Here are the communication and behavioral ground rules for working together.

TREAT TRUTH TELLING AS A PRECISE ART FORM

Truth telling resembles a martial art in that it takes tremendous discipline; it's not just a punch here or a jab there. Please note that telling the truth does not mean saying everything you are thinking, or adding every nuance to explain, defend, or justify yourself. The question in back of your mind at all times is "How can this forward the situation and make a positive difference?" When you tell the truth, especially when you are angry or disappointed, remember that you are not meant to spill your guts or set up a situation where, as in a contest, you have gathered votes to prove that your way is the best way. Once you begin to say "and furthermore, Robert and Sarah and Michael all agree with me," you have moved out of essential truths into the area of debate. My observation of truth telling is that the sentences are short; they don't run on and on into rambling paragraphs. They stay with the specific point, and there are not a lot of "furthermores" and "therefores." Each truth sentence is around seven to twelve words, and when you finish, it is critical to take a breath and maintain a few moments of quiet to let the impact of the words settle in.

Here is an example of truth telling that initially created a schism and then was rethought several days later to open the way for relationship progress. At an off-site held with a very angry leadership team, the boss started out by saying, "This is my truth. I am the leader here, and I don't intend to change. I know many of you don't like my style, and therefore I suggest you vote with your feet and leave. You see, you can stay and follow my directives or go elsewhere in the company or to another company. If you want change, it is you who will change, not me." Needless to say, the air in the room was thick with discontent and depression, even though you could argue that the boss had, in fact, told the truth.

With some private coaching after that absolutely awful first off-site day, the boss began to listen differently. This is the way he started on the last morning of the retreat: "First, I want to apologize. I was wrong to set up such a confrontational challenge when we first met. I did it to protect myself. I knew there were many things that were not working with our team. Yet what I did was an old knee-jerk way of reacting so I could feel safe. However, not only was there a lack of safety for me, there was no room for dialogue and no safety for any of you to tell your truth. I am now willing to really listen, and if I begin to defend or justify myself, I give permission for anyone in the room to raise your hand, and I will be quiet." There was a collective sigh of relief in the room. The meeting ended with a tremendous amount of real work getting done and surprisingly little time spent talking about emotions.

MAKE SURE THAT WORK IS NOT A REHAB FACILITY

You can offer to give others your suggestions, but then you need to back off. If the patterns of other folks get too much in the way at work and your conversations don't help, then HR, mentors, performance improvement plans, and termination are the next viable alternatives. Often there is such a strong desire to help people grow and change as you begin to be pattern aware that too much time is given to the process of "helping." The rule of three is a good one to follow. If by the third time you have to go over the same retread territory and there is no viable change, then please take action to the next level with a different type of intervention, as just discussed. Your part is to be committed to continued truth telling and active listening.

Robert Sutton, Stanford professor of management and author of *The No-Asshole Rule,* has little tolerance for those not willing to change and grow. He challenges us to make sure the work environment does not become a depressing place filled with disrespect because we are willing to ignore rudeness and power games by looking the other way. Continued bad behavior, like any other addiction, has no place in the work setting. It is helpful to tackle areas of contention through the use of dialogue. Sutton puts it well: "Saying smart things and giving smart answers are important. Learning to listen to others and to ask smart questions is more important."[1] The idea is not to turn the conversation into "point-counterpoint," but to make sure you let the other person have his or her say without interrupting, and then respond. High-level leadership is about exploring and probing for new perspectives rather than staying locked into old positions. The capacity to observe and include emotion-laden content rather than ignore or discount it is at the crux of powerful and creative dialogue. People need to be heard and respected in getting out their side of an issue, just as you too have a right to your say. However, if there is no willingness to do things differently, more explicit action is required. Just remember that rule of three!

Listen for Emotion and Repetition

Dialogue is a truly interactive process, and you can really sense what is going on by checking your own physical responses. If you feel your gut area tighten, pay attention; if your heart begins to race, pay attention; if you feel queasy, uneasy, or conflicted, pay attention. We do pick up cues from each other, and if you have a sense of discomfort, you can be pretty sure that the other person or persons are feeling variations on the theme. Continually ask yourself what you are experiencing as the conversation develops. My business clients are usually receptive to the idea of active and empathic listening, yet they admit they are not sure what to listen for or how willing they are to trust their physical reactions. What you are listening for are key words or phrases that tend to repeat and repeat. You may hear, "I don't feel I am being included" or "Why am I always the last to know?" or the always popular "It was his fault, her fault, their fault." Once, twice—again, by three times you can bet you have a pattern to contend with. Phrases or words that tend to repeat have a strong "feeling tone" to them. Trust your gut and follow your hunches. As you listen, you may notice that the speaker's tone is often out of alignment with his or her spoken words. Here it is important to trust your "inner hearing" or what I call the BS detector. When someone says "It really doesn't matter" or "I'm not upset" and in your head or your gut you hear the BS buzzer go off, trust it more than the words.

One colleague recently told me about his company's new COO, who was so lacking in integrity that the business was at a standstill.

> This jerk started a power battle with one of the senior VPs that is so obvious, there is a lottery to see how long either the VP will stay or how long the COO has before he is booted out. The COO took credit for an idea of mine and blamed the VP for blocking it. I reminded him that it was my idea and that in fact he had been the one to block it. At that moment he had a bad "malfunction in his falsehood manager" and played the worst game of "CYA" you could imagine. Unfortunately, when words and actions are that much out of alignment, it sets up the domino effect, and more than half of the best producers have their resumes on the street. And that includes me.

BE OPEN TO OUTCOME, NOT ATTACHED TO IT

Being clear and decisive does not in any way keep you from changing your perspective and following a new direction. Therefore, before you commence with your first open-ended question, know the direction you want to go. Be clear: Is this a fact-finding time, a time to learn more about how the other person thinks and feels, or a time to reassess how you will work together? It is not enough to merely say, "I am frustrated with the lateness of your projects, and I just want you to get your work done"; it's just not that simple. Remember, no one is going to come up to you and say, "Hi, my name is Tony. I used to be a procrastinator, and now I have transformed into a realizer. So, what do you want done?" The more you think through what you want as an outcome—think it through in minute detail—the more it becomes possible for you to get what you want. This is especially true when you have done your own inner work to release old, outmoded patterns in your own life.

Listening for Verbal Cues

Here is what Kevin did when he was newly promoted in a company based in Cheshire, England. He had to talk with a direct report who had filed a grievance about being in a "hostile work environment."

When Corinne entered Kevin's office, she didn't want to say much and sat staring straight ahead. He did his best to make her comfortable, yet he knew they had to explore how they were going to work together and why she saw this work environment as hostile. They came to an agreement that if at any time during their discussion she felt uneasy, she would come back with a union representative.

During their talk, she kept addressing the fact that she felt "isolated" in the office. As Kevin told it later, she used this word over and over, yet it made no sense. She worked in a large room with cubicles, and at lunch would go off with several colleagues to the cafeteria. He was not sure what to do with his gut feeling that the word "isolated" was a key to the source of the problem. He chose to wait for another opportunity before bringing it up. Please remember as you become sensitive to talking with others about patterns that it is all in the timing. Helping someone recognize what is to you annoying, repetitive behavior may be a revelation to him or her. So be as strategic with this information as you would be with acquiring a new company.

Several weeks later, Kevin and Corinne met again. Corinne was more relaxed, although cautious. Kevin found an opportunity to ask her about the sense of isolation. He stated that he was curious how her working in a large, open office and having lunch with her friends connected with her feeling of isolation. And then he became quiet. Corinne hesitated and took a gulp of air before she launched into a very intense story.

"It doesn't have to do with you, Kevin, or the office. I guess it is stuck back with your predecessor, Pietro. He was a 'Don't bother me' type of boss. And no matter what I had to say or what I needed, I was always brushed off with a 'Sorry, I'm busy' attitude." Corinne got really quiet, and Kevin again sat and waited.

Another gulp of air, and she continued. "I don't know why I'm going to tell you this. I don't talk about my personal life to most people, yet somehow I want you to know." Again quiet, and then she plunged into her story. "When I was seven, my parents were killed in an automobile accident. My twin sister and I were put into a foster home, since there were no other relatives who could take us. It was hard because it was a 'stiff upper lip,' never-talk-about-anything-emotional household.

"It was okay until I was twelve, and there was a group of us walking along a country lane on our way home from school. A car veered out of control, and my sister, who happened to be on the outer side of the group, was hit and died later that day."

Again a long silence as Kevin took in the magnitude of what he had just heard, and Corinne sat with the memories.

They both shifted in their chairs, and Corinne continued:

Life was dark for me after that. My foster parents, in typical English fashion, told me we would all just have to get on with it and put this behind us. I had no one to talk with, and I felt so isolated. I made a decision then that when I became an adult and had more control over my life, I would never be put in the background when I had something to say.

And that leads to Pietro. He was like my foster parents. Just shut up and produce. Don't ask questions and be the good little soldier. I attempted to explain to him that I wasn't getting enough direction to complete some of my job responsibilities, and he just brushed me off. I am not demanding, but I'm not willing to pretend everything is hunky-dory when it's not. I lived that throughout my growing-up years.

Kevin and Corinne made a pact that if he was overly busy and she really needed to speak with him, she would use the word "isolation" and that would get his attention. And it worked. Corinne dropped her suit with the union, and she and Kevin have had an excellent working relationship for nearly four years.

There was one extra benefit. Kevin's company always held meetings with its sister company in Sweden. Until Kevin became her boss, Corinne would never attend the overseas meetings. She had never talked about her fear that one of her three children might be hit by a car or that some other tragedy would happen and she would not be available. About six months after their initial truth-telling meeting, Corinne told Kevin she was willing to go to the next off-site in Stockholm. The two celebrated with a glass of schnapps the first night at dinner.

CHANGING CONVERSATIONS WITH ACTIVE AND EMPATHIC LISTENING

The table below is a list of sound bites for you to consider so that you can begin to practice listening for the patterns. After several months, you will start to get the clues in warp speed and to see where your direct reports, peers, and those to whom you report are simmering in old, outmoded patterns. You then can be a great ally in simply pointing out what you observe and opening to an authentic dialogue. The key here is your willingness to be both honest and vulnerable yourself. (The right-hand column provides comparable sound bites that you might hear from those who have transformed a destructive life pattern into its positive equivalent.)

SOUND BITES

Super-Achiever	Creative Collaborator
"I just had the greatest idea, another great idea (they come to me all the time), and I want to share it with all of you in my company."	"It's great when we get together and come up with fabulous ideas. Jane and I figured out a great way to save the company tons of money."
"I just came back from my Stanford executive program, the one that only takes ten of the most advanced business high-potentials in the country, and I want to share what I learned with you."	"I'd love to share what I learned at Stanford so we can discuss how to use these new ideas here at work."

Super-Achiever (cont'd)	Creative Collaborator
"I know I am the right candidate for the promotion. No one here has the credentials to do the job like I do."	"In the past, I was so busy getting ahead that I never took time to collaborate, and now I know that I can support whoever gets the promotion."

Rebel	Community Builder
"Can you believe he was so demeaning to her at the meeting? I'm going to tell her to get back at him by complaining to HR."	"In my old pattern, I would have loved to stir things up; however, it's a waste of time, so I'll talk with him privately about my concerns."
"This organization is all talk and no follow-through. I'm going to start a petition for a real change management initiative that I'm going to lead."	"I want to find a way for us to solve the issues that cause us to derail change initiatives. I don't want to work against everyone anymore; now I want to work *with* everyone."
"You can't argue with a fool. I know a great lawyer who can advise us on what action to take."	"In the past I would have gotten a group to complain to the district manager. I'd rather see if we can create a plan together."

Procrastinator	Realizer
"Stop getting yourself in a tizzy. I'll have it done tomorrow, or maybe the day after, or sometime next week."	"I know I have a tendency to rush at the last minute and can see how that has caused so much angst, so I cleared my schedule to get it done today."
"You need to chill out. This pressure is going to make you sick, and I'm not taking responsibility for your health."	"I'm giving up my last-minute adrenaline rush. It really adds pressure for you, and I know that's not fair."
"I don't know why you are making such a fuss. The team has everything under control, and I'm just doing what they tell me."	"My pattern of procrastination was a way to keep me safe from criticism, and all it did was bring on more upset than it was worth."

SOUND BITES *(Continued)*

Clown	*Humorist*
"I have a private line to the Godfather, and these jokers are on my list."	"The wind is up, the sails are billowing, and with great intention we can survive this mess. Okay, everyone push!"
"He's going to be the first one voted off the island."	"Let's hear the musketeer cheer: All for all and all for all and all for ME. Now we're cooking."
"I thought *Sex and the City* was just on the tube. Can you believe what she was wearing?"	"Vive la difference, except when it's too low cut. Guess I'll talk to her about it on the phone."

Persecutor	*Visionary*
"Did you see what that stupid jerk did? Wait until our meeting, and I'll tear him a new one."	"We're going to take a deep breath, reevaluate the situation, and find the pony that by god is in the manure pile."
"How dare you criticize my directive. I'm your boss, and you just do what you're told."	"Every opinion counts, so let's get the basics in place and then jam and jive with all the creativity I know is in this room."
"What were you thinking when you planned that trip? It will cost the company a fortune. No, you can't go. It's time for you to get with the program or get out."	"I know you can come up with an amazing strategy that will make the trip really pay for itself."

Victim	*Explorer*
"It always happens like that. She is addicted to telling me what I did wrong, and I can never, ever please that witch."	"I'm so tired of being the victim. I'm going to throw caution to the wind and give her this plan I developed."
"Why is it that every good idea I have gets trashed?"	"I hate to be evaluated, yet I'll never get to a new place unless I ask for feedback and not see it as an attack."
"He has a great talent for making me feel worthless, and I can never have a good comeback when he bashes me."	"I just signed up for a course in emotional intelligence, and I'm excited to begin to explore why it's so easy to intimidate me."

Rescuer	Mentor
"She really needs my help. She will come unglued under the barrage of complaints about her new IT initiative."	"Let me help you by asking some questions so you have a better sense of how to handle this complex new complaint program."
"Don't bother him; he is really tired. Just tell me what your comments are, and I will be pleased to tell him when he's rested from the trip."	"Let's gather all the comments and develop a plan with him after the board meeting. He'll be more receptive if we have our ducks in a row."
"I will take it up with HR and senior management. You really don't have to worry; I'll make sure everything gets handled."	"I believe we can have a great meeting, and you can be the chair, once we put together the key areas of concern in question form to get company buy-in."

Drama Queen or King	Storyteller
"If this chaos continues, I'm going to have a nervous breakdown and then nothing will get done."	"When I get stressed, I just want to yell and blame. Instead I think I'll take a walk and clear my head so I can be of value for the meeting later."
"Can you believe he embarrassed me in front of the whole team? I have not slept in a week, I'm so upset."	"What he said was highly inappropriate. I've put time on the calendar to talk with him rather than be angry and demand an immediate apology."
"If you ever, ever talk to me like that again, I will get you fired. I am so upset, I can't face anyone who was at that meeting."	"Let's come to an agreement about how we can support each other at meetings. I get really upset when I see people discounting others, and I know we can work together to avoid ugly scenes."

Martyr	Integrator
"I didn't even go home last night. I slept on the sofa in the reception room. And as usual no one even said 'Thank you.' It doesn't pay to give of yourself."	"I love to work hard, and I usually don't ask for help, which is kind of stupid. With us all working together we can get this project done in warp speed."

Sound Bites (*Continued*)

Martyr (cont'd)	Integrator
"Because of the way I'm treated here, I'll never, ever be happy."	"My old pattern says 'Carry the burden and do it myself,' except it's breaking my back. Gosh, maybe that's why so many people have aching backs."
"I'm only doing the work of ten people, and you want me to do what?"	"I have a pattern of over-giving and then I ask for your firstborn in return. A better idea is to distribute work more evenly from the git-go."

Pleaser	Truth Teller
"Of course I'll take your dog to the groomer, and then I'd love to get flowers for you to give to your wife. Anything else?"	"I always love to help, yet the truth is that some of your requests do not really fit my job description, and it is best for me to tell you No up front."
"I'll cancel my plans; they really weren't important anyway."	"I know this is important, but I have other plans tonight. In the past I would have cancelled and stuffed my anger; not anymore. So I'll handle your request tomorrow."
"Whatever you want! Yes, of course your requests are doable, and I love to make sure you are happy."	"Remember when you would ask and I would say 'Whatever'? Well, those days are gone, and we will both be the better for the truth."

Avoider	Initiator
"There is no reason to talk about the cramped quarters here. We're growing, and people should just be grateful they have a job."	"I am not willing to let this matter just sit and simmer. Even though it is always uncomfortable for me to be in a conflict situation, let's talk!"
"What you just said is totally beside the point. Just concentrate on what I tell you, and you'll be just fine."	"I apologize for walking away before; it's an old habit that creeps back every now and then. I want to schedule a meeting soon so we can get to the bottom of the issue."

Avoider (cont'd)	Initiator
"You are like a broken record bringing up the same old stuff. If I haven't answered you by now it's because what you say is irrelevant."	"It is apparent that you don't feel heard, or you would not keep bringing up this subject. Let's set a team meeting and get these concerns aired and cleared."

Denier	Trust Builder
"The shipping department is great. Just because everyone quit, you think there's a problem. Everything is really fine."	"The shipping department is a mess. I like to ignore these guys; they are so demanding, and I become a wimp. Let's talk it through with them and find a solution."
"I haven't noticed that gas prices are going up."	"I hate change, so I pretend it away. I can understand your request to work from home one day a week. I wonder if we'll ever get gas prices to stabilize."
"We're just one big happy family in this company. I never hear anyone complaining."	"I hate to spend the money, and I wish there was an easier solution. Sometimes I become an ostrich, and that only makes the problem worse. Let's call in an architect today."

Splitter	Peacemaker
"I see how bad his behavior is, but if I were you, I would just ignore him. I've already told him you are upset, so just lay low."	"It is better if I am out of the middle of this issue. When you both sit down together, I am available to meet, but only if we're all there."
"He told me that he was very upset with your behavior at the meeting last week, but don't let on I told you."	"If you want to tell me something, I cannot promise to keep it a secret. I can only promise to use discretion, and I will tell someone only if it will help the situation."
"Promise if I tell you what she said, you won't get in the middle of it. I do hate when people don't get along."	"As we prepare to go into these difficult talks, I'd like you to remember this Rumi poem: 'Somewhere out beyond ideas of right-doing and wrong-doing, there is a field. I'll meet you there.'"

You don't have to wait for a formal discussion to begin listening for patterns. Look for other opportunities to continue developing your listening skills. Lectures, films, and parties are all great places to practice listening for life patterns.

The Martyr Revealed and Then Transformed

Let's take a specific pattern, that of the martyr, and walk through a real-time situation where talking about the pattern and its impact helped a team begin to redesign itself. Once the pattern was named, right out in the open, it lost its power, and the possibilities of a new type of team integration became obvious.

When the senior executives of a toy-importing company met to talk about the tugs and pulls happening with their newest acquisition, there was a tendency to see the acquired company as filled with naysayers and procrastinators. The CEO, annoyed with the newcomers, would make caustic comments about them to his leadership team; after all, he had known this group for years and felt safe to let off some steam. Although no one would say anything during meetings, off line they would complain to each other about his poor behavior. The CEO continued to whine while everyone else stayed quiet. Something had to give. The stalemate caused folks to make excuses to avoid meetings. That was until Ramon held up his hand when the CEO started his now familiar ramble.

Ramon began to speak about the undercurrent in the room, and there was a sigh of relief. He turned to the CEO and shared his observation. The CEO, his friend, was stuck in a rut, and unless he was willing to "move past the past" and give up the need to talk about what wasn't working, they would never get to what *was* working. They were simply going to revisit and revisit and revisit. The great things they expected from the acquisition would never materialize. Ramon used an image of a magnet that was so strong that it kept pulling them into the past.

Initially the CEO was quiet and looked irritated. Ramon gave several examples and then admitted that he too felt like a martyr, over-giving and getting little in return. The acquisition had not been what they expected, and the disappointments were real. He asked for others to speak up. Yes, they were all frustrated, yet the deal was sealed. The question was how they were going to move forward even though it was enticing to stay at the place of recriminations and vindictiveness.

The CEO looked around the room and said, "I think I got it. By God, I think I got it. I had to prove that those guys were not up to our caliber. I was so pissed off that they didn't jump in with all hands on deck, and I wouldn't blame it on my leadership, so I had to blame them."

This was the turning point. "Next time I go to that self-indulgent place of complaining, anyone in this room is welcome to look at me and say 'There goes the magnet again!' And if I see the old pattern returning, I'll give the 'magnet sign.'" And with that, he made a fist and pulled his hand in a backward gesture. It got the point across.

Years later, a new hire asked a seasoned employee, "What is that funny gesture that I see folks make during meetings? Is it some kind of secret obscenity?" The response was, "In a manner of speaking, it is. It reminds us that living in the past and creating enemies are a waste of time.

THE IMPORTANCE OF SYSTEMS THINKING IN THE WORKPLACE

The true key to transformation, as I have said before, is to look at life holistically and think about how the parts of the system connect rather than merely to look at superficial problems. Just about every company I work with still has frustrations about the silo mentality, no matter how many matrixed teams there are or how many solid- and dotted-line reporting structures have been put in place. The silo mentality sets up nonporous boundaries and limits cooperation between the various parts of an organization. In every company, there are patterns and rigid roles being played without thinking through either the short-term or especially the long-term implications. These patterns constitute the office politics that is often called "The Gotcha Game" and take up more of the day than any of us prefer. We will continue to play this interactive, win-lose game until enough of us say "Stop." Once enough of us become determined to take responsibility to become emotionally and socially adept and pattern aware, it is then and only then that we can change the game to win-win. I acknowledge that staying committed to changing your behavior, day in and day out, requires lots of elbow grease. That's why it helps to remember that you are part of a larger system in which some people and situations will inevitably push your buttons. The more conscious you are of the interplay of patterns, the more you can make choices that will benefit you as well as those around you. This is how being part of a system helps us help each other. We can change ourselves and thus participate in changing our work environments by using the skills of dialogue: telling the truth, finding a balanced way to respond, checking our emotions, and thinking holistically.

This approach works in all types of organizations, wherever people gather together to achieve something they deem of consequence. I would like to share one example from a sports team, where winning and losing are obvious to players and fans alike, and certainly have an impact on the bottom line—the number of people who show up in the stands game after game.

This team had several super-achievers, one or two martyrs, a very obvious clown, a drama king who was often grist for the gossip mill, pleasers, a procrastinator, a couple of "no problems here" deniers, and an avoider coach who hated—yes, deeply hated—any form of conflict.

At the beginning of the season, the team was marked for success. They performed and were applauded. And then something happened; that "something" was a magazine article. One of the super-achievers was crowned "the one," and it was suggested that the team's success really belonged to him and him alone. Other magazines picked up the theme, and reporters as well as cute young "groupies" gathered outside the stadium to, well, just to talk to him, to get a glimpse of him and be able to say, "I saw him in person."

The coach thought it would blow over. After all, the media are fickle, and there would be another superstar soon enough. He would not heed the warning signs that these big, strong basketball stars were no longer a cohesive team. They went onto the court wearing the same color uniforms, yet the ability to trust and be trusted was gone. Soon the drama king was arrested on a DWI, and the procrastinator was always late for practice.

Fast-forward three months to a team meeting after the coach had received some coaching for himself. He admitted he had run from the conflict, yet it was not going away. When he told his truth, he opened the way for others. This "simple" act of personal accountability for his own behavior created an opening for others to speak up. A major breakthrough came when the anointed superstar spoke. He had not coveted the attention; he said that he felt like an outcast with these guys who had been his great buddies on and off the court. It took time, many more meetings to clear the air, and more truth telling, but slowly, as each began to see how his specific patterns interfaced with the others, the tension diminished, and their cooperation on the court improved.

This team is an example of an ancient saying attributed to Buddha: "Imagine that every person in the world is enlightened but you, they are all your teachers, each doing just the right things to help you learn patience, perfect wisdom, and perfect compassion." If we could all see each other as teachers and see ourselves as lifelong learners, we could all play on the winning team!

PATTERN-AWARE LEARNING

Up to this point, Chapter Seven has been about dialogue, active listening, asking questions that can lead your colleagues to their own answers, and telling the truth to each other in ways that enhance, not harm. I've talked about finding ways to work together so we can all win. Here is an example from my own life. Years ago when we were just at the beginning of our pattern exploration days, my company had a wonderful administrative assistant who was fashioned from angel cloth. She was dedicated and reliable, and welcomed everyone to our retreat center as if he or she owned the place.

Nothing lasts forever, right? After tax season one year, when the returns were coming in the mail, Lisa asked if she could meet with Herb and me. She had a twinkle in her eye, and I must admit it made me nervous. As we settled into one of the conference rooms, she leaned toward us with anticipated joy, ready for us to share in her good news.

"You know, Sylvia and Herb, how you encourage everyone to find their paths and stretch to their highest goals?" I already did not like the flavor of this conversation. She continued. "Well, you have been very generous to me, and I have been saving money for the first time in my life. And I decided that if I got enough money back from the IRS, I was going to return to school and get my master's degree. And I think working here has given me the courage to step out into the unknown, and I not only got enough money, I can go to one of the universities in the San Francisco area, and that has always been my dream."

Lisa stopped. She was smiling a massive smile, and she waited. Herb was, as Herb always is, enthusiastic and encouraging. I, in contrast, looked over at Lisa, burst into tears, and said eloquently, "You can't do that!" They both looked at me in shock.

If that moment could have had a title, it would have been "PDA" as in "Pretty Damn Awkward." Lisa, following my lead, also began to cry. Herb then took charge and said quietly, "Sylvia, you can't tell Lisa she can't go back to school. I know you really don't mean that." He then asked Lisa to let us have a few minutes alone. "What's up?" was all he said before the tears started gushing again. "I need her" was all I could muster.

It took us a few powerful minutes for me to compose myself and understand what had just happened. For me, even though Lisa was giving us six weeks' notice, news of her imminent departure was still sudden. I had not expected her to leave for, well, forever. Herb had me look at my tendency (we didn't even talk about patterns back then) to get "antsy" when someone in my life was going on to his or her next adventure. It didn't take long, and through my tears I observed and understood that my father's sudden death from a heart attack when I was fourteen was lodged in my nervous system. Lisa had become like family to me. And voilà. Here was someone who was leaving me, just as my father had, without my buy-in.

It was the first time I had a clear understanding of how the powerful patterns from our childhoods play out at work. We invited Lisa back into the conference room, and I was able to tell her what I had just put together. I could wish her well and listen to her exciting plans and be there with her, even though a part of me sat for the rest of the day with the sadness of the fourteen-year-old girl who, instead of going to school on a Tuesday, stayed home to help with the plans for a funeral.

The next day, I was emotionally grounded enough that I asked to be in charge of Lisa's farewell party. If Lisa's departure had been left unconfronted and unresolved, it would have been marred with undercurrents of hurt and resentment; instead, she left on such an upbeat note that years later, with her master's completed and a burgeoning career in psychology, she would call and tell us she could still hear our voices cheering her on.

What I can offer to help as you make the commitment to transform your work and therefore your life is the following list of ten guidelines to keep in mind as you continue to help yourself and your colleagues. We call them your pattern-aware learning (PAL) list.

1. **Be ultra-observant of what you say and how you use words.** As we saw in this chapter, certain words or sentences are pattern indicators. If you tend to say things like "I never have 'me' time," think martyr. If you begin a sentence with "She [he] is always the problem," think avoider. Using the word "scared" frequently, think victim. To change your patterns, focus on changing what you say.

2. **Become more familiar with your gut.** There is a sensation—tightness in the gut area, maybe even a sense of nausea—that allows you to know that you are in the realm of patterned reactions. You can find a quiet place, put your hand on your stomach, press slightly, and simply ask yourself whom a given person in your office reminds you of, or where there has been another situation resembling this one. Then write down what has shown up. Don't judge it, although this can be hard to avoid. Our tendency is to see such an exercise as so much foolishness. It isn't.

3. **Change your position in conversations and meetings.** This is a pattern-interrupt method. If you tend to speak up first, go last. If last, speak up first. See how it feels to find a place somewhere in the middle of the group conversation. Doing so will automatically force you to see the situation, hear the discussion, and feel the impact from a different vantage point. Remember, any time there is even one small change in a system, the whole system begins to change.

4. **Practice truth sentences.** These are short sentences of seven to twelve words that really get to the core of a truth and are thus felt deeply in the body as they are uttered. Truth sentences have the potential to transform relationships with your colleagues by beginning honest, meaningful dialogue. Say them before a mirror and then say them for real.

5. **Probe beyond the obvious.** By holding back on your thoughts and listening more closely to others, you can gain more insight into your own patterns. Ask questions that begin with "What," "When," "Where," "How," and "Why." When you get a response simply say "Tell me more" and then stay quiet and listen again. Also, don't be afraid to leave space for silence. There is a great deal going on in the stillness. Let it become part of your communication style.

6. **Get a "pattern-busting buddy."** It is important to get feedback from someone you trust and with whom you feel safe. In this case, it is better to make sure that this is someone *not* in your family and also not one of your closest work colleagues. The ideal buddy is one who will listen and then give you feedback on what you are saying—kind of like a talking mirror. When you request time with this talking partner, make sure you set a time limit. As you practice pattern busting and truth telling, remember that it is not about spilling your guts. Rather, you are practicing a disciplined way to see yourself and the world you are helping create.

7. **Keep an icon on your desk or on your computer screen.** This is a visual touchstone to remind you of the important work you are doing to clear the past so that you can live in the present. On my desk, I have a small soap sculpture of a sumo wrestler that represents the power of patterns to contend against our best efforts to overcome them. My little sumo guy reminds me that once a pattern is transformed, it becomes small and manageable. Other examples: a pleaser who has the song "I'm Just a Girl Who Can't Say No" on her iPod; a procrastinator who has the song "I'm Late" from *Alice in Wonderland* on his computer. Find your own icon, and remember: keep it light and whimsical.

8. **Keep a journal.** Short entries only—no more than two paragraphs. At the end of each day, write about one key encounter and its impact. Do not go back and reread. At the end of two to three months (no more), go back and read all the entries. Use a highlighter to track the reemergence of patterns and also to track where patterns have been transformed. Then burn the journal or throw it away, making a new commitment to effect changes in areas you want to work on. Start a new journal.

9. **Help others become aware of the larger system.** Sankofa Mapping and pattern observations are bigger than you are. Help others in your life understand this, and also help them appreciate their

role in the larger system. Put events in their proper perspective by acknowledging the influence of culture, historical circumstances, or other factors outside the family structure. Help others in your life unite around your story so that they can feel part of it and also see avenues for change and growth.

10. **Talk from the heart, while respecting others' discomfort.** The power of Sankofa Mapping derives from your own honest desire to be a change agent for yourself and others. Offer your family members, friends, and coworkers the surprise and wonder of observing patterns. At the same time, realize that folks will feel vulnerable and even confused at times. Remember that while you are discussing your history and patterns, you may also be unsettling theirs. Acknowledge their discomfort, offer hope, and extend your hand in true generosity of spirit.

TAKEAWAYS

- Dialogue trumps debate and casual conversation when it comes to effecting real and lasting change.
- The following are ground rules for dialogue at work: treat truth telling as a precise art form; make sure that work is not a rehab facility; listen for emotion and repetition; and be open to outcome, not attached to it.
- To develop new ways of listening and responding means thinking systemically, asking probing questions, and sharing your observations.
- Practice listening for clues to the other person's patterns— words and phrases that repeat, and vocal tone that does not match the words.
- Become a pattern-aware leader by constantly monitoring your inner reactions to the important relationships in your life.

CHAPTER EIGHT

CONNECTING THE DOTS

The man who can drive himself further once the
effort gets painful is the man who will win.
—SIR ROGER BANNISTER

On May 6, 1954, approximately three thousand spectators gathered at Iffley Road Track in Oxford, England, where winds up to twenty-five miles per hour began to subside just before the start of the event.

The race was historic, and the BBC commentator, Harold Abrahams of *Chariots of Fire* fame, took his time announcing that Roger Bannister had cracked the myth of the four-minute mile, winning the race in 3:59.4.

What was once deemed impossible has now become commonplace. Jim Ryan, who held the world record at 3:51.1 from 1967 to 1975, commented, "I'm surprised that so many have done it. In another way, I'm not. Time has proven that barriers like the four minute mile, the 16 foot pole vault and the 60 foot shot put were able to be surpassed with better training, better nutrition and a better understanding of what we were doing."[1]

Of course, most of us would place a high pole vault squarely in the realm of personally impossible, and, fortunately, that's not likely to hold us back at the office. Yet every organization has its own version of "don't even think about it" barriers, and like the world's most celebrated athletes, we get nowhere if we allow ourselves to be daunted by them. Not everyone has it in him or her to set the new world's record for company transformation. However, by working together, people can effect positive and long-term change. Remember, when any part of a system changes, the whole system begins to change. And just like the four-minute mile, new ways of communicating, relating, and behaving at work can quickly go from impossible to improbable to commonplace. Yet before the new way becomes commonplace, expect to enter the "funhouse" of pure, intoxicating, and dizzy-making change.

In this chapter, you take what you have learned about the hidden aspects of relationships and human interactions into organizational culture change. Remember, you've confronted change before; that means you can do it again! You have addressed your own accountability—by doing your Sankofa Map, confronting your patterns through PEPtalks, and learning the essence of dialogue by listening attentively and asking great open-ended questions. Once you become master of your own fate, you are ready to be part of a collective force to make your business environment the best it can be.

It's one thing to "own your own stuff" or talk with one or two colleagues; it's another order of magnitude to help change the dynamics that exist within the culture of the larger company. This is leadership at its best, and it takes a keen understanding of change and a steady hand to traverse the "chasm of chaos" inherent in the change process.

Taking on the role of change agent is not a task for the faint of heart; you have to be a risk taker to be a powerful leader. There are those who see well into the future, so far ahead of their time that they are often ridiculed, like the Wright brothers. They hang out at the most uncomfortable point, "the bleeding edge." Then the pioneers take charge and forge new territory with determination and vigor. Next are the early adopters who see a great idea and jump on it when major kinks have been smoothed out. Eventually, after the idea has been proven and re-proven, you get the mass market. And way at the old end point demanding that things forever stay the same are those who want to turn back the hands of time, those who can't give up the "good old days."

It's up to those who develop the awareness we have worked on here to take a leading-edge role in helping organizations change. I'm not suggesting that you lobby to add a section on Sankofa Mapping to your company's employee handbook. In fact I've already said that I do not believe that intact teams should work together on Sankofa Mapping. It is too personal and needs a different type of private setting. Even in our Total Leadership Connections program we do not have people from the same company in the same program (at best we have a maximum of two, and only with their personal permission). Instead, I suggest two more modest and incremental steps, which will be discussed in the remainder of this chapter.

First, gain an understanding of how to make the black hole of the work world—meetings—become more vital and timely. No more "Wish I weren't there," no more "What a waste of time that was," no more "Can you believe that was said." Second, help your company through communication malfunctions by creating an environment safe enough for employees to take risks and dare to do things differently. The key learning here is what every orchestra conductor knows: "It's all in the timing."

The overriding idea is that **the process of breaking through barriers in the workplace is nearly identical to the process of doing it with your family.** There is anxiety, stress, and a subtle yet potent demand to maintain the status quo, while at the same time there is an underlying yearning for change and growth. At the very least, commit to being an early adopter of pattern awareness and begin modeling the new behavior you would like to see in your organization. It's contagious. As for the "good old days" types, give them plenty of time and patience. And remember to give yourself the same.

Tapping into Team Power

A technology team I worked with had a strong leading-edge component. They were learning to integrate the basic tenets of emotional intelligence and pattern awareness into their company, as they also tackled the challenge of smoothing out operations with newly acquired international units. As they practiced expressing themselves with more adeptness, tension and eventually arguments broke out at meetings. In the past, they had just saluted and followed their marching orders. The "real" talking had been at breaks and off-line. Their boss, choosing to host a different kind of conversation, decided to stop controlling the flow of the meetings and started to embrace the confusion that comes with real change. It was a dicey time.

After one particularly chaotic session, Raj the VP of IT, wondering what he had gotten himself and his team into, pulled me aside and said, "Can't we just go back to the old command-and-control days? This is exhausting!" Several weeks later, the voice of this same gentleman was on the phone—not exhausted this time, but highly animated—telling me, "Finally I get it! I know it looks sloppy and like we are wasting time. However, I finally get what it means to let the group process work, and that there is a greater wisdom in the group mind." He continued,

> We spent forty-five minutes with ideas bouncing off walls. It was going nowhere fast. And to top it off the new COO had asked if he could sit in to observe the meeting. I was getting nervous. It didn't look good to someone who had no idea of what was really going on at the invisible level. I started to lose my nerve and was just about to go back to command and control when someone said, "Hey wait a minute. What if we send Dylan and Carl to India and then send a small team to Nigeria and . . ." Then someone jumped in to add their idea, you know, like the sax just picked up where the drummer was keeping the beat. It was amazing; within less than ten minutes we had a new and improved plan that would have taken us . . .

His voice trailed off and then he continued, "You know what? I don't think if we had done this in our traditional linear manner we would ever have gotten here."

Then with frustration in his tone he added, "What really got me ticked off, though, was the feedback from the COO, who said he thought I'd better learn how to run a meeting so it's not disorganized. I started to say something and then said to myself, "Screw it," he's a prove-it-to-me type, and he'll just have to learn this by watching it work."

What happened with Raj's team wasn't just a flash of inspiration from out of the blue. It was the result of many months of individual and team dialogue. It came from learning to look for the hidden agenda at the core of a meeting. It came about because the actors in this specific play called *The Technology Leadership Team* agreed to clear out their own blocks and look at the patterns that were limiting success, practice deep listening, ask open-ended questions, and trust the wisdom of the collective mind. They knew it would be chaotic and messy, and they were willing to play in this new arena of emotion and systems. Until now most of them saw improvisation as limited to the comedians on *Saturday Night Live*.

In his book *Group Genius,* Keith Sawyer states, "We're drawn to the image of the lone genius whose mystical moment of insight changes the world. But the lone genius is a myth; instead, it's group genius that generates breakthrough innovation. When we collaborate, creativity unfolds across people; the sparks fly faster, and the whole is greater than the sum of its parts."[2] When teams are thinking and acting from a systems perspective, especially when there is a foundation of trust and a willingness to listen and "jam" together, they can develop new products and solve old problems. By capitalizing on the creative energy of the integrated whole, it is possible to move mountains and even stretch time.

MEETINGS OF THE MINDS

As Raj found out, meetings are the perfect opportunity to put this theory into practice. Meetings are often called "the black hole in the business day." Think about meetings in general. Do you see them as productive or a waste of time? Do you feel you make an important contribution? Sometimes? Rarely? Never? Most meetings are agenda driven and stay with the linear left side of the brain, often excluding the intuitive right side. Yet it is the combination of the two that sets off creative sparks and bonds teams together.

So how can you and your company get the best out of the various meetings you have every day, and activate the creativity lying just under the surface? Please consider what you have already learned. **Staff meetings have all the emotional elements of a family gathering.** The patterns developed in the company are front and center, and no surprise—everyone is bringing his or her personal patterns into the room. You can't see them, smell them, or touch them, but just know they are there waiting to be recognized, wanting to be transformed.

Everyone has to learn to manage anxiety. Meetings that can establish a balance point between fact gathering and dialogue, between staying on the agenda and having free discussion, between creative conflict and contentious polarization will win. It is up to you to help those at the meeting accept the tension and not move to solutions too quickly just to avoid discomfort. Acknowledge the discomfort and ask for as many points of view as possible before making a final choice. You will find that staying with that edge of angst often leads to better long-range planning.

WORKING IN THE "UGLY MIDDLE" OF THE CHANGE PROCESS

I hope by now that you are beginning to understand that organizational change does not happen without the same stress and anxiety, the same courage and optimism needed to make changes within the organization of the family. There are rules to follow on this path of change and transformation, yet it is messy. In what I like to call "the ugly middle," it always becomes quite confusing. Keep in mind that as anxiety builds in your organization,

Gossip increases.
Paranoia increases.
Polarization of perspectives increases.
People feel overused.
People feel undervalued.
Cliques develop.
Humor is mean-spirited.
Physical ailments increase.
The "old way" looks better.
People want quick solutions.
People play retribution cards.
Old patterns return.
Patterns get bigger and *bigger.*

This is the time to put trust in the wisdom of the collective. During this difficult period, take comfort in the fact that you are only a part of the system; you are not the whole system!

You can be a catalyst along with your workmates. Learn to appreciate the gifts and challenges, the virtues and the baggage of your company as you move toward a higher level of teaming and collaboration.

When I was consulting with a global organization working out the kinks in the new merger of two giants in their industry, the anxiety and corollary power games were palpable. All the aforementioned attributes of the ugly middle were obvious. Although there would not be massive layoffs, and those seeking early retirement would get great packages, no amount of reassurance that all was well with the world could quell the fear that was rampant throughout the company. Everyone was grappling with his or her basic concerns around being accepted or rejected and finding a place in the new "family."

The frozen environment cost the organization untold amounts of money. The rumor mill was in full swing, and the excellent work ethic that had been apparent in each company prior to the merger fell by the wayside. Folks would say, "I'm not going to work myself to the bone; who knows where I'll be in six months?" or "There can be only one general manager job, and I better spend my time campaigning for the position" or "I'll just hang back and see what kind of package I can get."

Although a boatload of money had been allotted for the change management initiative, the program was traditional, safe, and superficial. One day, working with my breakout group of ten, on an intuitive impulse I asked them to talk about one or two important changes that had happened to them when they were children. Initially I got the usual "What the heck does that have to do with this?" I replied, for the umpteenth time in my career, "I'm not sure; let's just see where it goes."

What an eye opener! We missed cocktail hour and slipped into the resort dining room just in time for dinner. Much of the conversation had centered on folks who had done a lot of moving as children—from home to home, from country to country, from a two-parent family to one that included stepparents and stepsiblings, from safety to unsafety and the other way around.

By the time we joined the others in the dining room, everyone in our group had connected some vital dots between the ways his or her family had accepted or rejected the changes in living conditions and the anxiety that was at the core of the "merger mania" people were experiencing.

- A man born in York, England, had grown up living for long periods of time in New Delhi, India, with other short-term stops in between. He was the calmest of the lot. He was able to connect that his father, a scientist, had always moved for career enhancement, and each move was celebrated as a sign of success. He was ready for the next move, knew in his heart that it would be successful, and now saw the etiology of why he was so comfortable with the present process.
- A man from Italy had moved only once in his life, still lived in the same neighborhood as his parents and siblings, and was clear that his family came first. If asked to move, he would leave the company. Yet regardless of how much he espoused the value of his family over his job, he was torn up inside. He began to understand the tension he was feeling, and his desire to spread his wings had to do with the clash between loyalty to the family and loyalty to his personal desires.
- An American woman who grew up as an "army brat" saw frequent moving as a way of life and knew her husband and children would just go along without much pushback. She was very judgmental about anyone who made a fuss about potential changes. She judged people who were fearful of moving as weak and inadequate and was vocal about her feelings. Eventually she was able to admit that she always felt like an outsider because she never landed anywhere long enough to make close friends.
- A woman from Ireland who was the only child of elderly parents shared how her mother said they could not get along if she didn't live close by them and that her loyalty to her family was more important than any loyalty to her company. She saw those who moved around the globe without any difficulty as superficial and disconnected. This woman and the army brat ended up becoming close friends.

As time went on, this group became a small community in the vast sea of many thousands, and they all felt that their connection was extremely helpful. The deeper quality of their conversations made the work changes easier for them and also gave them tools to help their own teams. They stayed in contact long after the merger was put to rest.

Defining Boundaries

Does everyone immediately embrace the power of honest relationships and open communication? No. I've learned that what goes into our nervous system takes time to absorb, and each of us has our own internal clock that is not run by my preference for stories that are tied with lovely pink bows. That's one of the risks of being on the leading edge, and we all have to learn to enjoy the highs and tolerate the lows that come when we reach the limits of what is possible at any given time. It is not easy when someone is unable or unwilling to take the heat of change, to be in the crucible and permit the alchemy of change to occur. Not everyone wants to be or hang out with Indiana Jones.

One of my saddest memories is with a global company in the throes of a major reorganization. I knew many in the company were excited and ready to tackle the change initiative in new, creative ways. Yet what was coming down the pike was the same-old, same-old.

One quiet evening, before a group of several hundred was to convene, I was having a glass of wine with Claudia, the global VP of organization development. We were chatting away and talking about the pros and cons of standardized personality profiling.

Sitting in the gorgeous Tuscan countryside watching the sky darken and the stars emerge and twinkle, we were having a peaceful, pleasant dialogue. So I was confused as to why my stomach was in a knot. Nothing anxiety producing was going on. Nothing was obviously amiss, but something was wrong.

I mentioned my feeling of nervousness to Claudia and asked if she was feeling tense also. Her response and the soliloquy that followed were very powerful. "Sylvia, I'm always tense. Haven't you noticed that?" She was one of those tall, thin, cool women who was always dressed properly and in excellent taste. She never raised her voice. It was hard to imagine her using any off-color language even in moments of annoyance. So I merely nodded and she continued:

You once commented to me about my ability to never get upset when the CEO starts his wild yelling. You wondered if it ever bothered me, and I never said anything. Well, let me tell you why I can handle his bad behavior so easily and also why I'm always a ball of tension. Remember I told you I was divorced several years ago. The underlying reason was that my ex-husband abused me. I mean as in beat the crap out of me. He would go into a rage if dinner was ten minutes late or if I wore the red blouse instead of the blue one he told me to wear. I would, if I was fast enough, run into the bathroom at the top of the stairs and lock the door. On days I was not so agile, I would cower under the kitchen table and plead with him to leave me alone.

I was an abused wife, and I was lucky to get out alive and get my daughter out with me; she was fifteen at the time. I was also abused as a child. My older brother would beat me black and blue, and my parents would tell me to stop making such a fuss over nothing. I am from a classic denier and avoider family. And now you know why when you want to have people look at the patterns from the past I reject the notion as not proper for the workplace. It's too much to bear, and it would be even worse to have to share any of this with anyone.

We sat listening to the waiter taking an order from the table behind us. I finally found my voice: "So, what made you tell me this tonight?"

I believe in your work and yet it scares me. What I want is probably impossible. I want you to help me find a way to create a change and integration model for our organization without anyone ever having to reveal anything. I want a model that does not entail anyone having to feel anxiety or tolerate any stress. I want a model based on tables and charts and the best that science has to offer. I want people to be authentic and creative and work well together. And I want pure objectivity. Before I was the head of organization development I was a PhD chemist. Let's base this on chemical formulas and make sure none are meant to blow up. Okay?

It is impossible to get to truth through the level of detachment Claudia requested. She was not ready to move past her own fear and anxiety. I really liked her and wanted to help her. We talked at length about the essential point that you do not have to share the details of unhappy or painful past experiences at work, yet you do owe it to yourself and those with whom you work to at least acknowledge the patterns that developed from your life history and begin to make positive changes. When this type of accountable and authentic behavior becomes the norm in a work environment, it is enlivening and beneficial both for ongoing business relationships and for the bottom line. Sadly, I knew I would eventually disappoint Claudia, and, unfortunately, that prophecy came true. I was unwilling to facilitate the surface "feel-good" program she suggested, and she certainly did not want anything that would truly create deeper change. We soon parted ways, each feeling a sense of sadness that we were unable to find the better way to connect. Perhaps we will meet again in a future that has moved us both to another level of growth and possible collaboration.

Helping find the balance between too much involvement and no emotional connection is one of the jobs of the modern work culture. Please remember my caution: **work is not a rehab facility.** Yet if people are given the opportunity to find their own set point and are neither forced nor excluded from telling helpful parts of their personal story that have a purpose at the given time, real progress can be made for healthy team connections to occur. Willis Harman, a mentor who made an enormous impact on organizations, described his vision for future organizations in *Creative Work:* "Corporations that compete best have high levels of internal cooperation. Without gainsaying the virtues of competition in a free market, it is nonetheless apparent that the future belongs to those who can preserve those virtues while creating in their organizations and in society a climate of caring, cooperativeness, richness of meaning and quality of relationships."[3]

The Tension of Change

I would like to end with a story about what is possible when there is a willingness to embrace the new wave of organizational awareness that Harman has advocated. Changing the way we have been trained to see the split between our behavior at work and our behavior outside of work demands risk taking and steadiness in equal amounts. It requires a conviction that when people are offered a safe place to explore and options for new ways of tackling problems, their organization will experience growth, creativity, and ultimately bottom-line profit. The story I am about to tell you could be titled "The Perfect Storm."

The off-site was risky—actually, very risky. The regional director figured that if it didn't work, there was going to be a lawsuit anyway, so there was really nothing to lose.

On a rainy Thursday, six people were to gather, part of a sales team that worked together—or, put more directly, had to find a way to work together. I had consulted to the larger team of thirty for almost a year and had deep respect for them and for their director. Now, however, this subgroup was thrown together for a mission impossible.

Randall sat tall and straight. The ex-Marine was in perfect physical health and looked quite dashing in his blue cashmere sweater and crisply pleated slacks. He was already in the conference room when I arrived. He nodded and continued to write on his yellow legal pad.

He had agreed to the off-site because he was determined that justice be done and to placate his boss, the unit director who had given him so many opportunities for career development. He also knew that these two days would give him even more documentation for his lawyer. The lawyer, he told us much later, had coached him for the better part of a week so that the discrimination case they would bring against this major corporation would get them both big, big bucks.

The other five came in together after sharing a very tense breakfast. They knew that there had been inappropriate comments and that the offhand jokes had been meant to be funny and biting at the same time. They had agreed to use this meeting to set things right. They knew that if there really was a lawsuit they, or at least some of them, could lose their jobs. They also knew that their bonus was based on the collective success of all of them together.

On paper the company's high-minded policy was great. It was one that welcomed diversity and requested openness and fairness. The big question was, the menu may sound great, but how can we be sure the meal is as good as the menu?

The problems started the month before the Christmas party. Everyone was welcome to bring a significant other, a date, even a son or daughter. Randall went to Marianne, the unit director, and asked if he should bring his partner to the party. Marianne said, "Of course." And Randall said, "Marianne, I mean my 'life partner.'" She smiled and said, "I will be delighted to meet him." And that was the end of that. Or so they thought.

Randall arrived with Grant, a VP of marketing from a well-known computer company. As Randall told it later, he felt his back stiffen when several people looked over and lowered their eyes in disgust.

The new business environment was meant to be color and gender blind. Yet it is impossible to mandate people to be kind and caring; that comes from another place than directives. There is a powerful scene in the movie *Mississippi Burning* when the wife of a member of the Ku Klux Klan is no longer willing to be loyal to the past, to what she had been taught. She states to the FBI man on the case of the missing white students from the north that by the age of seven, she had learned everything she needed to learn hearing her parents quote from the Bible to prove that segregation was part of life as it was meant to be.

So here we were on this very difficult day. Even in our seemingly "open" world, talking about cultural and religious prejudices that lurk just under the surface borders on impossible. Two in the group of this very talented sales team were devout Christians who had already voiced to everyone but Randall that they believed homosexuality to be against God; it says so in the Bible, and they can quote chapter and verse.

Randall was asked to begin. He told the team how hurt and angry he was. He talked about the nasty comments made behind his back, the hurtful innuendos, and the crass jokes about homosexuals just loud enough for him to hear. He talked about the frustrations of having to hide who he was and how disappointed he was when he brought Grant to the Christmas party and how ugly it had been. He wished he had stayed in his tight little cocoon and never said the truth. He wanted the team to work together and did not have a clue how to get past this awful impasse.

Nick was directly across from Randall. Initially he sat way back in his chair almost tilted to fall over. When Randall finished, Nick's head was leaning on his hands, and he was focused on Randall. He sighed and began to speak, haltingly and then with strength.

I never realized how similar we are, Randall. Before I explain the similarity I need to apologize. I was the one who told the fag jokes, and you are right, I would save them until you were in the room. It hit me just now as you were talking how much I hate—no, I take that back—how much I *fear* anyone who is different. When you were talking about your loneliness as a kid because you felt so unique, I could feel that same feeling in me.

No, I'm not going to tell you I am gay. I am going to tell you about being different. Not me; I was as nondescript as oatmeal. But my dad, oh my God was he different. He was in movies, not a major star, but on his way. We lived in Hollywood, and he would have these wild parties; they would last all weekend, nude swimming in a time when the world was still rather conservative, outlandish clothes like all these grown-ups were doing Halloween all year long, lots of drugs before most people knew how to spell marijuana. My mom left my dad because of the extreme behavior. Somehow he ended up with custody, and I had to live in this land of "different," and all I yearned for was *Leave It to Beaver*. So for me different means pain, and while you did nothing wrong by bringing Grant to the Christmas party, you were different and therefore a source of pain. And the only way I could counter the pain was by being the clown.

There was a deep silence. Nick said, "Again, I'm sorry. Now as I look at you I see a brother. I hope it's not too late to make amends."

Randall nodded. He was not ready for what he had just heard. He was ready for an attack, and the Marine in him was ready for a fight. The two men looked at each other, nodding their heads up and down until they both became embarrassed by the intimacy and looked away.

Janelle, whose Christian beliefs were deep and strong, had never heard about the personal struggles of someone who was homosexual. Haltingly she said, "Randall, I like you. I wish I didn't know you were gay. It is really hard for me not to judge you yet; I can really begin to understand your difficulties, and I don't want to add to your discomfort. I also apologize. I just want us to be able to work together."

Tyrone, who was the other devout Christian in the group, made a commitment to keep the personal part of their relationship as far away as possible from the business relationship. He also said he regretted making stupid comments and realized that he could only consider what was right for him and not condemn others. And then he too opened up. He shared that in spite of their religious differences, he too, as an African American, could relate to the feelings of being an outsider. He was relieved that Randall got all the "flak" of stupid, inappropriate jokes. That had been his position in prior jobs. And then he looked at his colleagues and said, "My God, when are we ever going to get past the hatred of the past?" He stood up, and I wondered if this meeting was too much for him and he was going to leave. Instead he walked to Randall and put out his hand; when Randall went to shake it, they both instinctively reached out to give each other a hug. We all sat and soaked it in.

Alex, who was the most neutral of the group, who never took risks, took one. He invited Randall to bring Grant to meet his wife and join them for dinner at his home. He sat huffing after that statement as if he had just run the four-minute mile.

And finally, just before we were going to break for a late dinner, Nanette spoke. Perfect Nanette, in her stunning designer dress, her shoes and purse highlighted by her flawless makeup and precise speech.

Randall, thank you, thank you. I haven't said anything until now. I find you easy to work with, and homosexuality has never bothered me. I grew up in a liberal home, and differences are fine. What made an impact on me was that the split I see you having to live with is the same for me. You see, I have a split between corporate Nanette and after-work Nanette. I grew up as a gymnast, and I was preparing for the Olympics when I injured my back, and that career was over.

What I did learn in all those years of training and competition was to be superficial, plastic, and profusely polite, a real pleaser. And what I learned was that love meant performing. So somehow along the way I became great at competition, jealousy, and striving to be the best salesperson in the company. I was jealous of you because you know how to sell better than anyone I have ever met, and I had to find a way to put you down and make jokes so you would seem little. I forgot how to have fun, how to be spontaneous. The after-work Nanette would go home, change clothes, and go to whatever funky club and drink and dance until dawn. The after-work Nanette and the corporate Nanette have one thing in common: they are both little and mean-spirited people who never really care about anyone else. I too am sorry, and I too want to find a way for all of us to work together.

I know that this team's story may sound a bit too dramatic, too Hollywood. Listen, as I sat there even I found it hard to believe. It was truly a perfect storm. All the forces were in place to make this meeting with this specific group of colleagues happen as it did. No one was forced to speak, yet they all did, they all risked being real. A safeguard had been put in place. People had permission to talk or just to listen. There was no forced communication, and there was an agreement that the meeting could end early if the discussion became too difficult.

You may be uncomfortable with the strong dichotomies in the group. You may not agree that they should have talked about these very personal issues at a work meeting. You may even feel there should have been retribution for prior bad behavior at work.

For me, this narrative transcends the specific issues of homosexuality, fundamentalism, racism, avoidance, and perfectionism, and touches a core of the human dilemma: that we are all so much more alike than we are different, and that with the time and space to find the commonalities, we can make great progress in all our relationships. And this group did make great progress, winning sales awards and, more important, finding a new humanity in themselves.

How do we know when real change is happening? Sometimes it is in the sudden shift from disagreement to agreement. Sometimes it comes in waves of genuine listening and genuine dialogue. Often it happens when people are willing to work together with honesty, even if there are deep disagreements. In every off-site I facilitate, there is a desire for more trust, more authenticity, more creativity, and more connectedness. All this is possible so long as there is room for truth to surface. It is this search for truth and meaning—for finding new ways to see each other, to hear each other, to experience each other—that sets us free.

Ultimately this book is about freedom, a new kind of personal and professional freedom. It is about the complex and liberating feeling you get when you take conscious responsibility to individuate, to become less influenced by old, tattered family or organizational patterns. In loosening the ties that bind, you become stronger and more capable of handling the anxiety that inevitably shows up when you step into uncharted territory.

Individuation is a lifelong process. It begins with consciously naming the patterns that have run our lives and then taking action steps to redesign relationships with the people who matter most to us. We can all learn to stand steady in the tension between homeostasis and growth. In the midst of that tug and pull is life-enhancing creative energy. Once we begin the process of listening and discussing, once we take ownership of the process of shaping and reshaping our lives, we gain a sense of presence. Then we cannot ever be bought; we are unwilling to sell out to cajoling, to bribery, to empty promises. We become authentic.

And this, dear reader, is where the book ends and your next step into your own life begins. I hope you will make good use of the tools you found beneficial here. Take them to help you on your journey. Take them to help you at work and at home. The next step on your evolutionary path is to observe, understand, and transform what no longer serves your health and well-being. I wish you deepened knowledge as you soar to new heights. Bon voyage!

Takeaways

- The process of breaking through organizational patterns and barriers is nearly identical to the process of breaking through the family patterns and barriers that have limited success.
- When in meetings, team members who are able to use a combination of logic and intuition can help drive the process more efficiently and gain results that are of a higher caliber than ever expected.
- Our tendency to want to solve problems quickly is partially driven by our need to alleviate anxiety.
- Group members will establish mutual trust only when they are willing to create a safe environment where they can speak the truth without judgment or blame.
- You achieve freedom when you take conscious responsibility to individuate, both on a personal and on a professional level.

APPENDIX

FILMS OF INSPIRATION

As you embark on your Sankofa action plan, it is helpful to watch films that show the power of patterns and how both fictional and real people have taken the hard road to make change happen. I recommend the following:

Changing Lanes. How our patterns create battles of wills and what it takes to move us beyond our own self-absorption.

Freedom Writers. This film shows how one woman can challenge an establishment filled with deniers and avoiders who claim that "nothing can really change here" at an inner-city school.

Gandhi. This film explores how a whole country can make change happen when one man is willing to be a truth teller rather than a pleaser, and an initiator rather than an avoider. It shows how a man's legacy transcends time and has a deep impact on the world.

The Kite Runner. This beautifully written book is now a film that takes us deep into the culture of contemporary Afghanistan and shows the power of legacies, loyalties, and secrets as they play out from one generation to another. It also shows how small changes are enough for transformation to occur.

The Life and Death of Peter Sellers. The troubled private life of the man behind the actor and how family patterns repeat.

Living in Conflict. This documentary by Mikayla Lev explores the lives of five Palestinian and Israeli artists and how they have transcended their historical roots to find meaning in connecting and in using the expressive arts for healing and hope.

Mandela: A Revolution in Four-Part Harmony. This exceptional documentary about the end of apartheid in South Africa shows the power of people like Nelson Mandela, who chose to be an integrator and help his country move into a new world order with a minimum of bloodshed.

Real Women Have Curves. A coming-of-age story that takes us inside the family dynamics of change versus homeostasis.

Sankofa. Ethiopian filmmaker Haile Gerima encourages people to face the emotional roots of their past. While on a photo shoot in Ghana, Mona, a self-absorbed black fashion model, is challenged to look beyond the present and engage emotionally with the sufferings of her ancestors. The message is that you need to *feel* the past, rather than intellectualize or avoid it, if it is to be included in the tapestry of your life.

Water. This film portrays the plight of a child in present-day India who is married and widowed at eight years old and sent to a home where Hindu widows must live in penitence. The director, Deepa Mehta, would not be silenced, even though extremist groups waged a campaign of riots and arson to shut down the production. Mehta is an explorer willing to consider how the impact of radical traditional thinking limits dialogue.

Recommended Reading

Books that inform both intellectually and emotionally help you maintain a clear view of how patterns operate and how to be a change agent in making your workplace one of truth and integrity. I recommend the following:

Alfred and Emily, by Doris Lessing. This book is partly a daughter's memoir. The Nobel Prize–winning author, now in her late eighties, takes a novel approach to reviewing her parents' lives and shows how the crises of war affect relationships.

A Death in the Family, by James Agee. This book is an American classic that shows the impact of death in a family as told through the eyes of six-year-old Rufus.

The Family Crucible, by Augustus Y. Napier. You will discover the general patterns that are common to all families—stress, polarization and escalation, scapegoating, triangulation, blaming, and the diffusion of identity—and you will gain a vivid understanding of family dynamics.

Flawed Advice and the Management Trap, by Chris Argyris. Too often, advice about change is overly simplistic and does not consider the underlying patterns that keep us from doing what we instinctively know is good for us. The author offers new ideas on how to accomplish business change.

The Fortune at the Bottom of the Pyramid: Eradicating Poverty Through Profits, by C. K. Prahalad. Collectively, the world's billions of poor people have immense entrepreneurial capabilities and buying power, and we have much to learn from those at the bottom of the pyramid.

Freakonomics, by Steven Levitt and Stephen Dubner. This book argues that many apparent mysteries of everyday life don't need to be so mysterious; they could by illuminated and made even more fascinating by our asking the right questions and drawing connections.

The Hidden Connections: Integrating the Biological, Cognitive and Social Dimensions of Life into a Science of Sustainability, by Fritjof Capra. This book suggests that for us to sustain life in the future, the principles underlying our social institutions must be consistent with the organization that nature has evolved to sustain the "web of life."

Iconoclast, by Gregory Burns. This book gives valuable information to help us better understand the workings of the brain, how to set aside fear, and implement fresh ideas.

Leadership and the New Science: Learning About Organization from an Orderly Universe, by Margaret Wheatley. This book explores the connection between modern leadership and the tenets of scientific disciplines, including quantum physics, biology, chemistry, and chaos theory.

Leadership Without Easy Answers, by Ronald Heifetz. An innovative management book that helps shed new light on current issues affecting organizations most—order and change, flexibility, planning, and innovation.

The Legacy Guide: Capturing the Facts, Memories and Meaning of Your Life, by Carol Franco and Kent Lineback. This book takes you through life stages to uncover long-forgotten memories and discover their significance. It helps you clarify what really matters and gain perspective.

Social Intelligence: The New Science of Human Relationships, by Daniel Goleman. This book describes what happens to our brains when we connect with others and shows how relationships have the power to mold not only human experience but also human biology.

Toward a Psychology of Being (3rd ed.), by Abraham Maslow. A world-renowned psychologist looks at the essence of human behavior as intrinsically good and optimistic. Written before the term *social capital* gained importance, this book underlines the desire of human beings to be loving, creative, and trustworthy.

Transparency: How Leaders Create a Culture of Candor, by Warren Bennis, Daniel Goleman, and James O'Toole. This book explores why the containment of truth is the most dearly held value of far too many organizations, and suggests practical ways to achieve openness. Written for any organization—business, government, and nonprofit—that must achieve a culture of candor, truth, and transparency.

Trust: The Social Virtues and the Creation of Prosperity, by Francise Fukuyama. Communicating a brilliant understanding of the context of economics and culture, this book explains the vital importance of social capital as the leveraging point for business success in the emerging global economy.

A Whole New Mind, by Daniel H. Pink. Just as information workers surpassed physical laborers in economic importance, the workplace terrain is changing yet again, and power will inevitably shift to people who possess strong right-brain qualities.

The Wisdom of Crowds, by James Surowiecki. Whereas our culture generally trusts experts and distrusts the wisdom of the masses, this book argues that "under the right circumstances, groups are remarkably intelligent, and are often smarter than the smartest people in them."

The World Is Flat, by Thomas Friedman. Friedman is not so much a futurist, which he is sometimes called, as a "presentist." His aim in this book is not to give you a speculative preview of the wonders that are sure to come in your lifetime, but rather to get you caught up on the wonders that are already here.

NOTES

Chapter One

1. Carter McNamara, *Field Guide to Consulting and Organizational Development* (Minneapolis, Minn.: Authenticity Publishing and Consulting, 2005).
2. Aristotle, *Metaphysicia,* ed. Richard McKeon (New York: Random House, 1941).
3. Pitirim Sorokin, *Social and Cultural Dynamics* (New Brunswick, N.J.: Transaction Publishing, 1941).
4. Debra Hammond, *The Science of Synthesis: Exploring the Social Implications of General Systems Theory* (Norman: University of Oklahoma Press, 2003).
5. Michael Mandizza and Joseph Chilton Pierce, *Magical Parent–Magical Child* (Nevada City, Calif.: In-Joy, 2003).
6. Edward Lorenz, *The Essence of Chaos* (Seattle: University of Washington Press, 1996).
7. Margaret Wheatley, *Leadership and the New Science,* 3rd ed. (San Francisco: Berrett-Kohler, 2006).
8. Shoshana Zuboff, *In the Age of the Smart Machine* (New York: Basic Books, 1989).
9. Daniel Pink, *A Whole New Mind* (New York: Riverhead Books, 2005), 1.
10. Mark Poster, *Critical Theory of the Family* (New York: Seabury Press, 1978).
11. Salvatore Minuchin, *Families and Family Therapy* (Cambridge, Mass.: Harvard University Press, 1981).
12. Ivan Boszormenyi-Nagy and Geraldine Spark, *Invisible Loyalties* (New York: Routledge, 1973).
13. Murray Bowen and Michael Kerr, *Family Evaluation* (New York: Norton, 1988).
14. David Barlow, *Abnormal Psychology* (Belmont, Calif.: Thomson Wadsworth, 2004).
15. Malcolm MacFarlane, *Family Therapy and Mental Health* (New York: Haworth Press, 2001).

16. Walter Vandereychen, *The Family Approach to Eating Disorders* (Costa Mesa, Calif.: PMA, 1989).
17. Robert Holman Coombs, *Handbook of Addictive Disorders* (Hoboken, N.J.: Wiley, 2004).
18. Interview cited in Associated Press, "Novelist William Styron Dies at 81," November 2, 2006, www.msnbc.msn.com/id/15521076.
19. Leonard Sagan, *The Health of Nations: True Causes of Sickness and Well Being* (New York: Basic Books, 1987).
20. James Lock, *Anorexia and Family Therapy* (New York: Guilford Press, 2002).
21. Mark Young, *Counseling and Therapy for Couples* (Pacific Grove, Calif.: Brooks-Cole, 1997).
22. Michael Yapko, *Hand-Me-Down-Blues* (New York: Macmillan, 2000).

Chapter Two

1. H. Kitaoji, "The Structures of the Japanese Family," *American Anthropologist* 73, no. 5 (1971): 1036–1057.
2. Russell Thornton, *The Cherokees: A Popular History* (Omaha: University of Nebraska Press, 1992).
3. Jean Houston, *The Possible Human,* 2nd ed. (New York: Tarcher, 1997).
4. Quoted in Dan Millman, *Living on Purpose: Straight Answers to Universal Questions* (Novato, Calif.: New World Press, 2000), 4.
5. Dennis Koslowski, interview on "Prisoner 05A4820," *60 Minutes,* CBS, March 25, 2007.
6. Aldous Huxley, *Island,* Perennial classic ed. (New York: HarperCollins, 2002).

Chapter Three

1. Michael Kinsman, "Conflict on the Job a Major Issue for Most Workers," *San Diego Union Tribune,* December 24, 2006.
2. Kinsman, "Conflict on the Job a Major Issue for Most Workers."
3. "HR Most Likely to Fall Out over Issues at Work," *Personnel Today,* June 12, 2007.
4. *Boston Globe,* "Office Idiots, Survey: Irritating Co-Workers Are No. 1 Source of Stress in the Workplace," July 26, 2006.
5. Bradley James Wright, "Health Care Expenditures and Stress," *Journal of Occupational and Environmental Medicine* 50, no. 3 (2008): 316–323.
6. Shelly Garcia, "Changing Workplaces Mean Conflicts Get Attention: Managers Spending More Time Handling Squabbles," *San Fernando Valley Business Journal,* February 5, 2007.

7. *Press Association Regional Newswire-East Anglia,* "Workers Clash on a Weekly Basis," June 7, 2007.
8. *Daily Yomirui,* "Survey Finds Workplaces Rife with 'Power Harassment,'" February 13, 2000.
9. Eric Kandel, *In Search of Memory* (New York: Norton, 2007).
10. Richard Brown and Pilar Milner, "The Legacy of Donald O. Hebb," *Nature* 4 (2003): 1013–1019.
11. Malcolm Gladwell, *Blink* (New York: Little, Brown, 2005).
12. Daniel Goleman, *Emotional Intelligence* (New York: Bantam, 1997).
13. Amy Edmundson, David Garvin, and Francesca Gino, "Is Yours a Learning Organization?" *Harvard Business Review,* March 2008.
14. Julia Flynn Siler, *Wine Wars* (New York: Gotham, 2007).
15. Barbara Smit, *Sneaker Wars* (New York: Ecco, 2008).

Chapter Four

1. Piers Steel, *Study on Procrastination* (Calgary, Canada: University of Calgary, 2004).
2. Michael Ruane, "Lincoln Urgent in Lost Letter to General," *Washington Post,* June 8, 2007, A3.
3. Rodd Wagner, *The Elements of Great Managing* (New York: Gallup Press, 2006).
4. Morton Thompson, *The Cry and the Covenant* (New York: Buccaneer Books, 1991).

Chapter Five

1. Warren Bennis and Joan Goldsmith, "Self-Defined Leadership: Looking Back to Effectively Lead Forward," *Member Connector* (International Leadership Association newsletter), September 2001.
2. John-Dylan Hayes, "From Genotype to Phenotype: Systems Biology Meets Natural Variation," *Science* 320 (2008): 495–497.
3. Darwin Porter, *Brando Unzipped* (New York: Blood Moon, 2006).
4. Porter, *Brando Unzipped.*
5. Richard Sewall, *The Life of Emily Dickinson* (New York: Farrar, Straus & Giroux, 1974).
6. Daniel Siegel, *The Developing Mind* (New York: Guilford Press, 2001), 12.
7. Tom Robbins, *Still Life with Woodpecker* (New York: Bantam, 1990).
8. Cited in Bob Minzesheimer, review of *The Bond: Three Young Men Learn to Forgive and Reconnect with Their Fathers,* by George Jenkins, Sampson Davis, and Rameck Hunt, *USA Today,* October 3, 2007.
9. Monica McGoldrick, *Genograms,* 2nd ed. (New York: Norton, 1999).

Chapter Six

1   Carl Jung, *Modern Man in Search of a Soul* (New York: Harcourt Brace, 1939).

2. Robert Johnson, *Owning Your Own Shadow* (San Francisco: Harper One, 1993).

3. John Rewald, *Post Impressionism: From van Gogh to Gauguin,* Rev. ed. (London: Secker and Warburg, 1978).

4. Doris Kearns Goodwin, *A Team of Rivals* (New York: Simon & Schuster, 2005).

5. Warren Bennis and Patricia Ward Biederman, *Organizing Genius: The Secrets of Creative Collaboration* (New York: Basic Books, 1998).

6. Mihaly Csikszentmihalyi, *Flow* (New York: HarperPerennial, 1991).

7. Helen Keller, *Light in My Darkness,* 2nd ed. (London: Chrysalis Books, 2000).

8. Ron Powers, *Mark Twain: A Life* (New York: Random House, 2005).

9. Robertshaw cited in Randy Erickson, "Humor in the Workplace," *Commerce Now,* May 1995. (Available at www.drhumor.com/workplace)

10. Emily Rubin, "Ethical Products Marketing," *Ethical Corporation,* March 2006.

11. Amy Bloom, "Women of the Year: Eileen Fisher," *Ms. Magazine,* Winter 2003.

12. Louis Fischer, *The Essential Gandhi,* Reprint ed. (New York: Vintage, 2002).

13. Margot Morrell and Stephanie Capparell, *Shackleton's Way: Leadership Lessons from the Great Antarctic Explorer* (New York: Viking, 2001).

14. Betsy Morris, "Richard Branson: What a Life," *Fortune,* September 22, 2003.

15. Azim Khamisa, *Azim's Bardo—from Murder to Forgiveness—A Father's Journey* (San Diego, Calif.: Rising Star Press, 1998).

16. Nelson Mandela, *In His Own Words* (New York: Little, Brown, 2004).

17. Thich Nhat Hanh, *Keeping the Peace: Mindfulness and Public Service* (Berkeley, Calif.: Parallax Press, 2005).

18. Thich Nhat Hanh, *Keeping the Peace,* 20.

19. Bill Moyers, *Journalists as Truth-Tellers,* speech presented at the Ridenhour Prize awards ceremony, Washington, D.C., April 3, 2008. (Reprint of speech available at www.thenation.com/doc/20080421/moyers)

20. Cited in Janet Ward, "Philadelphia Mayor Ed Rendell: 1996 Municipal Leader of the Year," *American City & County,* November 1, 1996, http://americancityandcounty.com/mag/government_philadelphia_mayor_ed/index.html.

21. Jim Collins, *Good to Great* (New York: HarperCollins, 2001).
22. Deepak Chopra, "Dalai Lama," *Time*, May 12, 2008, www.time.com/time/specials/2007/article/0,28804,1733748_1733757,00.html.
23. *San Francisco Chronicle*, "Man Gets Prison Term for Attack on Rosa Parks," August 8, 1995.
24. Gregory Bateson, *Steps to an Ecology of Mind* (Chicago: University of Chicago Press, 1972).

Chapter Seven
1. Robert Sutton, "15 Things I Believe," from his Work Matters blog, http://bobsutton.typepad.com/my_weblog.

Chapter Eight
1. James Dunaway, "From Impossible to Commonplace," *Track and Field*, May 4, 2003.
2. Keith Sawyer, *Group Genius* (New York: Basic Books, 2008), 7.
3. Willis Harman and John Hormann, *Creative Work* (Indianapolis: Knowledge Systems, 1990), 143.

About the Author

Sylvia Lafair, PhD, is president of Creative Energy Options, Inc. (CEO), a global consulting company focused on optimizing workplace relationships through extraordinary leadership. With a doctorate in clinical psychology, Sylvia, who was a practicing family therapist, took her talents into the work world and has revolutionized the way employees react and teams cooperate. People are not only finding new ways to relate and innovate but also taking skills home for more rewarding family time.

Always an adventurer, Sylvia has spent her life uncovering the basic building blocks of relationships. Along with her husband, Herb Kaufman, Sylvia created programs to invite leading-edge teachers to help business and social service professionals explore the newest advances in health, wellness, and spirituality. They hosted a stellar collection of thinkers, including Deepak Chopra, Elizabeth Kübler-Ross, Matthew Fox, Huston Smith, Herbert Benson, Robert Bly, David Whyte, Joseph Chilton Pierce, Willis Harman, and many others.

Believing in experiential learning, Sylvia and Herb took business leaders to hike the Inca Trail, to walk in the Amazon rain forest, and to study with Native American elders in New Mexico.

Delving into the complexities of conflict, Sylvia and Herb created the Center for Intercultural Dialogue to explore the human dynamics between Israelis and Palestinians through the use of the expressive arts. Sylvia has taught in Europe, South Africa, and has begun a leadership program in Ghana.

In all her journeys to "the heart of the matter," Sylvia has sought out "that which connects us" to bring this perspective into the business world. She has developed such intriguing educational programs as The "Gotcha!" Game: Decoding Office Politics; Get the But out of Your Yes: Effective Communication Skills; Ouch!: Resolving Conflicts at Work; and The Creative Edge: Team-based Innovation. CEO's flagship program, Total Leadership Connections™, uses the tools of pattern-aware learning to help individuals understand how behavior patterns developed at home and repeated at work can derail success and how to transform them into productivity, purpose, and profit.

As a workshop leader or keynote speaker, Sylvia engages audiences with her natural storytelling ability. She weaves her knowledge of what makes a business successful into real-life stories about workplace cultures. Her thought-provoking messages leave audiences with information to take back to the office and immediately put into practice. She has written numerous articles for trade publications and national magazines.

Sylvia and Herb divide their time between Santa Fe, New Mexico, and White Haven, Pennsylvania, headquarters of CEO with its private retreat facility, the Country Place Retreat and Conference Center. Sylvia enjoys spending time with her children and grandchildren; she is especially fascinated watching them all "stand on the shoulders of the past."

Sylvia can be reached through her Web site, www.patternaware .com, by e-mailing Sylvia@ceoptions.com, or by calling (570) 636-3858.

INDEX